Þe Wohunge of Ure Lauerd

EARLY ENGLISH TEXT SOCIETY

Original Series No. 241

hereliíaste þ þe blod yrang ut at
tine finger neiles as haiþes
bileueþ ybunde ledden wyh ⁊
dimede unridelio rug ⁊ o schul
dres ⁊ bifore þe pines buffeted ⁊
beten. Siden bifore pilat hu þu
þi naker bunde faste to þe pi
ler. þ tine mihtes no phy ider
prenche sta ya dintes. þer þu yes
for un luue yid eno to skepe þi
unge þya þ ti luuelicke liches mih
te beo to torn ⁊ to rent. ⁊ al þi
blisfule bodi streamed on a birre
blod. Siden o þin heaued yet set
te te crune of scharpe þornes.
þ yid eaurich þorn y nagu ut
te reade blod of þin heali hea
ued. Siden sette buffeter ⁊ to
dunet iþe heaued yid þe wd set
de þ wyal ear i honde swen
won hoker ringe. Al þat schal
tu don: Vu mih lutte mai to
brecke min ehne floyen al o ya
tet. A nu is mi lesing demd for
to deren. A nu mo ledes hi ford
to munte caluarie to þe qualm
stoye. A lo he beres his rode up
on his bare schuldres. ⁊ leſ ſu
duntes drepe me þ tai þe dun
chen. ⁊ yrasten þe ferd yard syt

þe woyard ti dom. A lesuo hu
mo folhes te þine frend farih
che yid remmig ⁊ soike. þine
fend hokerliche to schome ⁊
yundre up o þe. A nu haue þai
broht him yuder. A nu raute
þai up þe rode. Setd up þe yar þ
tro. A nu na cnes mo mi lef
J nu drinen ha him up yid
skepel ⁊ yud schurges. A huh
ue iſor reoy de þ seo mi mi lef
mo up o rode. ⁊ hya to draheþ
hiſ elimes þim a ilus bodi
euch ban telle. A hu þya nu
driue ir nene neiles þurh þi
ne soreli onder i to hard rode
þurh þine sirolicke set. A nu
of þa honde ⁊ of þa fet sya lu
ueli streames te blod hya rey
li. A nu bede hami leoſ þ seid
þ him yristes: aisille surel al
ir þinge drinch menged yid
galle his hing britrest. Eſya
hale drinch iblod letinge sya
sur ⁊ sya bitre. bote ne dunkes
he hit noht. A nu skere iþu set
up on al þi ya ha eken schome
⁊ businer. Lataen þe to hoker
þer þu o rode hengest. þu mi
uneucke lef þer þu yid strahte

Þe Wohunge of Ure Lauerd

EDITED BY

W. MEREDITH THOMPSON

Published for
THE EARLY ENGLISH TEXT SOCIETY
by the
OXFORD UNIVERSITY PRESS
LONDON   NEW YORK   TORONTO

UNIVERSITY PRESS

Great Clarendon Street, Oxford OX2 6DP
United Kingdom

Oxford University Press is a department of the University of Oxford.
It furthers the University's objective of excellence in research, scholarship,
and education by publishing worldwide. Oxford is a registered trade mark of
Oxford University Press in the UK and in certain other countries

© The Early English Text Society 1958

The moral rights of the authors have been asserted

Database right Oxford University Press (maker)

First Edition published in 1958 (for 1955)
Reprinted 1970

All rights reserved. No part of this publication may be reproduced,
stored in a retrieval system, or transmitted, in any form or by any means,
without the prior permission in writing of Oxford University Press,
or as expressly permitted by law, or under terms agreed with the appropriate
reprographics rights organization. Enquiries concerning reproduction
outside the scope of the above should be sent to the Rights Department,
Oxford University Press, at the address above

You must not circulate this book in any other form
and you must impose this same condition on any acquirer

Published in the United States of America by Oxford University Press
198 Madison Avenue, New York, NY 10016, United States of America

British Library Cataloguing in Publication Data
Data available

Library of Congress Cataloging in Publication Data
Data available

Original Series, 241

ISBN 978-0-19-722241-6

TO

E. M. T.

PREFATORY NOTE

FOR this edition I am indebted to the kind unfailing stimulus and advice of Professor J. R. R. Tolkien, who, wearing his own ring of power, is present in most of its best parts only. I also wish to express sincere thanks for assistance of various kinds from Mr. R. W. Burchfield, the indefatigably helpful Secretary, and Dr. Mabel Day of the Early English Text Society, Mr. Joseph Harris and the late Principal W. C. Graham of Winnipeg, Professor Angus McIntosh, my pupil Mr. Rudolph E. Habenicht, and my martyred German 'mutti', Frau Lilli Goldschmidt.

Acknowledgement is gratefully made to the authorities of the British Museum and of Lambeth Palace Library for permission to print the manuscripts represented here and to reproduce a page of MS. Cotton Titus D. XVIII as the frontispiece.

W. M. T.

21 January 1957

CONTENTS

British Museum MS. Cotton Titus D. XVIII, f. 131ᵛ	*Frontispiece*
PREFATORY NOTE	vi
INTRODUCTION	
The Manuscripts	ix
Orthography	xii
Problems of Origin and Literary Relationship	xiii
Form and Style	xxii
Language: Phonology	xxix
Accidence	xli
Dialect, Textual History, and Date	li
Abbreviations and Chief References	lx
Note on the Text	lxii
TEXT	
On Ureisun of ure Louerde [L]	1
On wel swuðe God Ureisun of God Almihti [N(U)]	5
On Lofsong of ure Louerde [N(Lo)]	10
On Lofsong of ure Lefdi [N(Le)]	16
Þe Oreisun of Seinte Marie [R]	19
Þe Wohunge of ure Lauerd [W]	20
NOTES	39
GLOSSARY	51
INDEX OF NAMES	79
APPENDIX	80

CORRIGENDA ET ADDENDA

PAGE

7 line 93, change *?* to *;* (*MS ?*)
42 n. 28 (line 2), change *et* to *þet*
57 under *efne adj.* remove *N(U)72,L61*
58 add *euene n.* 'resources' *N(U)72,L61* (*ON efni*)
60 under *gostlich* add *adv. L45*
65 under *liuien* (line 3) change *liuee* to *liuiee*
73 under *tuðe* add *or v.s.imper.* '*grant*'? (OE *tȳðian?*) *N(Le)85*
76 under *went* (line 2) change *wended* to *wendeð*

INTRODUCTION

THE MANUSCRIPTS

THE manuscripts of the texts presented here are all of the early thirteenth century.

1. MS. Lambeth 487 consists of 68 folios in vellum, 7 × 5¼ inches, written in single column. It contains the seventeen so-called Lambeth Homilies, a version of the *Poema Morale*, and a piece listed in the table of contents (by Sancroft) as *A devout praier to or Savior*, which Morris renamed *On Ureisun of ure Louerde*. This is an incomplete version of the same work that is found in full form in MS. Cotton Nero A. XIV, and there called *On wel swuðe god ureisun of God Almihti*. An inserted note by J. P. Gilson tentatively dates the Lambeth manuscript between 1185 and 1225; the *Ureisun* (ff. 65ᵛ–67ʳ), however, is in a somewhat later hand. It may have been added to fill up a few spare leaves at the end of the manuscript. It has been suggested that the manuscript may have been one of a group that came to Lambeth from Lanthony Priory, Glos., but there seems to be no certain evidence on the point.[1]

2. MS. Cotton Nero A. XIV consists of 131 folios in vellum, 5¾ × 4½ inches, written in single column. The manuscript contains the N version of the *Ancrene Riwle* (ff. 1–120ᵛ), *On god ureisun of ure lefdi* (ff. 120ᵛ–3ᵛ), and *On wel swuðe god ureisun of God almihti* (ff. 123ᵛ–6ᵛ), the two untitled pieces called by Morris *On Lofsong of ure Lefdi* (ff. 126ᵛ–8) and *On Lofsong of ure Louerde* (ff. 128–31), *The Apostles Creed in English* (f. 131–1ᵛ), and twelve lines of Latin verse ascribed to St. Bernard, followed by a paragraph of Latin prose. According to Miss Day, the manuscript is probably of the second quarter of the thirteenth century, and is the work of two scribes: the one wrote out the *Ancrene Riwle*, the other the remainder of the manuscript. The last of numerous marginalia by Richard James, Sir Robert Cotton's librarian, is written in dull reddish ink on f. 123ᵛ beside the *Ureisun of God Almihti*, and reads *Monachi inventores hymnorum B. Mariæ*, apparently with

---

[1] R. M. Wilson, 'The Provenance of the Lambeth Homilies', *Leeds Studies in English*, iv (1935), 39 (where Lanthony is mistakenly said to be in Worcestershire).

x *Introduction*

reference to the previous piece. Miss Day suggests that the manuscript may once have belonged to Winchcombe Abbey.[1]

3. MS. Royal 17 A. xxvii consists of 98 folios in vellum, $6\frac{1}{2} \times 4\frac{3}{4}$ inches, and is in two parts. The first part (ff. 1–70ᵛ) is an early thirteenth-century manuscript containing almost all of the 'Katherine Group' (*Sawles Warde* (not so named), *Katherine*, *Marherete*, *Iuliane*) and a fragment of the *Lofsong of ure Lefdi* there called *Þe Oreisun of Seinte Marie* (f. 70–70ᵛ). The second part (ff. 71–97) is an early fifteenth-century collection of hymns and prayers. The first part and possibly both parts came from the Theyer library. The name Iohanes Theyer is written on a piece of vellum attached to the front fly-leaf (numbered f. 1*), and again in the upper margin of f. 70ᵛ. The *Oreisun* was probably included to fill up the folio left vacant at the end of the thirteenth-century manuscript, and represents the second of three hands therein.[2]

4. MS. Cotton Titus D. xviii consists of 148 folios in vellum, $6\frac{1}{8} \times 4\frac{7}{8}$ inches, written in double column, in a fifteenth-century hand to f. 13ᵛ, thereafter in script of the first half of the thirteenth century. It contains a *Liber Alphabetarius*, some Latin poems, versions of the *Ancrene Riwle* (with two missing folios), *Sawles Warde*, *Hali Meiðhad*, and *Katherine*. Preceding the last is the unique text of *Þe Wohunge of ure Lauerd* (ff. 127–33). On f. 148 is a list of some sixty bishops and saints.

The manuscripts employ the usual letter-forms, abbreviations, and punctuation of the period. After questions the sign ⸵ occurs in W (transcribed as ? in this edition) and the contemporary interrogation mark resembling a modern ? on its side occurs in N, though the practice is not entirely consistent. These are evidently derived from the liturgical *punctus interrogativus* as distinct from the *punctus elevatus* which normally separated main divisions of a sentence.[3] The latter in these manuscripts is (⸵); but the dot (.), which regularly indicates the end of a non-interrogative sentence, could also take the place of every other mark of punctuation.

[1] Mabel Day, *The English Text of the Ancrene Riwle*, ed. from Cotton MS. Nero A. xiv, E.E.T.S., o.s. 225, pp. xii f.   [2] Mack, pp. xiii f.

[3] Peter Clemoes, *Liturgical Influence on Punctuation in Late Old English and Early Middle English Manuscripts*, Occas. Papers 1, Dept. of Anglo-Saxon (Cambridge, 1952).

The Manuscripts xi

Though our L and R texts do not have the *punctus interrogativus*, R. M. Wilson notes a similar usage (not reproduced by Morris) elsewhere in L.[1]

Erasures, gaps, blurs, expunctions, deletions, additions, and other corrections are indicated in footnotes to the text. Such are particularly common in N: in N(Lo) two whole lines (43, 81) are omitted and added in the margin; in N(Lo) and N(Le) there are numerous erasures. In some places, as between 17 and 18, 34 and 35 in N(Lo), clipping of high and descending letters may point to erasure after the text was written, but of what is indeterminable.

As usual in this period, word-division is not seldom erratic, as in *swotes melles* N(Le) 21, *alsikerof* N(Lo) 131, *alforlesede* W 88. Less arbitrary is the frequent separation of prefixes, usually without hyphens, as in *bi foren* N(U) 150, *bi leaue* N(U) 24, *i liche* N(U) 142, *i uorðed* N(U) 145, *i loked* N(Le) 20, *uor driuene* N(Lo) 49; the joining of pronoun and verb, or verb and pronoun, as in *iseo* W 599, *iwile* W 53, *nabbich* N(Lo) 79, *schuldi* W 551; or of preposition with a following word, as in *iblodleting* W 521; *ifihte* W 150, *ofluht* W 335, *orode* W 317, *ipe* N(Lo) 139, *ipine* N(Lo) 167, *ipinge* N(U) 34.

Otherwise crowding is most apparent at line-ends in the two-columned manuscript of W, and on f. 70ᵛ of R where lack of space probably caused the abrupt ending in the middle of a sentence.[2]

[1] Op. cit., p. 40. For the rhetorical aspect of the punctuation, see pp. xxvi f.

[2] At the ends of lines, cramping (or haste ?) in original or copy is probably responsible for errors of various kinds: (i) Clipped spellings: *drihti[n]* W 149, *weasch* (for *weasche*) N(U) 114 (see note to line), and possibly *underfo[n]* N(Lo) 140. (ii) Other errors at word-ends: *neh* (*h* expuncted) W 202, *hauei* (*i* expuncted) W 292, *purch* (= *purh*) N(Lo) 17. (iii) Repetitions: *ne ne* L 78; and from one line to the next: *up/po*, W 284–5, *pe/asch* (for *weasche*) N(Lo) 47–48 (see note to line); and possibly *li/licunge* N(U) 45–46 (though *li* on recto anticipates *licunge* on verso of the folio, the only instance of this), and *deren/nedes* W 570–1 (but see note to line). (iv) Various other errors: *wah* W 279 (see note to line), *Girre* (= *gure* ?) W 480, *Ewa* (= *Twa*) W 520, *phi* (crossed out) W 564, *to-ðe* (= *soðe* ?) N(Le) 61, *p̃et* (*pet* ?) L 30, *to to* (= *to pe* ?) L 62, *bodi* (for *blodi* ?) L 94, *nab ich* (for *nabbich*) N(Lo) 80. (v) Possible but unusual forms (in the texts concerned) occurring only at line-ends: *fant* W 323, *heawed* (= *heaued*) N(Lo) 121. Mistakes are less common at the beginnings of lines, but occur—e.g. confusion of similar letters in *poure* (= *poure*) W 352, *plod* (= *blod*) W 545.

xii *Introduction*

ORTHOGRAPHY

The orthography in the four manuscripts, like that of AB, is largely based on late OE., but modified both by subsequent development and by the influence of French. In most cases orthographic and phonetic features are closely connected and will be treated together in the Phonology.

Punctuation is sporadic: most consistent (and related to sentence structure) in R and W, sometimes quite arbitrary in L.[1] Capitalization varies: in W and N, where capital and small letters usually differ in form but not size, capitals sometimes appear within sentences. In L and R they are used with more discrimination. Parts of compounds are separated or joined or (rarely within lines) hyphenated. At line ends, hyphens are absent in L and R, infrequent in N, frequent but sporadic in W.

In all manuscripts *wyn* (p) is used for *w* (except for two spellings, *halwi*, *schadwe*, with the letter-form *w*, in L). It is used for *u* in native diphthongs, normally in W and R, occasionally in N (as *fowr*, *nawt*, *nowðer*, *rewli*); but *u* also occurs (as *naut*, *nouðer*, *treulac*): W has *mildeu*, W and N have characteristic AB *euch(e)*. In diphthongs of foreign origin, practice varies: AB regularly and N sometimes use *w*, as N *lowe* (ON. *lágr*), *sawter* (OF. *sautier*), beside *abaundune* (OF. *a bandon*); W regularly and L (in one instance only) have *u*, as W *chaumbre*, *poure*, *ribauz*, L *sauuin* (OF. *chambre*, *povre*, *ribauz*, *salver*). Conversely *u* represents *w* in *qu* (see below) and in L *hua*. Confusion of *w* and *u* is seen in N *heawed* (for *heaued*), *haweð* (for *haueð*), *wtewið* (for *utewið*). Confusion of p and *p* is seen in N *uwward* (for *uppard*), N, L *spetnesse* (for *swetnesse*), and probably in N *spetunge* (for *swetunge* ?), and *pe* (crossed out) N(Lo) 47: confusion of p and *þ* in L *þat* (for *wat*).

As in AB, R and W write *þ* initially, ð medially and finally; N has ð in all positions, but rarely initially. L has *þ* in all positions, ð very rarely. Exceptionally *d* is written for ð, as N *leued* pl. pr., *predðe* (for *wreððe* N(Lo) 39), L *derf* (for *ðerf*), R *oderhwiles*: ð represents *d* in N *wiðe* (for *wide*), L *goð* (for *god*). Use of *th* for *t* occurs in W *scarioth* and L *wiþ uthen* (an error).

[1] See p. xxviii below.

Orthography

For *þet, þat*, all manuscripts frequently have *ꝥ*: for *þur(u)h*, N frequently has *þ̄*.

For the variation of *c/k*, *f/u/ue*, *ʒ/g*, and the arbitrary addition or dropping of initial *h*, see the Phonology.

For *cw*, AB has *qu* only in *quoð*: a few other *qu*-spellings (*monquellere, quemen, quene, querfaste, quiddet*) occur in L, N, and W (but not R). Vocalic *v* (for *u*) is used initially a few times in W and N (as *vnderstonde, vpo, vuele*); consonantal *v* appears twice, in N *tovel* (= *to uvel*), *vif*. W has *ph* for *f* in Lat. *prophete*.

Continental *z* occurs only in two French plurals: N *sacremenz* (beside *sacremens*), W *ribauz*. An unfamiliar form of *r* may have caused the scribe of L to write *dieope* for *drope*, similar confusion of *i* and *r* being frequent in the *Lambeth Homilies*.[1]

For the variant spellings of vowel sounds, see the Phonology. The most frequent correction in N (in the whole manuscript) is the addition of interlined *o* after *e* in words like *de⟨o⟩re, he⟨o⟩uen* (see footnotes to text). Elsewhere N incorrectly writes *eo* for *e, o*, and *ea* (see p. lvii below). In W, *o* is not always easily distinguished from *a* or *e*: *strong* 455 and *werlde* 18 might be *strang* and *worlde*.

Examples of various other (sporadic) orthographic developments and errors are shown in the glossary.

PROBLEMS OF ORIGIN AND LITERARY RELATIONSHIP

The *Wohunge*, the *Ureisun* (in two versions, N(U) and L), and the *Lofsong of ure Louerde* belong to a large body of religious literature, written for (and perhaps, in some cases, by) devout women, which looks back to St. Æðelwold's translation for nuns of the *Rule of St. Benedict* in the late tenth century, and more immediately results from the religious revival in the twelfth century. They derive particularly from the tradition of the mystical marriage of the Heavenly Bridegroom with Holy Church or the human soul—above all the soul of the religious who renounces earthly desire—that had come into English chiefly through Latin writings of the renowned doctors of the church,

[1] C. Sisam, 'The Scribal Tradition of the *Lambeth Homilies*', *R.E.S.*, N.S. ii (1951), 110.

xiv *Introduction*

St. Anselm, St. Bernard, Hugh of St. Victor, and others. This tradition also found expression, variously, in works to which our texts are closely related: the *Ancrene Riwle* and the so-called 'Katherine Group' of virtuous homilies and virginal legends. But the *Wohunge*, the *Ureisun*, and the *Lofsong* have very distinctive qualities of their own. They and the *Lofsong of ure Lefdi* (in two versions, N(Le) and R) are the only religious *prose* lyrics in the early thirteenth century or before Rolle and the later mystics. They are closely related in language, substance, and manner; and may be called appropriately the 'Wooing Group'.[1]

The *Lofsong of ure Lefdi* is the very free translation of a Latin poem *Oratio ad Sanctam Mariam* by Bishop Marbod of Rennes (1035–1123).[2] The others of the group, so far as is known, are original; but original in the medieval sense of free expression within a tradition and a current phraseology. This characteristic led various scholars of the past to regard them as mere paraphrases or as pastiches of *plagiaten* and *geraubten gedanken*. Thus Morris described the *Wohunge* as 'a lengthy paraphrase of a portion of the seventh part of the *Ancren Riwle*',[3] viz:

ȝif heo is forto ȝiuen.' hwar meiht tu biteon hire betere.' þen up on me.' nam ich þinge ueirest.' nam ich kinge richest.' nam ich heixst ikunned.' nam ich weolie wisest.' nam ich monne hendest.' nam ich monne ureoest.' . . . nam ich alre þinge swotest ⁊ swetest. þus alle ðe reisuns. hwui me ouh forto ȝiuen luue.' þu meiht i vinden in me.[4]

This does indeed resemble lines 252–62, which summarize most of the preceding part of the *Wohunge*:

Þenne þu wið þi fairnesse. þu wið richesce. þu wið largesce. þu wið wit ⁊ wisdom. þu wið maht ⁊ strengðe. þu wið noblesce ⁊ hendeleic. þu wið meknesse ⁊ mildeschipe ⁊ mikel debonairte. þu wið sibnesse. þu wið alle þe þinges ꝥ man mai luue wið bugge.' haues mi luue chepet.

---

[1] This designation is chosen because these pieces are all concerned with wooing (praise and, especially, supplication); and all, except N(Le) and R, with mystic love. Moreover, the *Wohunge* itself is the finest of them. *On God Ureisun of ure Lefdi* (also in N) is not here included, because it is in rhymed and metred couplets, and is in other ways very different from this group.

[2] *Carmina Varia* VII in *Patr. Lat.* clxxi. 1651. See Appendix. Marbod's connexion with England is apparent from his having written epitaphs on Lanfranc and Anselm and addressed poems to Matilda (consort of Henry I) and to Ermenegard, 'uxori Alani, Britanniae ducis'.

[3] *Specimens*, i. 124.   [4] AR 181/10 f.

Problems of Origin and Literary Relationship xv

There are many incidental verbal similarities (pointed out, where they occur, in notes to the text); but no other passage of such length, either in the *Riwle* or the other related writings, corresponds so closely with any of the 'Wooing Group'. However, lines 625-34 of the *Wohunge*:

ȝette ȝif þ i mi luue bede for to selle. ⁊ sette feor þer upon swa hehe swa ich eauer wile.' ȝette þu wult hit habbe ⁊ teken al þ tu haues ȝiuen.' wiltu eke mare. ⁊ ȝif i þe riht luuie. wilt me crune in heuene wið þe self to rixlen werld in to werlde

might certainly bring to mind the following (or vice versa):

ȝif þin luue is so to sullen.' ich habbe ibouht hire mid luue ouer alle oðre ... and ȝif þu seist. þet tu nult nout leten þer on soliht cheap. auh wultu ȝet more.' nem hwat hit schule beon. Sete feor oþine luue. þu ne schalt siggen so muchel. þet ich nulle ȝiuen ðe. uor þine luue.' muchele more.... Wultu welden al þene world.... ich chulle makien þe mid al þis. cwene of heouene.¹

Earlier in the *Riwle* there is a typical crucifixion which could virtually be put together out of bits and pieces of the *Wohunge*,² and has strong kinship at least with lines 43-57 of the *Lofsong of ure Lefdi*. Thus:

þencheð euer inwardliche up o godes pinen. þet te worldes weldinde wolde uor his þrelles.' þolien swuche schendlakes. ⁊ hokeres. buffetes. spotlunge. blindfellunge. þornene crununge. þet set him iðet heaued.' so þet þe blodi streames urnen adun. ⁊ bileaueden his swete bodi ibunden naked to þe herde pilere. ant ibeaten so.' þet tet deoruwurðe blod orn adun on eueriche halue.³

Indeed a number of the most striking utterances in our texts have their counterparts elsewhere. For example:

(1) Nis na trewe ifere þe nule naut scottin in þe lure. ase in þe biȝete. (L 59 f.)

nis he neuer god feolawe ... þet nule scotten iðe lure.' ase eft iðe biȝeate. (AR 163/24 f.)

¹ AR 181/23 f.
² e.g. *herteliche þenke þat i for þe luue of þe polede schome ⁊ bismere. and schomeliche spateling* (406-9), *schendlac* (393), *buffetes* (461), *⁊ haðfule hokeres* (371), *(þe) þ demere art of werlde* (377-8).... *Siðen o þin heaued wes set te crune of sharpe þornes. þ wið eauriche þorn wrang ut te reade blod* (481-4). *Siðen bifore pilat hu þu was naket bunden faste to þe piler* (473-5), *⁊ beten* (473), *⁊ al þi blisfule bodi streamed on a Girre blod* (479-81).
³ AR 83/8 ff.

(2) Ne wene nomon to stihen wið este to þe steorren. (N(U) 76 f.)
ne wene non mid este: stien to þe steorren. (AR 165/26 f.)

(3) al þ pinende pik. ne walde ham þunche bote a softe bekinde bað. (W 42–44.)
a ueat . . . wið pich . . . warð hire ase wunsum as þah hit were a wlech beað. (J(B) 673 ff.)

(4) te sunne were dosk ȝif hit to þi blisfule bleo mihte beo euenet. (W 50–52.)
for aȝein þe brihtnesse ⁊ te liht of his leor. þe sunne gleam is dosc. (SW 26/246 f.)

If we add to these similarities of subject-matter and phraseology, the nearness in date, the affinities of dialect, and the existence of numerous manuscripts of the *Riwle*, it seems probable that the 'Wooing Group' may have been influenced by it. But there is no proof of this. Influence of the saints' lives in the 'Katherine Group' and, to a less extent, of *Hali Meiðhad* and *Sawles Warde* might also be claimed, if not so convincingly; and the *Wohunge* has been called 'the thoughts and prayers of Juliene written out at large'.[1]

Moreover, the several pieces of the 'Wooing Group' (other than as parallel versions) not infrequently echo one another, where perhaps some common sources are involved. For example:

(1) ase wis ase a drope of þine deorewurðe blode. muhte weaschen awei alle folkes fulðe.' ase wis liues louerd þeo ilke fif wellen of þine blisfule bodie sprungen ⁊ striken dun strundes of blode. weasch mine fif wittes.' of alle blodie sunnen. (N(U) 110 ff.)

ase wis ase a drope of þine deorewurðe blode þ tu o rode scheddest were inouh to weaschen alle folkes fulðe. þeo sterke stremes ⁊ þet flod þet fleaw of þine wunden. moncun uor to helen.' clense ⁊ weasch mine sunfule soule þuruh þine fif wunden iopened o rode. wið neiles uor driuene ⁊ seoruh fulliche fordutte. hel me uorwunded þuruh mine fif wittes wið deadliche sunnen. (N(Lo) 43 ff.)

(2) þi deað.' a deadie in me flesches licunge.' ⁊ licamliche lustes. and makien me liuien to þe ðet ich muwe seggen wið seinte powel ðet seið. Ich liuiee nout ich.' auh crist liueð in me. (N(U) 120 ff.)

ði deað adeadie þe deaðliche lustes of mine licame. . . . ⁊ euer liuie to þe. þ ich muwe siggen wið seinte powel þet seið. ich liuie nout ich.' auh crist liueð in me. (N(Lo) 60 f., 67 ff.)[2]

---

[1] d'Ardenne, p. xliii.   [2] See note to N(Lo) 60–64.

Problems of Origin and Literary Relationship xvii

(3) ȝet ase halewen weneð. þet [s]oðe blod rune. was in his ereste. nimunge in þe feste bindunge. þet tet blod wrong ut et his eadie neiles. (N(Le) 61 ff.)

i þin earst niminge ... hu ha þe bunden swa hetelifaste þ te blod wrang ut at tine finger neiles as halhes bileuen. (W 463, 467 ff.)

These recurrent parallels undoubtedly indicate the emergence of a native tradition with a somewhat conventionalized phraseology, much influenced by Latin writers and by the *Song of Songs*. There are thus many more or less corresponding passages in popular clerical writings such as Anselm's *Meditations*, Bernard's twentieth Sermon on the *Song of Songs*, and Hugh of St. Victor's *De Anima*. For example:

Tu es Deus meus vivus, Christus meus sanctus, Dominus meus pius, rex meus magnus, pastor meus bonus ... dilectus meus pulcherrimus ... lux mea verax, dulcedo mea sancta, vita mea recta ... portio mea bona, salus mea sempiterna, misericordia mea magna ... spes mea firma, charitas mea perfecta ... exsultatio et vita mea beatissima sine fine mansura.[1]

which corresponds in a general way to much that is in the opening lines of the *Wohunge* or the *Ureisun*; but not verbally, and not to the extent that it must be regarded as a source, though there is no way of determining whether the author(s) had it in mind or not. Vollhardt, who studied this problem, did not find any closer parallels than this, but he did show that, in places where the *Riwle*, &c., correspond with the 'Wooing Group', there are often possible Latin parallels to be found.[2]

Similar parallels might be found in other vernacular literatures of the period, especially in Anglo-Norman. However, the discovery of parallels, enlightening as it may be as to the strength of a tradition, is very different from the discovery of sources. Apparent sincerity and independent artistic merit give the 'Wooing Group' the stamp of originality. If direct sources are ever discovered for others of the group, it is safe to assume that these sources have been handled with the freedom and improvisation, within the native idiom and tradition, which characterized

---

[1] Anselm, *Med.* XVIII in *Patr. Lat.* clviii. 798; cf. *Med.* x ibid., p. 762.
[2] W. Vollhardt, *Einfluß der lateinischen geistlichen Litteratur auf einige kleinere Schöpfungen der englischen Übergangsperiode* (diss., Leipzig, 1888)

English devotional writing from Ælfric onwards. Skilful assimilation of this kind is apparent from a comparison of the *Lofsong of ure Lefdi* with its source (given here as an appendix) and then with the other works of the group. As Professor Tolkien has said of *Sawles Warde*, 'it is not novice translation-prose at all'.[1]

The pieces of the 'Wooing Group' represent the increasing preoccupation with the Passion and with the possibilities of mystical communion which was a part of the emotionalizing of Latin Christianity which had been proceeding since the eleventh century; and they illustrate 'the realistic, pathetic manner ... coming into fashion in the thirteenth century'.[2] According to Miss Allen, English mysticism was especially characterized by its interest in personal devotion, more than in metaphysics or visions, and that devotion less concerned with the cult of the Blessed Virgin so popular in the thirteenth century than with that of the Holy Name of Jesus. The *Lofsong of ure Lefdi*, though addressed to the Virgin, is not concerned with her cult. It is a plea for her intercession,[3] contrasting the sinfulness of the speaker with the passion and triumph of Christ. It closely resembles much of the *Wohunge*. The *Ancrene Riwle* and the 'Wooing Group' also represented the beginning of the use of terms proper to the worldly conception of knightly character and courtly love to express more spiritual conceptions—such words as *gentilesse*, *hendeleic*, *largesce*, &c., which in this way became elevated.[4]

However, in addition to these similarities, there are also great differences. The 'Wooing Group' differs markedly in kind and degree, or both, from the monitory and domestic parts of the

[1] Tolkien, p. 113.

[2] H. E. Allen, 'The Mystical Lyrics of the *Manuel des Pechiez*', *Romanic Rev.* ix (1918), 162.

[3] What Miss Allen calls 'the familiar and realistic appeal to her maternity, which was the latest development of all' is present in these pieces (ibid., p. 164).

[4] This blending may reflect increasing disapproval of courtly love—by adapting what one could of it to religious use. But cf. ten Brink (*E.E. Lit.* i. 200): 'Divine love (*die Gottesminne*), in the mediaeval sense, became a new theme in English literature, before secular love-poetry ... could take root there.' Similarly G. R. Owst, *Literature and Pulpit in Medieval England* (Cambridge, 1933), p. 16: 'In its first beginnings, indeed, the religious love-lyric in this country may well have been a direct product of homiletic fervour, rather than a mild imitation of worldly love-songs.'

Problems of Origin and Literary Relationship xix

Riwle, from the miraculous narratives of the 'Katherine Group', and from homiletic tracts like *Sawles Warde* and *Hali Meiðhad*. It has little of hell's terrors or the loathsomeness of human life and functions; and it does not seek to confound 'fifti scolmeistres' with 'flowinde wettres of wittie wordes'.[1] It is meditative and emotional rather than logical—the *Wohunge* seems less logical than it actually is. The use of the first person gives the whole group an intimacy which these other works inevitably do not possess.

In a word the 'Wooing Group' is lyrical. Taken together, these little 'mystical rhapsodies' are all, like the *Ancrene Riwle* and the 'Katherine Group', related to native pre-Conquest traditions in prose and verse. But they are also closely related to the contemporary (verse) lyric with its Franco-Latin background; and it is significant that the principal home of the lyric in the thirteenth century was also in the West.[2] The following is typical:

> Iesu, of loue soth tocknynge,
> þin armes spredeþ to mankynde,
> þin heued doun-boweþ to swete cussinge,
> þin side al openeþ to loue-longynge.
>
> Iesu, when ich þenke on þe
> ant loke vpon þe rode-tre,
> þi suete body to-toren y se,
> hit makeþ heorte to smerte me.[3]

Of the pieces in the 'Wooing Group', the *Wohunge* and the *Ureisun* are most alike. In the latter, however, the emotion seems less intense. There is less of ecstatic mysticism, more of the 'long wone of gostlich elne'. 'Woa is me þet ich am so freomede wið þe' is its despairing cry. Possible influence of the *Poema Morale* on these prose lyrics would best be seen here. The *Lofsong of ure Louerde* is similar, but more reserved and conventional, possibly because of a more allegorical view of the mystic marriage. The *Lofsong of ure Lefdi*, despite its Latin source, reads like another

---

[1] K 521, 687/8.

[2] 'There is intimate relation of the vocabulary and formulas (alliterative and other) in A and B both to the westerly lyric, whose little world lay between the Wirral and the Wye, and to the specifically alliterative verse.' Tolkien, p. 116.

[3] *Dulcis Iesu memoria* (MS. Harl. 2253), ll. 57–64, given in Horstmann, *Yorkshire Writers*, ii. 15.

version of the confessional part of the *Ureisun* and the crucifixion in the *Wohunge*.

These pieces are an important part of the background of later mystical writing in England, in general and somewhat in particular too. For instance, Morris described the late thirteenth-century *Luue Ron*[1] as 'a poetical version' of the *Wohunge*,[2] apparently because it similarly presents Christ as the ideal *leman*, who is fairest, truest, richest, joyous in appearance and living in a dwelling full of bliss—thoughts which indeed need not have come from the *Wohunge*. Otherwise the impersonal, rather cold and severe *Ron* is very different in style and tone. Much more convincing evidence of the popularity and influence of the 'Wooing Group' is found in *A Talkyng of þe Loue of God*[3] which Konrath showed to be a pastiche, of which the first part is paraphrased from the *Ureisun of God Almihti* and the last part from the *Wohunge*.[4] As Miss Allen says, 'The whole development of English mysticism may turn out to be indicated in the genealogy of the *Talkyng of the Love of God*.'[5]

Already in the early thirteenth century the desire for mystical communion ranges from the literal realism of earthly passion:

wið him þu schalt wealden, as wið þi were iwedded, world buten ende, heuenriche winnen. Eadi is his spuse, hwas meidenhad is unwemmed, hwen he on hire streoneð; ⁊ hwen ha teameð of him, ne swinkeð ne ne pineð.[6]

to fantasies of more ethereal rapture:

let me beo þi leouemon ⁊ siggen ase heo seið. leof wið þi luft erm. þ is. wið þine worldliche ȝeouen hold up min heawed ðet ich þuruh to muche wone ne falle i fulðe of sunne. ⁊ leof wið þin riht erm. þ is in heuene wið endelease blissen biclupe me abuten.[7]

The mystical marriage is symbolical; but whether, in any particular instance, the *himmelsbraut* is a particular woman, or man

[1] ed. Morris, *Old Eng. Misc.* (E.E.T.S., o.s. 49, 1872).
[2] *Specimens*, i. 124.
[3] Ed. M. Salvina Westra, The Hague, 1950.
[4] M. Konrath, 'Eine übersehene Fassung der Ureisun of oure Louerde, bez. Ureisun of God Almihti ... und der Wohunge of ure Lauerd', *Anglia*, xlii (1918), 85 f.
[5] H. E. Allen, op. cit., p. 187.　　　　[6] HM (T) 55/586 ff.
[7] N(Lo) 119 ff. Of N(Lo) Wells nevertheless says 'In its ardor, the piece largely loses the spiritual in the physical' (*Manual*, p. 528).

Problems of Origin and Literary Relationship xxi

(the soul in either sex being feminine), or humanity as a whole, or Holy Church, or the world, or any complex of these, is often very difficult to decide.[1] Yet the question of authorship is closely related to this decision.

It is not known who wrote any of the pieces in the 'Wooing Group'; and, since no external evidence of their authorship has been discovered, conjectures (and there have been quite a few) have had to rely on internal evidence of a rather general kind. The most interesting conjecture is that of Einenkel:[2] that the preponderance of enthusiasm and fantasy over thought and the 'innigkeit' bespoke feminine (and spontaneous) composition— whether by one or more women (and by whom) he was not sure. However, noting that the three anchoresses of the *Riwle* are told 'ȝe habbeð of þeos blissen iwriten on oþer stude',[3] he asked if the *Wohunge*, at least, might not be the work of one of them. We should then infer (from the *Wohunge*) that she was a woman of privileged birth (because of her skill in reading and writing), who suffered some sharp reversal, was deserted by kith and kin,[4] had constantly to struggle against world, flesh, and devil because of a passionate nature—whose authorship would also indicate a cultivated religious milieu. Many other suggestions have been offered.[5]

[1] Morris, ten Brink, and Vollhardt considered that the allegorical aspect was uppermost in these works, Einenkel (in view of his theory of authorship—see n. 2 below) that it was not. In paraphrasing the *Wohunge*, the *Talkyng* has: 'þou ... robbedest helle.' and laddest out þi deore léef. *þat is monnes soule*'—but the italicized words have no counterpart in the *Wohunge*.

[2] E. Einenkel, 'Eine englische Schriftstellerin aus dem Anfange des 12. Jahrhunderts', *Anglia*, v (1882), 265 ff.

[3] AR 187/15.

[4] *borne breðre hauen me forwurpen* (W 244 f.); but even this is conventional. Both Margaret and Juliana are *forwurpen* for their faith by parents.

[5] Vollhardt sought to show that qualities Einenkel thought feminine could be found in Latin parallels written by men. Morris (*OE. Hom.*, pp. ix, x): 'From internal evidence I am convinced that "The Wooing", in its *original* form, was by the same author as the "Ancren Riwle", &c.' d'Ardenne (p. xliii): 'If X [the hypothetical author of the contents of MS. Bodley 34] wrote all B, he certainly also wrote the *Wohunge*.' Hall (ii, p. 505) proposes one author, Gilbert of Sempringham, for the whole of MS. Titus D. xviii. Wilson (*Sawles Warde*, p. xl): 'Every single student of the texts must make up his own mind on this point [of authorship], and he can hardly hope to convince anyone else that his own point of view is necessarily correct.' This would apply here.

Although the authorship cannot be determined, recent studies have added greatly to our knowledge of the western culture which produced so many important works concerned with women. That there should emerge therefrom a gifted woman writer—though not necessarily one of the three anchoresses—is by no means impossible in an age which idealized saints like Margaret, Katherine, and Juliana, and in real life produced Hildegard of Bingen and Elizabeth of Schönau. Whoever wrote the *Wohunge* has left it strongly marked with individuality, immediacy, and an almost complete independence of conventual surroundings, earthly intercessors, and hierarchical orders: marked with a passionate elevation which has much less of the sense of sin than most of the related writings, and a self-absorption of will and heart leading to the all but entire self-forgetfulness which marks the true mystic. These qualities would indicate, to those who sense them, that it is unlikely that the *Wohunge* was written vicariously, or that it is chiefly an allegory; and that it is likely that it was written by a gifted woman.

She would later have passed it to some *leue suster* for the latter's comfort and edification. Did she then try to repeat herself with less success ? Or did one or more sisters, with less art, try to imitate her ? Either conjecture might account for the *Ureisun* and *Lofsong* addressed to *ure Louerde*. The *Lofsong of ure Lefdi* is less strongly marked by feminine authorship and might have been written, though not necessarily, by a man. These possibilities must be noted: but, because of the many conventions and the many parallels, they are possibilities only.

FORM AND STYLE

As meditative and emotional prose lyrics, the 'Wooing Group' have something of the free improvisation of the usual *bussgebet*. But they are enough alike to indicate certain conventions of content and, apparently, of structure. The *Ureisun*, for example, is not divisible into parts, yet it amplifies a discernible pattern of development, thus:

Salutation: Iesu soð god soð godes sune . . . &c. (N(U) 1 f.)
Invocation: aliht mine þeostri heorte . . . &c. (15 f.)

Form and Style

Confession: woa is me þet ich am so freomede wið þe . . . &c. (20 f.)

Contemplation of the Passion: hu þu streihtest þe for me on þe rode . . . &c. (47 f.)

Aspiration unto mystic love:
hwi ne worpe ich me bi tweonen þeo ilke ermes . . . &c. (48 f.)
hwi ne con ich wowen þe. wið swete luue wordes . . . &c. (86 f.)

Petition to the Virgin for her intercession:
help me englene cwene of heouene . . . &c. (130 f.)

Final supplication:
a iesu hwuder schal ich fleon . . . bute to þine rode ? (162 f.)

The *Lofsong of ure Louerde* is wrought out of the same elements (except the petition to the Virgin), and the *Wohunge* contains all these and more. In each of the three pieces addressed to *ure Louerde*, the impulse to mystic union provides an emotional and structural climax. In the *Lofsong of ure Lefdi* this is absent: but a parallel spiritual ascent is implicit in the vision of 'syon þe heie tur of heouene' in the last lines of the work.

That the *Wohunge* is not merely derivative but an achievement of independent art is nowhere more evident than in its well-knit form, of which the sections are marked off by the refrain-like prayer:

A iesu swete iesu leue þ te luue of þe beo al mi likinge.

The method probably owes much to homiletic tradition: after orderly exegesis of Iesu's qualities as perfect lover, there is much in what follows that suggests the *applicatio* and *peroratio* of the sermon. The piece lends itself to systematic outline:

A. Salutation and preliminary *expositio* of what makes any man 'love-worthy' (1–32).

  B. Iesu excels every man in 'love-worthy' qualities (32–262):
     Feirnesse (32–55)—Refrain.
     Richesce (57–77)—Refrain.
     Largesce (79–105)—Refrain.
     Wisdom (107–17)—Refrain.
     Strengðe and *Hardischipe* (119–58)—Refrain.
     Gentilesce (160–94)—Refrain.
     Meknesse and *Mildschipe* (196–215)—Refrain.

xxiv   *Introduction*

      Sibnesse (217–51)—Refrain.
      Summary (252–62).

C. But Iesu, *tat kidde keiser cruned in heuene*, has spiritual qualities surpassing all these (262–546):
    He has championed the speaker's soul against her foes (269–308).
    He has taught her to endure poverty, shame, and pain (308–553):
      Poverty, through his life on earth (317–64)—Refrain.
      Shame, through his revilement and degradation (365–437)
      —Refrain (slightly elaborated).
      Pain of body and soul, through his crucifixion and death (440–553).

D. Conclusion (554–644):
    Petition to the Virgin (554–68).
    Personal surrender and identification with Iesu in his love and Passion (568–619).
    Summary of the whole *Wohunge* (619–34).
    Refrain (much elaborated, 635–44).

(E. Envoy to 'mi leue suster', 645–58.)

In spite of this methodical structure, the *Wohunge* gives the impression of warm spontaneity. It moves forward with ever-increasing intensity to a climax where pathos, horror, devotion, and submission are all compact. At the conclusion, describing the agonies of the Passion with strong realism, the writer changes suddenly into the present tense[1]—not merely the historical present, or the artifice of prosopopoeia—for she has so identified herself with the Christ as to experience his sufferings anew. The style is sometimes diffuse and repetitive, but beneath it thought and emotion are full of movement and life.

The whole 'Wooing Group' belongs to the tradition of rhythmic, alliterative prose which is found in the 'Katherine Group' and derives its patterns ultimately from the late Old English prose of such works as Ælfric's *Lives* and Wulfstan's homilies.[2] Its rhythm results from an ever-varied interweaving of phrases, now strictly parallel, now less symmetrical, with a musical adjustment of the

---

[1] 491 f.
[2] See Angus McIntosh, 'Wulfstan's Prose', *Proc. Brit. Acad.* xxxv (1949), 109 ff.; R. W. Chambers, *The Continuity of English Prose* (E.E.T.S., o.s. 191A, 1932); D. Bethurum, 'The Connection of the Katherine Group with Old English Prose', *J.E.G.P.* xxxiv (1935), 553 ff.

Form and Style

rise, fall, and flow of sentences, enforced and enriched by alliteration, and generally clarified by the semi-rhetorical punctuation used. The opening lines of the *Wohunge* are noteworthy in this respect; and might be rearranged to show the patterns more plainly:

Iesu swete iesu.

mi druð.
mi derling.
mi drihtin.

mi healend.
mi huniter.
mi haliwei.

Swetter is munegunge of þe þen mildeu o muðe.

Hwa ne mei luue þi luueli leor?
Hwat herte is swa hard þ ne mei to melte
iþe munegunge of þe?

Ah hwa ne mej luue þe luueliche iesu?

Writing of this sort is prose, not verse; and attempts to scan similar pieces as poetry have produced distortion.[1] The fact is that there are passages (like that just quoted) in which there can be found a fairly regularly recurring stress;[2] yet to read them with the measured movement of verse is to destroy their otherwise

---

[1] See Wilson, *Sawles Warde*, p. xl f. Einenkel printed *Katherine* in four-beat couplets, to be associated, he argued, with the metres of Laȝamon and the OHG. poet Otfrid. Wagner put *Sawles Warde* into 1,072 lines of similar kind, representing, he said, 362 variants of five basic rhythmic patterns. O. Victor (*Zur Textkritik u. Metrik der frühmittelenglischen Katherinenlegende*, Bonn, 1912) claimed that the punctuation was to divide this sort of prose into more or less regular metrical units. Schipper (*Hist. Engl. Versification*, pp. 85 f.), Luick (*Anglia Beiblatt* xxiii (1912), 228), and Hall (op. cit.) are among those who argued against such views.

[2] In W, one or two metred and rhymed couplets do occur—in all likelihood fortuitously: *wið þi blod þu haues me boht. ʏ fram þe world þu haues me broht* (578 f.) may recall a favourite verse. *Lauerd hwat mai i ȝelde þe for al þ tu haues giuen me* (582 f.) translates the Psalmist. *For hwen ... pine* (599–602) is much more debatable. The antistrophic clauses, each ending with *me* (637–42), may be intentional rhetoric, but need not be regarded as poetry. Comparison of W with more measured parts of the *Talkyng* based on it makes the prose quality of the former very apparent. See Westra, op. cit., pp. xxii, xxiii.

natural modulation as prose. But mainly they do not exhibit the phrase rhythms of poetry—the *tendency* to conform to a line length—and to divide them thus leads to great complexity and syntactical dislocation. The punctuation chiefly marks off segments of a prose phrase rhythm, which as a rule are syntactic units as well.[1] Such apparently is what the author of the *Talkyng of þe Loue of God* meant in saying that 'Men schal fynden lihtliche þis tretys in Cadence. After þe bigynninge. ȝif hit beo riht poynted.'[2] It is to be read, he says, 'esyliche and softe. So as men may mest in Inward felyng. and deplich þenkyng. sauour fynden.' The prose of the 'Wooing Group', such as the passage just given from the *Wohunge*, with its alliterations and other blending of soft sounds, suggests oral reading of a similar kind.

This passage will also serve to show that the 'Wooing Group' has been influenced by the practice of Latin and probably by the study of classical rhetoric as an inevitable part of medieval education. There is no doubt that, from Alfred onwards, the development of English syntax towards the kinds of stylization that make for clarity and cogency benefited greatly from this influence—and yet remained remarkably idiomatic and native. It is possible that in the 'Wooing Group', as in the *Talkyng*, 'so complete a treatment of the chosen themes suggests regard for the principles of rhetorical *inventio*'[3] also in some general way. Since classical rhetoric (or *dispositio*) provides fearsome names for most of the fortuitous nuances of speech, one may discern in the short phrases at the opening of the *Ureisun* (L): *iesu soð god. soð mon* a polyptoton; *soð mon. Mon Meidene bern*, an anadiplosis. Analysis of this kind is extremely interesting; but it hardly leads to the con-

[1] The punctuation is most clearly related to stylistic patterns in N, R, and W. In L, it is often confused and confusing.

[2] See Margery M. Morgan, 'A Treatise in Cadence', *M.L.R.*, xlvii (1952), 156 ff., and Skeat's note on the rhythm of *De Octo Vitiis* in Morris, *OE. Hom.*, pp. 329 f. Cf. W. 651–3: '*carpe* toward iesu ⁊ seie þise wordes.'

[3] Margery M. Morgan, '*A Talkyng of the Love of God* and the Continuity of Stylistic Tradition in Middle English Prose Meditations', *R.E.S.*, N.S. iii (1952), 103. See also Agnes Mary Humbert, *Verbal Repetition in the Ancrene Riwle* (Washington, 1944), and Bethurum, op. cit. Concerning the 'Katherine Group', Miss Bethurum says: 'In the matter of style, there is no influence from the Latin accounts. The Latin lives are not without the customary devices of rhetoric, but they have no correspondents in English' (p. 563)—a rather extreme view.

Form and Style

clusion that these pieces exemplify 'a unified system of rhetoric'; and I think the question must be left open whether they were exercises in rhetoric at all. Rhetoric they have; as has all impassioned utterance. Their style is the style of a school, of their day, and of their ancestry. It was already old in its devices, which had probably long since become largely an unconscious element in literary technique.

The diction of the group is derived from a literary medium both educated (rather than learned) and highly conventional. It is for this reason chiefly that they have so many verbal similarities with related works. Descriptive and alliterating tags such as *lastelese lates, lufsum leor, heaðene hundes, kid keiser, wode wulues*; doublets such as *beih ⁊ buh, meknesse ⁊ mildschipe, weole ⁊ wunne, wit ⁊ wisdom*; catch-phrases such as *godd of alle god ful, mine heorte eihen, schuppere of alle schaftes*—familiar to all readers of the literature of this period—appear and often reappear. But, on the whole, the 'Wooing Group' is less conspicuously dependent on verbiage of this kind than the 'Katherine Group'. Passages like

hwi ne worpe ich me bi tweonen þeo ilke ermes so swiðe wiðe to spredde. ⁊ i openeð so þe moder deð hire ermes. hire leoue child for to bi cluppen? ȝe soðes. (N(U) 48–52)

and:

A swete iesu þu oppnes me þin herte for to cnawe witerliche ⁊ in to reden trewe luue lettres. for þer i mai openlich seo hu muchel þu me luuedes. (W 546–51)

illustrate the fresh unhackneyed use of words, most of which had served Englishmen for religious expression since Anglo-Saxon days. Yet much of the vocabulary, so far as we may judge, is also rare or new;[1] and, considering the size of these texts, the proportion of foreign words, Latin, French, and Norse, is noteworthy evidence of cultivated authorship.

On the whole, the style is very different from that of the *Ancrene Riwle*. The latter is less rhythmic and alliterative, more

---

[1] According to *O.E.D.*: (1) the following words are first recorded in our texts: *dunchen, druggunge, moder-sune, nacnes, rattes*; (2) the following occur only here: *biclaried*(?), *bekinde, todunet*; (3) the following, in appearing here, are earlier than first instances of them listed by the *O.E.D.*: *A* interj., *cwedli, heht* pp., *hendeleic, lahter* meaning 'subject for laughter', and *mades* pt.

xxviii *Introduction*

learned and plain, with a fondness for citations, exempla, overt moralizing, scholastic interpretations, bestiary motifs, and metaphors—so different that it could hardly be from the hand that wrote any of the 'Wooing Group'.[1] The 'Katherine Group' is different again. Yet all these works represent varieties of that West Midland prose which transmitted the literary impulse of pre-Conquest England to the next century and beyond. As Chambers said, 'It is strange to reflect how our English prose has been handed down to Tudor times, from the days of King Alfred and Abbot Ælfric, not by clerks working in the royal chancelleries, but through books originally written to be read in lonely anchorholds or quiet nunneries: retreats like those of the three sisters of the *Riwle*, or the sister to whom *The Wooing of our Lord* was addressed.'[2]

LANGUAGE

The study of the language is in two parts:

1. In the Phonology and Accidence the four manuscripts are treated together in order to show more clearly their linguistic affinities and divergences. Developments consistent or not consistent with AB, or widespread in ME., are noted. Since these are all mixed texts, OE. origins given in the Phonology are early enough to indicate sources from which divergent developments, when they occur, have sprung. Quotation of forms is illustrative only, since all forms in these texts are listed, with their frequencies, in the Glossary.

2. The following section on Dialect, &c., summarizes the most significant evidence thus accumulated; and, from this and other kinds of evidence, attempts to weigh and identify the different linguistic ingredients in each of these texts, taken separately.

Since the particular antecedents of AB and its close relationship to the language of the Vespasian Psalter (VP) have been extensively studied by Tolkien, d'Ardenne, and others, reference will simply be made to their work, where necessary. In no one of the present texts can the language be derived entirely from OAB.

[1] There are two examples of the practice (frequent in the *Riwle*) of following a Latin quotation with a long free-construed rendering (W 403 ff., 581 ff.).   [2] Op. cit., p. cxxxii.

Language

The abbreviations W, N, R, L refer specifically only to the texts in this volume. Usually the first three of these are consistent with the remainder of the manuscripts from which, in each case, they are taken. But the L text, *On Ureisun of ure Louerde*, is in a different hand from the pieces that precede it in MS. Lambeth 487 and represents a somewhat different scribal tradition.

PHONOLOGY

Vowels in stressed syllables

OE. *a* before nasals

Before nasals the norm for all these texts and for AB is *o* (as *moni, hond, longe*), but in W, where *o* : *a* = 6 : 1, the *a*-forms are frequent enough to suggest the admixture of another dialectal element. Here Class III strong preterites always have *a*.

The preservation in N and R of *þen(e)* acc. s. (deriving from OE. forms with æ, *e*, beside *o*) occurs also in AB. The similar forms *hwen, þen,* adv. were widespread in ME.

NL *þeonne* adv. is probably influenced by ME. *heonne* (OE. *heonan*); W *eorn* pt. is a misspelling caused by *eorðe* in the same line.

Angl. *al*+consonant

Probably all the forms in these texts are to be referred to Angl. *al* (as *alle, cwalm*), not WS. *eal*; since when lengthened, as before *ld*, we have *a* [ā] beside the later development of *o* [ǭ] which is normal in N and occasional in L (as *halden, monifald,* beside *biholdeð, twofold*).[1] AB has *a*-forms only.

OE. *a* in open syllables

Normally *a*-forms (only) occur in these texts, and were widespread in ME. There is no trace of the characteristic *ea* of AB (and VP): hence we have here *atol, gladien*. Since this *ea* did not appear in AB before *l*, or gutturals *k, h, (ʒ), x*, the *a* in forms like *baluful, schal, make, drahe*, is consistent with AB.[2]

In N *scheadewe, schea*- probably continues OE. *scea*- with *e*

---

[1] In *monifald* and *twofold* the last syllable does not bear full stress.
[2] d'Ardenne, §§ 2(i), 4, 5 (n. 2).

Introduction

indicating the palatal quality of the consonant; N *ischeapen* may be similarly explained.

Prim. OE. æ

This presents difficulty since in some areas, including parts of OMerc., Prim. OE. æ became *e*, while in early ME. texts, wholly or partly of other origin, variation between *e* and *a* spellings may be due simply to orthographic attempts to represent unchanged OE. [æ].[1]

AB, N, and R normally write *e* which is probably the sequel of Merc. *e* for Prim. OE. æ (as *feste, efter, þet*). L normally has *a* (as *faste, after, þat*) which is probably characteristic of this text's non-AB ingredient in which OE. æ > *a*.

Dialectal admixture is probably indicated by the occasional appearance in N of non-AB *a*-forms (as *blase, hwat, was*); in L of AB *e*-forms (as *hwet, wes*), though *wes* was widespread. N and L also have a few forms with *ea* (as N *weaschen*, L *eafter*) which may be blends. Most mixed is the language of W, which uses both *e* and *a* in the proportion of 1:2 (as *hefde/hafde, wes/was, hwat*).

The sequel of OE. æ irregularly developed is seen in L *steapes* (OE. *stæpe*), where N aberrantly has *steopes*.

OE. *ear*+consonant

In LOE., *ea* of any origin > æ, and is thus one of the chief sources of [æ] in OAB (where normally older Prim. OE. æ had > *e*: see above); but the *ea*-spelling was regularly preserved in AB. Thus AB has *bearn, dear, hearde, hearm*, &c., while in N and L the normal spelling is *e* (as N *bern, erm, herde*, L *bern, derf*). Probably all these spellings still represent [æ].

Dialectal admixture is more apparent in R and W. The norm of R is *a* (as *dar, harde, harm*) which probably represents a development of [æ] > [ɑ], as in the case of L *a*-forms from Prim. OE. æ (see above);[2] but R also has occasional *e*-spellings (as *bern*). In W, the proportion of *a*- to *ea*-forms is 14:5 (as *hard* beside *bearn, earmes*), which no doubt indicates mixture of dialect to some extent; yet most of its *a*-forms are possible in AB (as *scharpe*,

---

[1] Mack, p. xxxv, n. 3; d'Ardenne, § 1.
[2] d'Ardenne, § 3, n. 3.

Phonology

toward): after *w, ch, sch, ʒ, a* appears normally in AB[1] and in all these texts. The verb form *art* is also regular in AB, R, W, and L, but *ert* is the only spelling in N and occurs (once) in L.

OE. *a* in reduced stress

In some cases *a* appears where OE. has *a* instead of *æ*, probably owing to low tone or lack of stress. Thus we have *ac* (Merc. *ah*) 'but', *haueð* (Merc. *hafað*) 'has'.

Front Mutation of Prim. OE. *a/æ*

Front mutation of Prim. OE. *a* and *æ*, as sources of the above developments, appeared in these texts and in AB normally as *e* (as *men, tellen, heriede, ʒerde*); but occasionally in AB and R, and once in W, we have *eal* representing *æl* the mutation of Angl. *al* (as W *wealdes*). In W *wearnen* (OE. *wærnen*), *ea* probably represents a more opened *e* before *r*+cons. (as rarely in AB, especially in OF. words like *mearci*):[2] the other manuscripts have forms of *wernen*.

Aberrant forms: W *igedered*, pp. is from OE. *gaderian* but with the stem vowel of OE. -*gædere* (< **gædyri* < **gaduri*). W *forwariede* is an AB form with *a* from *wari* adj., or from OE. **wærigan* (related to *wergan*). W and AB *lahhen* is probably from OAngl. **hlæhhjan* with *æ* retracted to *a* (instead of breaking) before *hh*, and then mutated to *æ*; or it may be from *hlæhtor*, n. W and AB *schuppere* represents either the spread into other dialects of WS. forms of religious words, or the independent development elsewhere of *e* > *y* between *sc* and *p*: even Orm has it.

L *suggen* and N *siggen* (beside W and N *seggen*: OE. *secgan*) show a modification of *e* between *s* and *cg* (as between *s* and *l*, cf. *suluen*, where LWS. *se* > **sie, sy*). *Suggen*, which points to an unrecorded LOE. **sycgan*, frequently occurs in texts written in or copied from WM. (e.g. Laʒamon's *Brut*), but AB has *seggen*. *Siggen* shows raising of *e* to *i* as in MKent. *zigge* (Ayenbite).

OE. *e*

Where breaking or mutation is not involved, OE. *e* remains in all manuscripts (as *efne, help, wel*) and in AB.

---

[1] Ibid., § 2(ii).   [2] Ibid., § 3(b).

N *freomede* adj. (OE. and L *fremede*) probably imitates numerous regular *eo*-forms in this text.

OE. *eo* from breaking and back mutation

In AB and all these texts except W, the normal spelling is *eo*, which probably represents the sound [ö] in ME. (as *eorðe, heorte, seolf, heouene*). In W the spelling *e* is about twice as frequent as *eo*, and dialectal admixture is clearly seen in such variants as *herte/heorte, heuene/heouene*. In N, *e*-forms also occur rarely (as *heuene* beside *heouene*, where the spelling *heuene*, like N *orðe*, may be due to accidental omission of a letter).

The *eo* also appears in Anglian, from back mutation, in the present stem of strong verbs of Classes IV and V (whence AB and N ʒ*eouen*); and, already in OE., sometimes occurred before smoothing consonants by analogy (whence VP *wreocan* and N *wreoke*); but such forms are not found in W. Otherwise, where smoothing had taken place, *e* remains (as VP, AB, and N *werc*).

After the consonant *w*, various changes had occurred in LOE. The form *wor* appears in all these texts in *world*, also in N *worpe*. The specifically AB form *warpe* which is due to an alteration of conjugation (see d'Ardenne, p. 169) appears in L and elsewhere in R (as M(R) 33/5); but VP has *aweorpan*. The mixed language of W presents *world/weorldes/werld*.

OE. *eo* from older *io* produced by breaking or back mutation is treated in the same way (as AB and N *seoððen*, AB, R, N, L *cleopien*, W *swepes*).

AB and W *suster* is from LOE. *swuster* with loss of *w* before the rounded back vowel *u*. N *suluen/seoluen* are from OE. variant forms *sylf/seolf*.

OE. *i*

OE. *i* is unchanged (as *bindunge, blisse, hit, is, milce*) in AB and all these texts. However, *wi* frequently became *wy* in LOE.: this type is represented by regular *wult* (beside *wilt* in W only), though here the further change of [wy] > [wu] may have taken place.

L *leuede*, 1 s. pt., may be an error, or may point to influence of

Phonology

2, 3 s. pr. in *io* in the antecedents of this dialect; but L has *liueð*, 3 s. pr.

OE. *ir*+consonant

When this group was originally followed by *i* or *j*, Merc. usually had forms without breaking, as OE. *girnan* 'to desire', beside *georn* 'eager' (cf. VP *afirran, hirtan*).[1] This type is represented by N ʒ*irneð*; but W has ʒ*erne* inf.

After *w*, Merc. had *wy*, the mutation of *wu* from earlier *wiu (as in VP *wyrsian*): to this type probably belong AB, R, and N *wurðe*, W *wurði*, N *iwursed*.

OE. *o*

OE. *o* is normally retained in AB and all these texts.

A characteristic tendency for *wo* > *wa* is seen in AB and R (M 33/2) *iwarpen*, pp. (but VP *aworpen*). Similar *a*-forms, of OE. origin, appear in AB and these texts: *wrahte* in R, L, and W is probably of Mercian development (cf. Corp. Gloss. *gewarht*); R and W *walde* was widespread in both OE. and ME.[2]

Beside regular forms for OE. *sorg*, N also has *seoruwe, seoruhfulliche*, where the *eo* is obscure in origin but widespread in ME. Also, errors in the use of *eo*, rarely *oe*, are found in N and L (as N *ibeoren*, L *neose*, N *noese*).[3] Levelling accounts for W *wurpen*, pp., N *iwurden*, pp., W *schulde*, R *schuldi*.

Prim. OE. *u*

For OE. *u*, AB and all these texts regularly retain *u* (as *bunden, hundes, lusti, sune, schuldres*). However, for greater legibility, *o* may appear for *u* before *u, n, m* (as N *louien*, L *loue*, N and L *come*, beside *luuie, luue, cumen*, respectively).

In AB and all these texts except W, the front mutation of *u* is regularly [y] spelt *u* (as *cusse, munegunge, sunne* 'sin'); and in many of the *i*-forms that occur (as *drihtin, king*) the *i* was widespread in ME. In derivatives of OE. *kyni*- (as W *kinebearn*), AB itself has *i*. In W the ratio of *u*:*i* (< OE. and ON. *y*) is approximately 3:2, and the mixture of dialects is clearly seen in the

---

[1] Luick, § 139. [2] d'Ardenne, § 12.
[3] See Orthography, p. xv.

xxxiv *Introduction*

variants *cunde/kinde, sunne/sinne, hule/hilede*: cf. W *monkin* beside N and R *moncun*.

W, N, and L *swuch(e)*, beside N *swich*, L *swilc*, derive from OE. variation in *swylc, swile* (also *swelc*). N and AB *studen* is from OE. *styde* (a variant of OE. *stede*) which appears to have been mainly used in the west. N *sunegi* (other forms in N, L, and R) is a late alteration of *sungin* (OE. *syngian* < **synnigian*) probably modelled on variations like *mynegian, myngian* in OE. (See d'Ardenne, p. 166.)

OE. *ā*

For OE. *ā* (VP *ā*), AB, R, and W regularly have *a* (as *cnawe, fan, gan, gastli, lauerd*). This use of *a* was conservative, for the sound had already shifted towards *o*, as indicated by the infrequent *oa*-spellings in R and W, but not in AB (as W *þoa*, R (M 9/9) *roa*). However, the *a*-forms in W are also consistent with its non-AB ingredient. In L, *a* also predominates, but the numerous *o*-forms are among the clearest indications that it too is a mixed text (as *gaste, hali, nan, swa*, beside *gostliche, louerd, no* (adj.), *swo, aore*). N regularly has *o*, occasionally *oa* after *w* (as *bihotest, holi, louerd, hwoa, woa*); but also has occasional *a*-forms (as *bihat, halewen, hwam*).

W *heali* (for *hali*) is an error probably caused by following *heaued*. W *lo!* shows an aberrant development not infrequent in exclamatory words: in this case the vowel of *loca*, imper. sg., may have exerted some influence.

For OE. *ǣ²* (VP *ǣ*, front mutation of Prim. OE. *ā*), the sound [ę̄] was probably retained in AB and in the AB or dialectally similar ingredients in these texts. Here AB has spellings with *ea*, less frequently *e*.[1] R has *e* in newer, *a* in older forms. W has *ea:e:a* in the ratio of 5:4:3, of which some of the *e*-forms and all the *a*-forms are non-AB. Thus, in W, *dealeð, earst, healend, leaue* are AB forms; *clenli, erst, leueð, lafdi* are non-AB. In L, *e*-forms predominate, but some of them and various *ea*-forms indicate an ingredient close to AB. Thus *ei, flesch, ear, healen, leafdi* are AB forms; *er* adv., *hele* n., are non-AB. In N, *e* is the normal spelling, but, infrequently, *ea* also occurs (as *leafdi*).

[1] d'Ardenne, § 20.

Phonology

The *a* in L *isprad, tospradde*, pp., results from shortening. W *gaðˇ*, 3 s. pr., is due to levelling and, at this time, is probably an easternism: AB preserved the mutated form *geaðˇ* (VP *gǣðˇ*). Exceptional reduction is seen in AB, W, and N *euch(e)*.

Prim. OE. $\bar{æ}^1$ (WGmc $\bar{a}$)

AB and all these texts regularly have *e*-spellings, representing [ẹ̄] derived from OE. non-WS. *ē* (as *dede, drede*, v., *nere, strete, þer*).[1] In a few words, *ea* for $\bar{æ}^1$ was fairly widespread in Midland ME. (as W *offeard*, L *þear*): see note to W 131.

OE. *ō*

Unmutated OE. *ō* was retained in AB and all these texts (as *blod, lokin, moder, soðˇ, stod, to*). N, L, and R *swote*, N and L *swotnesse* are unmutated forms (beside *swete, swetnesse*, with mutation).

N *weopinde* may result from the double labial influence of *w* and *p*; but the excessive use of *eo* in N (as *biheouede*) makes this doubtful. R *te* (for *to*) results from weakening in ME.

Prim. OE. *ū*

Unmutated OE. *ū* was retained in AB and all these texts (as *adun, bur, hu, ifuled, schrud, þu*). W and L *bote(n)*, for *buten*, is due to shortening.

For the front mutation of Prim. OE. *ū*, AB and all these texts except W regularly write *u*, indicating [ȳ], as *fulðˇe, lutel, prude*. In W, northern and eastern unrounding to [ī] is evident in twice as many *i*-forms as *u*-forms (as *hid, kid(de), unrideli*). In certain western texts *ui* represents [ȳ], as possibly in N *cuiðˇ* (OE. *cyðˇ*), but W *huide* is probably a blend form, though *ui* occurs elsewhere in T (as *bruide*, HM(T), 17/165).

Prim. OE. *ēa*

Since AB and all these texts present the older *ea*-spelling and the newer *e*-spelling (as *deaðˇ, eadi, heaued, reaues*, beside *cwedli, deðˇes, edi, reftes*), it is likely that both represented the same sound [ẹ̄]. Here AB, R, and W are the most conservative:[2] even in W,

[1] Ibid., § 19.   [2] Ibid., §§ 21, 22.

xxxvi *Introduction*

ea-forms are twice as numerous as *e*-forms. In AB, *ea* > *a* after *ch, sch,* and *ȝ* (as L *schawen*, W *ȝapliche*): hence W *cheap,* N and W *scheawe(n)* are probably not AB, though the *e* could merely indicate the palatal nature of the consonant (but cf. N *schewen*). In the past tense of strong verbs of Class II, AB has *ea* by levelling in such forms as W *cheas* (the analogy is with other Class II verbs with different initial consonant). In *þah, þauh,* and possibly in *chapmon,* the *a* is to be explained by shortening.

For (1) the front mutation and (2) the smoothing of OE. *ēa,* AB and all these texts regularly write *e,* probably indicating [ē]. Thus: (1) *bileuen, iherd, onlepi;* (2) *ek, heh, teken.*

OE. *ēo, īo*

Except before *c, g, h* (and sometimes before *w*), AB and all these texts (except W) and all WM. at this time regularly write *eo,* evidently to represent [ö] (as *beon, þeodest, feont, heo, deore, preo, peostri*), and the few divergences (as L *þester*) are aberrant. In W, however, *eo:e* occur in the approximate ratio of 3:5 (as *beon, bleo, deore, deouel, freoliche, leof,* beside *beden,* pr. pl., *bifel, dere,* adj., *deuel, fredom, lef,* adj.).

The front mutation of *ēo, īo* did not take place in the antecedents of these texts.

New diphthongs

ai, ei (OE. *ě* or *ǣ* before palatal *g,* or before *h*) both probably have the same phonetic value: [ęi] or [æi]. In AB and R *ei* is the regular spelling, except in some words from ON. and AN. In the other manuscripts (and in most ME. dialects) the two spellings were apparently interchangeable; but generally the north and east preferred *ai,* the south and west *ei.* In N, *ei* predominates. In L, the distribution of *ai, ei* is about equal. In W, the ratio of *ai:ei* is approximately 4:3 (as *aihwer, fairnesse, dai, mai, nailet;* from ON., *þai;* from AN., *mesaise;* beside *eihwer, feirnesse, mei, neiled; þei; eise*).

Vowel+*w*. The change of OE. *w* > *u* before consonants and finally (an important source of diphthongs in common early ME.) is only rarely expressed in the conservative orthography of AB. In this respect R and W are similar to AB. L and N, however,

Phonology xxxvii

have *u* as a frequent variant of *w* in the spelling of these diphthongs (as N *icnoulechie, nout, nouðer, soule, treoue*, L *naut, nouðer, saule*; beside N *nowt, treowe*, L *cnawlechi, sawle*). W *mildeu* is exceptional in this text.

Glides before *ʒ* and *h*. In N only, *i* after front vowels and *u* after back vowels are frequently developed before *h* (< OE. *g, h*), as *deih, eihen, eihsihðe, heihschipe, streihtest, auh, ismauht, inouh, abouht, pauh*. This development is of southern origin, not common so early, and Jordan (§ 97, Anm. 1; § 121) names N as the first manuscript in which it occurs.

Other new diphthongs from AN. (see *ai, ei*, above) include *au* (< AN. *a*+nasal, as *chaumbre, abaundune*; < AN. *al*+consonant, as W *ribauz*, L *sauuin*), where AB has *a* (as L *abandun*, N *saluen*), never *au*.

Vowels in weakly stressed syllables

Most of the developments are AB and common ME. practice and need not be dwelt upon, but the following may be noted.

Weakening to *e*, probably [ə], occurred especially in unstressed syllables (as in *drope, fikel, sune*) including many inflectional endings (q.v.). But when the vowel in question bore or had recently borne secondary stress, the original spelling was often preserved (as *licame, toward, -leas*). The vowel *i* was preserved in the adj. endings *-i* (< *ig*), *-lich*, and in the noun endings *-schipe, -inge*: *u* was preserved in the noun ending *-unge* and in the superl. ending *-lukest* (LOE. *-lucest*).

Loss of *e*: (i) *er* and *re* closely approached each other in pronunciation, tending to [r̩]. Hence there is much confusion in the distribution of these (as *froure, luðer, oðre, bettre, betere*). (ii) After *i, ei, u* (= [y]), primarily or secondarily stressed inflectional weak *e* was lost phonetically though sometimes restored by grammatical analogy. Its loss is most regularly seen in Class II (*a*) weak verbs. (See Accidence.) Thus: *seið, buð, leafdi, lokin*. (iii) *e* is occasionally lost in other circumstances, as in *earst*.

Addition of *e*: (i) Adverbs and prepositions in adverbial usage frequently add an *e* not found in OE. (as *hwaremide, ine, ofte*); (ii) *e* of various origin appears in compound words (as *baldeliche, mildeliche*); (iii) Between a consonant and *w*. This is usually *e*, but *o* finally in AB, and *e/u* interchangeably in N, as N *folewen, foluweŏ, haluwen, halewen, buruwen, scheadewe*; or both *e* and *u* in *i-boreuwen* (a blend). Similar glides between *r* and *h* are seen in *puruh, seoruh-*.

Consonants

OE. *c*

OE. front *c* is normally written *ch*, probably [tš], in all manuscripts except W. The spelling *c* which sometimes occurs at the end of words in L (as *ic, leoflic*) probably indicates the same sound by graphic economy or preservation of archaic spellings, but the latter are not common in L. In W, *ch* also is normal where the front *c* is preserved (as *lich* 'body', *luueliche, penche, misliche*), but in some forms a *k* of dialectal (eastern or north-eastern) origin appears (as *like* 'body', *luuelike, penken*). In W, OE. suffixal *-līc(e)* often appears as *li*, possibly through influence of ON. *-lig(r)* (as *fleschli, luueli, rewli*). This occurs, though rarely, in AB.

OE. back *c* [k] is usually spelt *c* before back vowels, consonants, and finally, *k* before front vowels only. Here again W agrees and diverges (as *caldeliche, cnawe, wac, kempe, wrekes*, but *kalde, wak, pik*). For OE. *cw*, the spelling *qu* very infrequently occurs (as *quiddet, quemen, quene*); but in AB and elsewhere in R, *q* appears in the (originally Latin) abbreviation *qŏ* which represents both Lat. *quod* and ME. *queŏ*. For OE. back *cc* [kk], the spelling *ck* occurs in W *wicke*, N *i-licked*; *k* in L *liked* ('licked').

OE. *sc* is normally written *sch*, probably [š], in all texts; but L has occasional *sc*-forms (as *felawscipe, holscipe, scomeþ*). For *flesch*, numerous variant spellings occur (as N *flech*, L *flehs, flehces*, W *fles*).

OE. *g*

(*a*) OE. front spirantal *g* was weakened in LOE. to [j] which became vocalized before consonants or finally (as in *forwariede, seide, halewei* (cf. N *healewi*, L *halwi*), *mei*). Initially the sound [j] was spelt with *ȝ* (as in *ȝiuen, inȝong*). The OE. prefix *ge-* has become *i-*. In AB and L *murhŏe* there is an instance of the retraction of front *g* to a back sound. In N *selhŏe* (which is also frequent outside these texts), it must be assumed that the *h* represents

Phonology

an actual sound, and is due possibly to the analogy of such words as *murhðe*, or the influence of adjective *sǣlig* through some unrecorded LOE. form as **sǣligð*. In L *unwurhþ*, the *h* must be regarded as erroneous.

(b) OE. front stop *g* occurs only in *ng* and where lengthened. In these cases the spelling remained *ng, gg* (as *i-mengd, buggeð, suggen*). Probably the sounds [ndž], [dž] are usually indicated; but when a consonant immediately follows, as in *i-mengd*, it cannot be certainly determined whether [ndž] or [ŋg] is intended. (See d'Ardenne, Lang. § 31, p. 195.) The change of [ŋg] > [nk] is seen in N *strencðe*, beside W *strengðe*, both forms of OE. origin.

(c) OE. back *g* had become a stop initially and in *ng* (as *gold, gastli, sprungon, strong*), and in secondary contact with *n* or other dentals (as *munegunge, i-suneged*). Medially its development varied in these manuscripts: it remained a spirant in all manuscripts but N. In L, this continued to be spelt ʒ (as *aʒen, maʒe, eʒen*) except in *stihen* (< OE. *stīgan*) and *lahe* (< ON. *lágr*). In AB, R, and W, the *h*-spelling is regular (as *ahen, drahe, wohunge*). In N, the OE. spirant regularly became *w* (as *owe, muwe, wowen*) except in *stihen* (< OE. *stīgan*), *eihen* (< OE. *ēagan*), and *muhen* (< OE. **mugan*). Finally, it was unvoiced in LOE. and written *h* which is retained (as *deih, arh, steih, buh*): this also occurred when it preceded a voiceless sound (as in *eihsihðe, felauhschipe*).

OE. *h*

Initially *h* normally remained an aspirate, but was lost from OE. *hl, hr* (as *leor, louerd, ream*). The confusion in the use of *h* in N and occasionally in L, shown by its frequent omission where required etymologically (as *oli, uni, aueð, abbe*, beside *holi, huni, haueð, habbe*) or insertion where not required (as *ham, hende, helles-hwat, hure,* for *am, ende, elles-hwat, ure*), is notable. Whether it is due to a native English dialect tendency or purely scribal habits (possibly influenced by French) is difficult to determine. Finally and before *t*, OE. *h* represented a voiceless spirant which was retained (as *ah, ahte, dohter, i-strahte, þah*). For *iht*, there are a variety of spellings in N (as *riht, rith, ritht, nowitht, brithnesse, brihtte*, imper. sg.). Exceptionally in N, *wt* is written for *uht* (as *abowt*, pp.).

OE. d

OE. *d* normally remains. The AB unvoicing of final *d* to *t* is frequent in R, infrequent in W and L, not evidenced in N (as (i) *et* of pp.: R *i-fulet, i-maket, misloket*, W *chepet, demet*, L *bicluppet*; and (ii) various other forms: R *feont, ant* (N, L, W *and*), W *fant*, pt., L *towart*; beside N *i-fuled, i-maked, feond*, &c.).

OE. ð

ð > *t* following *d, t, s*: (i) finally in LOE. in 3 s. pr. (see Verbs, below); (ii) initially in pronoun, article, demonstrative, &c. especially after words closely connected grammatically. All manuscripts have *t* from these sources occasionally (beside more frequent *þ*). W has most *t*-forms (as *te*, art., *tat, ta*, pl., *tis, tu (artu), te*, pron., *ti(n), tai, tei, trin, tah, ʒette* < ? *ʒēt-þā*). Already in OE., ð sometimes > *d* before *l* (as *ladliche*). There was also a tendency for ð*m* > *dm* as in OE. *madmas*, and here in *eadmodnesse*.

OE. *f*

AB and all manuscripts except W occasionally write *u, v* for initial *f*, probably indicating that OE. *f* had become [v] (as N *vif, uor, i-uorðed*; L *uor* only). Initially in W and finally in all manuscripts, OE. *f* was retained and written *f* (as *for, fif, half, seolf*). Where OE. medial *f* was voiced, *u* is normally written (as *heaued, haues, halue, froure*), but where *u* might be mistaken as a vowel, *f* is used in N, *f* and *ue* in W and AB (as *hafde, hefdich, nauedes*): where medial *f* was not voiced, *f* remains (as *after, ofte, softe, reftes*). Rarely *w* represents [v], as in N *heawed, haweð*.

Loss of consonants

Final *n* is lost, normally before consonants except *h* only, from *min, þin, an* ('one'), but not without exceptions; and less regularly from *in, on*. On inflexions in *n*, see Accidence, pp. xlv, li, below; cf. N *heoueriche*.

Double consonants are sometimes simplified: (i) frequently in unstressed syllables (as N *uorʒiuenesse, i-borenesse*); (ii) before another consonant, as already normal in OE. (as N *sunfule*); (iii) rarely by mere graphic error (as N *nabe*, and possibly W *setis*: see note to W 504).

Phonology

Other losses include: *l* before *ch* (as *swuche, hwuch*); final *l* (as *muche, lute*); medial of three consonants (as *wurschipe*); various reductions (as *ei* < *eni, euch* < OE. *ǣghwylc*).

Addition of consonants

Consonants are sometimes doubled, especially before *r* (as *attri, bitter, bittre, bettre*): *gentiller* is probably modelled on native words with double consonants before comparative ending, and *frerre* probably imitates forms like *herre*. In many cases the doubling is casual and scribal (as in *hokerringe, oppnes, þurhhut*), or due to misunderstanding of a rare word (as *girre*: see note to W 480–1).

ACCIDENCE

Nouns

1. Classes

As many nouns occur only in the uninflected singular, they cannot be classified on the evidence of these manuscripts. From available plurals, however, four classes can be identified (irrespective of individual word origins):

I. Plurals in *es*. These include nouns ending in a consonant or weak *e* and some foreign nouns (as *earmes, bearnes, wrecches, hurtes*).
II. Plurals in *en* (as *blissen, fan, ȝeouen, honden, bonen, lawen*).
III. Uninflected plurals. These include mutated plurals and a few others (as *fet, men, frend, þing*).
IV. French plurals in *s* (as *lettres, princes, prisuns, sacremens, schurges*. In *ribauz, sacremenz, z = ts*).

Hesitation occurs in *þing*, pl., beside *þinges*. Absence of inflexion after numerals is seen in W *drinch*, N(U) *half*. In *breðre* (OE. *brōðru*), mutation has been extended from the dative singular. W *ehne*, nom. pl., possibly shows influence of OE. *ēgna*, gen. (N has *eien, eihen*). Class I is the largest. Class II is mainly derived from OE. feminine or weak nouns, but has received some additions—e.g. old short-stem neuters, originally with pl. in *u* (as N *limen*).

Introduction

2. Cases

There is evidence for three case forms in the singular and for one (rarely two) in the plural. Since the gen. s. and the whole of the plural usually have the same ending, there are generally at most three case forms in all for any one noun.

In the singular:

(a) The uninflected form is used for the nominative, accusative, vocative, syntactic dative, and fairly often after prepositions. Nominatives in *e*, not derived from OE. nouns in *e*, have usually either generalized *e* from other cases, especially in originally fem. nouns (as *blisse, bote, burðe, dede*); or weakened some other vowel ending to *e* (as *bale, kempe, strengðe, sune*). OE. nouns in (weak) *e* have usually preserved this *e* (as *demere, frendschipe, likinge*).

(b) The genitive ends normally in *es*. In semi-compounds such as *worldes froure, flesches pine, monnes help*, it is general and adjectival in sense. Expressions like *helle hus, soule hele*, were probably regarded as compounds rather than as survivals of OE. feminine genitives. Possibly *moncunne froure* N(Lo) 135 was modelled on such expressions. In W *moder sune* (beside N *moderes*) and N *feder luue*, the originally uninflected genitives were probably no longer felt as such.

(c) The inflected form in *e* is used in AB and all these manuscripts (especially N) after prepositions, but not obligatorily; thus W *muðe, worlde*, N *childe, deaðe, liue, monne*, L *blode*; but (also after prepositions) W *muð, world*, N *deað*. However, the evidence is usually not clear, since either the inflected or uninflected form is not presented. See also gen. s. and pl.

In the plural:

(a) Normally one inflexion (or mutation), according to class, is used throughout the plural in all cases. Evidence for a special case form after prepositions is lacking or insufficient: N and W have *þinges*, N and L *þinge*, after prep. beside W *þing, þinges* in nom./ acc. In cases where the nom./acc. pl. is formed with *en*, W has a number of forms in *es* after prepositions (as *blisses, hondes* (beside *honden*), *murhðes, pines, schomes, schuldres, sunnes, wundes*). Since the nom./acc. does not appear in W for these words, they may

Accidence xliii

well represent the use of the *es* inflexion throughout the plural of the north-eastern ingredient in that text, though the use of *es* after prep. in the case of *en*-plurals is a feature of AB. In AB and all these manuscripts (except occasionally in W), the *n* of the Class II plural ending is 'fixed'.

(*b*) The genitive plural is also normally *es*. But in AB and all these manuscripts there are occasional forms derived from OE. plural genitives: (i) strong, as in N *alre þinge swetest* (beside L *uor alle þinge swetest*), *alle helplease help* (beside L *alle helpleses help*) and W *surest alre drinch* where *drinch* is preceded by *þinge* crossed out; (ii) weak, as in N *englene quene*. The latter ending *ene* had become blended in AB with the OE. adjectival ending *en* producing an unchangeable ending *ene* with genitival-adjectival function, as in N *þornene crune*, and possibly W *irnene neiles*.

Adjectives

1. Classes

According to form, there are three classes:

I. Consonantal stems, capable of inflexion in *e* (as *soð*, *god*, *dead*).

II. Vocalic stems:

(*a*) With (strong) singular in *e*, uninflectable (as *eche*, *kene*, *riche*).

(*b*) With singular in *i* (< OE. *ig*), sometimes inflectable with *e* in N only (as *ani*, *edi*, *hali*).

III. Adjectives in *lich(e)* (< OE. *līc*) (as *leoflich*, *gastliche*, *freoliche*).

In N, *lich* and *liche* alternate in the singular without clear syntactic reasons. In L and W, *liche* is regularly invariable, but L has *leoflic* (twice); W occasionally writes *like* (as *semlike*, *luuelike*). W also has invariable *li*-forms (as *eorðli*, *fleschli*, *gastli*, and *luueli* as weak and as pl. adj. beside *luueliche*). In R (as here represented) there are no adjectives in *lich*.

2. Inflexion

(*a*) The only normal inflexion is *e*. It marks weak and plural forms of Class I in all manuscripts, and sometimes of Class II (*b*)

xliv   *Introduction*

in N only (as *eadie, blodie*); but absence of inflexion also occurs in the plural (rarely) and in the weak sing. (more often), especially in N (as *luft, riht, eadi*, all weak, and *rewŏful*, pl.). As in AB, strong adjectives after prepositions occasionally have *e*, particularly if the noun has no distinctive case ending (as N *wiŏ soŏe luue*, W *in alle blisse*). Rarely, this occurs in other oblique cases (as L *longe wone*, N *muchele menske*—both acc.). Inflexion is normally absent from predicative adjectives, except plural past participles which usually have *e* (unless plurality is sufficiently indicated, as in *fif wunden i-opened* N(Lo) 48–49, *i-strahte* ₸ *i-sprad* L 50, and probably *to-spredde* ₸ *i-opened* (MS. *i openeŏ*) N(U) 50, but cf. L 43).

(*b*) The possessive adjectives *min, þin* (only) are similarly inflected. With few exceptions the final *n* is dropped before consonants except *h*; and occasionally *ti(n)* appears after dentals. In N, *mine, þine* occur frequently after prepositions (as *of mine licame, aʒein þine brihte leore*), and a few times in other oblique cases (as *mine heorte, þine siker swetnesse*—both acc.). This occurs but once in L, twice in W, not in R. A few plural forms without *e* (as W *min ehne*, L *þin earmes*, N *min earen*) occur mainly before vowels and are explicable as phonetic elisions. Other possessives are regularly not declined; but W has *hise*, pl. (twice).

(*c*) OE. gen. pl. *ra* survives only in *alre* (once or twice in each manuscript). Adjectival *e* in *alle helplease help, alle folkes fulŏe, redlease red* is probably due to vague compounding rather than conscious genitive inflexion.

Adverbs

Adverbs are regularly formed by adding *e* and *liche* to adjectives. W (only) has numerous adverbs in *li* (as *clenli, cwedli, fulli, herteli*). Regarding adverbs in *eliche, eli*, see Vowels in weakly stressed syllables (above). All manuscripts have the form *ofte*; AB, N, and L have *ase*. The preposition *ine* (with adverbial *e < inne* ?) occurs frequently in N, and once in L.

Comparison

In AB, OE. adjectival *ra* and adverbial *or* are both represented by *re*. Hence the formal distinction between adjectives and

Accidence xlv

adverbs is lost in the comparative. Our manuscripts have *est* (< OE. *ost* and *est*) in the superlative, and interchange *re*, *er*, *ere* (see Phonol., p. xxxix) in the comparative (as *betere*, *bettre*, *herre*, *lengre*, *swetter*, *swettere*). Various other irregularities are treated under Consonants and Vowels in weakly stressed syllables, above. Forms in *lich(e)* are compared in AB with *luker*, *lukest*. Our manuscripts happen only to present superlatives (as L *leoflucest*, N *leoflukest*), but *luker*, *lukest* are the normal endings in T.

Pronouns and pronominal adjectives

1. Personal

All manuscripts have *ich*, *me*, *min*; *we*, *us*, *ure*; *þu*, *þe*, *þin*. L has *ic* occasionally. The reduced proclitic form *ch* occurs twice in N *ch-ulle* ('I will'). The reduced enclitic form *i* occurs once in W *schuldi*. W has *i* not limited to the enclitic form, beside less frequent *ich* in the ratio of 4:1. The 2nd pers. pl. occurs only in W in the form *ʒu*, after prep. (< OE. *ow* in reduced stress with *ʒ* from nom. *ʒe*).

All manuscripts have masc. *he*, *him* (dat. acc.), *his*; neut. *hit* (nom. dat. acc.). N has acc. *hine* once. In the fem. AB forms predominate, thus (as recorded): fem. sg. W, L *ha*, N *heo*; all manuscripts *hire*. L also has *here* (once). (N, R also use *þeo*: see Demonstrative, below.)

The plural forms are: nom. W, R *ha*, L *ha*, *heo*, N *heo*; acc. dat. W, N *ham*; possessive W, L *hare*, N *heore* (also *hore* before *horie* n.). W also has the forms *þai*, *þei* in the ratio of 4:3 compared with *h*-forms.

True genitives are rare. Grammatical gender is preserved rarely: W *ha* 423 (antecedent *herte*), N(Le) *hire* 8 (antecedent *soule*), R *hire* 6 (antecedent *sawle*). That *sawle* retained fem. gender may possibly be influenced by the fem. gender of Lat. *anima* and OF. *anme* (*âme*). However, since the fem. gender of *heorte* is peculiar to OE. and does not correspond to Lat. or Fr., it is a genuine survival of OE. gender (cf. *mine heorte* N(U) 79, which is similarly a probable survival of fem. acc.). Other instances are *hire* (antecedent *rode*) N(Lo) 14, *hire* (antecedent *sunne* 'sun') N(U) 14, L 12.

Introduction

(On the interchange of þ/t, and dropping of final n, see Consonants, p. xlii. On the declension of possessives, see Adjectives, p. xlvi.)[1]

2. Article, Demonstrative and Relative

(a) Derivatives of OE. sē, sēo, þæt

The article and demonstrative are difficult to distinguish, since texts do not record the differences of voice and emphasis which were no doubt distinctions in living speech.

Article

The article (unemphatic) is normally uninflected, though fuller forms sometimes occur without special emphasis. They are here treated as forms of the demonstrative. The usual form is indeclinable þe. However, þet occurs in some places, mostly before originally neuter nouns (as before N, R bern, N blod, uni (L huni), werc). Before nouns originally of other gender (as N flod, song), þet may belong to the demonstrative.

Demonstrative

Adjectival þet/þat rarely occurs in these texts, except in W where it occurs fourteen times. Other inflected singular forms (none in W) correctly preserve OE. grammatical gender (as masc. acc. þene before N deouel, erm, holi-gost, louerd, wei; before N deað after prep.; þen before R deouel; masc. gen. þes before N feondes; fem. acc. þeo before N hwile, R world). Inflected plural forms are W þa (þoa once), N þeo. On the difficulty of deciding whether these are emphatic or unemphatic articles, see above. The inst. s. forms of OE., no longer associated with the foregoing, survive as þi in W, N, L for-þi, þon in L wiþ-þon, þen in N wið-þen, and in W, N adverbial þe with comparatives.

Relative

þet and þe both occur as uninflected relatives. However, in our

---

[1] The origin of a in ha, ham, hare is disputed. It is frequently regarded as a development of eo in reduced stress. But since the a-forms are not limited to unaccented usage in AB, while the phonetic development of eo > o in that variety of English is very unlikely, this explanation may be doubted. An alternative explanation is that a is derived from the a in OE. fem. acc. sg. and nom. acc. pl. þā (cf. d'Ardenne, p. 156).

Accidence

texts, þe is rare, except in L where it is frequent. Otherwise it occurs once only in N and not at all in W or in our text of R.[1]

(b) Derivatives of OE. þes, þēos, þis

Þis is the normal form of 'this'. Other forms are: singular after prep., N þisse in iþisse (twice) beside iþis (once); plural N þeos (once) and þeors (an error probably due to following wordes), W þise, adj. pl. (three times).

3. Other Pronouns. See Glossary.

Verbs

1. Classes

(a) Strong

From the evidence presented, all manuscripts preserve seven classes and probably four stems, such as result from developments given in the Phonology, above. AB (R less often) preserves a separate stem for 2, 3 s. pr. and s. imper.; and both AB and R regularly form the 2 s. pt. from the pt. pl. stem. Neither of these features is clearly evidenced in any one of our texts. Compared with OE., the forms presented here show some irregularities:

Present stems

The vowel i in the present stem of W, N ʒiuen, N ʒif, imper. (beside N ʒeouen, L ʒeuest) is also widespread in ME., and is certainly in part at least due to a levelling of the i proper originally to 2, 3 s. pr. ind. The irregular a in the present stem warpe is a feature of AB (see d'Ardenne, pp. 169, 242), and occurs in L (beside N worpe). The u in N buruwen, pr. subj., cannot be referred to OE. beorgan, but is found widely in ME.—e.g. in Havelok (buruwen) and Ayenbite (bouerʒe) (see d'Ardenne, p. 146, under burhe). W wealdes, 3 s. pr., is unlikely to descend from WS. wealdan. It is more probably from the Anglian form of the weak verb wældan (with group lengthening of the stem vowel), and, if so, has the appearance of being an AB form. W lahhen is a common Midland form in ME., found in both AB and Orm. The

---

[1] Cf. Angus McIntosh, 'The Relative Pronouns þe and þat in Early Middle English', *English and Germanic Studies*, i (1947–8), 73–87.

vowel *a* may descend from an OE. *hlæhhan* with an aberrant development due to the combination of *hh* medially and perhaps to the sense of the word favouring retention of the vowels *æ, a*: or the *a* vowel may result from substitution of the infinitive vowel of other words of the same class (as *faran, scacan*, &c.) which are unmutated. W *wrihe*, inf., and N *unwrih*, imper., may represent the rare AB verb *wrihen* 'to protect', probably a re-formation from the 2, 3 present stem of OE. *wrēon*. ONthumb. actually had a form *wrīga*.

Preterite stems

N *i-seihe*, 2 s. pt. (for *i-seie*), appears to be influenced either in writing or speech by the 1 and 3 s. pt. forms. R *weorp*, pt., is an AB form associated with inf. *warpe* (N has *werp*, pt.). N *fleaw*, 3 s. pt., may be an error for *fleow*.

Past participle

N *i-beoren*, pp., is probably an error for *i-boren*. In N *i-wurden* and W *forwurpen, wurpen*, pp., the vowel proper to the pt. pl. has intruded into the pp., possibly aided in this case by the fact that *weor* of the inf. might also produce *wur*.

(b) Weak

All manuscripts preserve two classes, which, except for certain Class I verbs with historic vowel change, conjugate from one stem. Class III is no longer an organized class. As in OE., Class I has long stems originally or from doubling, and a few others (as *delen, senden, cluppen, sette, penche, buggen*). In AB the alternation of double and single stem consonants is systematically preserved in conjugation; but not in our manuscripts (as W *telles*, 3 s. pr., but *setis* (if sg., see below); N *streccheð*, 3 s., *buggeð*, 3 s., *biclupen*, inf., but *buð*, 3 s., *biclupe*, imper.). In Class II, AB sharply distinguishes: II (a) Originally long stems, with *i*-endings in present (as *fondin*), and II (b) originally short stems, with *ie*-endings in present (as *luuien*).[1] All our manuscripts show traces of this distinction, but none carries it through fully. All show some levelling of Class II to Class I.

---

[1] Class II also contains most verbs which are of new formation or of foreign origin.

Accidence

In W and N, the present of Class II (*a*) has regularly gone over to Class I (as W *loken*, inf., *cheape*, inf., *balde*, 3 s. pr. subj., N *folewen*, inf., *wowen*, inf., *clense*, 3 s. pr. subj.), except for four *i*-forms in N (*wilni*, inf.; *wilni* (twice), *halsi* (twice), *sunegi*, all 1 s. pr.), and a few others in which the *ie* of Class II (*b*) has been applied to long stems (as N *i-cnoulechie, adeadie*). L has a few more *i*-forms than levelled *e*-forms (as *lokin, folegi, salui*, all inf., *adeadi*, 3 s. pr. subj., beside *woge*, inf., *shawen*, inf.). R has *cnawlechi, halsi*, both 1 s. pr.

In N, Class II (*b*) is carefully distinguished (as *luuien, hopien*, both inf., *luuie, hopie*, both 1 s. pr., *gladien*, 3 pl. pr. subj., *wuniinde*, pr. p.); but in L and W levelling to Class I also occurs here (as L *loue*, inf., *loue*, 1 s. pr., *louende*, pr. p., beside *louie*, 1 s. pr., *luuiende*, pr. p.; W *luuen, pole, maken, schome*, all inf., beside *luuie, polien*, both inf., *luuie*, 1 s. pr. subj.): in W, *e*-forms are three times as frequent as *ie*-forms and are evidence of the eastern dialect ingredient in that text.

All manuscripts form the preterite of Class I in *de, te*; of Class II (*a*) and (*b*) in *ede*. W *mades* (see note to l. 82) and *reftes* are north-easternisms.

2. Inflexion

While each manuscript evidences varied agreement with AB, none has the purity and consistency of AB conjugation. In W, the admixture of WM. and NEM. is very clearly seen, and the latter greatly predominates. The following presents (only) the chief points of comparison. Final *n* of endings is usually stable in R and N, where its occasional loss from the pp. is in accord with AB practice (d'Ardenne, § 43, p. 199). It drops more often in L, and frequently in W (but *not* from the pp.), apparently regardless of following consonants.

Infinitive

Except for N *wilni* (once), AB *in* of weak Class II (*a*) is found only in L, where it outnumbers *en* (as *folegi, lokin, salui*, beside *woge, schawen*). In weak Class II (*b*) only W has *e(n)*, which it uses much oftener than the *ien* of AB and the other manuscripts (as W *luue(n), make(n), pole(n)*, beside *gladien, polien*).

Introduction

Present Participle and Verbal Noun

In W, the endings *ande* (beside *ende*, *inde*) and *inge* (beside *unge*) are contrary to AB practice.

Present

For indic. 2, 3 s. W has north-eastern *es* approximately five times as frequently as *est*, *eð* of the other manuscripts (as *abides*, *drinkes*, both 2 s., *cumes*, *spekes*, both 3 s., beside *seist*, *hengest*, *dealeð*, *leueð*). Contraction of 2, 3 s. is found in W and L only in *seist* and *seið*, where the vowel has been absorbed by the new diphthong *ei*. Contraction is frequent in R and N (as in AB) where the stem ends in *d* or *t* (as N *beot*, *scheot*, *stont*, *welt*). N, L *buð* 'buys' is an AB form descending from OE. (Angl.) *bygeð* (> *buieð* > *buið*): the sound [y] and the diphthong [yi] became identical, hence *buð*. On W *setis*, see note to W 504. Absence of inflexion in N, L *bihold*, 1 s. pr., is caused by the pronoun (*ich*) following. On N *weaschs*, *waschs*, see footnote to N(U) 114, N(Lo) 47, 48.

For indic. pl. W has entirely supplanted the *eð*, *ieð* of all the other manuscripts (and AB) by *e(n)*, *ie(n)* (as *singen*, *quemen*, *fainen*, *þolien*).

Sometimes *e* appears in imper. s. of Weak Class I in W (as *leue*, *leoue*, *lese*, *þenke* (beside *dred*, *þenc*): but L *helpe*, imper. s., is probably an error.

Preterite

The strong 2 s. pt. in W has received the form of the 1st and 3rd persons (as *band*, *bicom*, *bihald*, *cheas*, *seh*). All the other manuscripts have *e* with change of grade in the 2 s. For the weak 2 s. pt. W has north-eastern *(e)des* approximately 12½ times as frequently as *(e)dest* of the other manuscripts and AB. Absence of inflexion in W *lasted*, *spitted*, *streamed*, all 3 s., and *spitted*, pl., may be caused, in each case, by the next word beginning with a vowel.

Past participle

W (but not the other manuscripts) occasionally syncopates *e* of the pp. ending (as *born*, *to-torn*, *demd*, *cald*, *martird*). N *underfo*, though at the end of a line, probably shows loss of nasal frequent

Accidence

in AB before *m, n*. The following word is here *me*. On *heht*, pp., see note to W 99.

For the weak pp., AB and R normally have the ending *et*; L and W have both *et* and *ed*; N has *ed* only; in W *ed* is twice as frequent as *et*. The other manuscripts and AB drop the pp. prefix *i* (OE. *ge*) normally only before other prefixes and in attributive usage: W most often omits the prefix, regardless of circumstances. For the declension of participles, see Adjectives (above).

Verb 'to be'

Singular forms of *beon* are normally subjunctive in all texts, except in the following instances: Consuetudinal usage is expressed by *beo*, 3 s., in N (twice) and L (once); by *bið*, 3 s. (with *euer*) in N (once); by *beoð*, 3 s., in L (once). N also has *beo*, imper. s. (once). The pr. pl. is *beoð* in all texts but W, which has (only) *arn* and *narn* (once each). The form *aren* is found in AB (both A and B) but rarely. For variation of *was/wes* in W, see Phonology, p. xxxii. W *weren*, sg., is an error.

(For the other anomalous verbs and the preterite-present verbs, see Glossary.)

DIALECT, TEXTUAL HISTORY, AND DATE

The foregoing analysis has shown that, while these manuscripts differ considerably from each other, each presents evidence of variation unlikely or impossible in one dialect; and each, in several important features, agrees with AB. Also, the language of each manuscript can probably be explained as the admixture of not more than two dialects (AB+*x*); and, when variants occur, one of these, in nearly every case, is consonant with AB. Moreover, the non-AB elements in all manuscripts (except W) have many characteristics which at this time were likewise western and reveal affinities with *Laȝamon A*, the oldest version of the *Poema Morale*, &c. In W, the non-AB element is north-eastern and has much in common with the language of Orm.

The most important evidence (based on the spellings) is summarized in the following table. Although only the normal developments are shown, it is to be understood that *all* the AB features

Introduction

listed are found in each of these manuscripts (at least in isolated examples, as given in the Phonology and Accidence) unless the contrary is specifically stated. A question mark means only that a manuscript does not provide sufficient examples to prove that the spelling in question is its norm. In W, where both dialectal ingredients are most fully presented, there are often two evident norms; but these cannot always be distinguished in general terms.

Normal developments in spelling of AB, R, L, N, and W

OE.	AB	non-AB: Western	non-AB: North-eastern (W)
1. a+nasal	o all MSS.		a
2. æ	e R, N, W	a L, R, W	a
3. ær+cons.	ea not R, not N	e L, N; a R, W	a
4. ald	a R, W, L ?	o N, L ?	
5. $\bar{a}$	a R, L, W	o N, L	a
6. $\bar{æ}^2$	(i) ea L, W, not R (ii) e R, L, W	e N; a R	a^1
7. $\check{e}o$	eo all MSS.		e
8. $\bar{y}$	u all MSS.		i
9. medial back g	h R, W	$\mathfrak{z}$ L; w N	
10. final d	t R, not N, not L	d L, N, W	d
11. noun after prep.	$-e$ R, N		
12. pres. pl.	$-e\eth$ R, L, N, not W		$e(n)$
13. $-ed$ of pp.	$-et$ R, not N	$-ed$ L, N, W	$-ed$
14. pres. of Wk. II (a)	i-endings R, L, not W	$-en$ L, N, W	$-en$

[1] i.e. a due to shortening.

This table must be read in conjunction with the detail presented in the Phonology and Accidence. It inevitably over-simplifies (e.g. a < OE. æ is in some words north-eastern, in others western but non-AB, in still others found in AB itself); it omits many minor developments of importance in establishing kinship with AB; and it is not concerned with the proportionate relations of dialectal ingredients. But it does show striking similarities: of the fourteen features listed, all but no. 10 are found in L, all but nos. 3, 10, and 13 are found in N, all but nos. 12 and 14 are found in W—either as normal developments or at least as sporadic occurrences.

These relationships are further indicated by evidence of other

Dialect, Textual History, and Date

kinds. The orthography of these manuscripts is that of the period; but in all (either normally or sporadically) there is some measure of the conservatism and of the special characteristics of AB, as *a* for the already rounded sound < OE. *ā*; *ea* for the development (prob. [ę̄]) of OE. *ēa*, p for [w]; *þ* initially, *ð* medially and finally (except in L); occasional *u* for initial *f* (except in W); &c.

The words themselves are very significant. AB has not a special vocabulary of its own: but it does employ many words not found or rarely found elsewhere at this time, and many more words which appear in it in highly characteristic forms. Of the former, we have in our manuscripts: W *dosk*, W *girre* (for *gure*), W *hetelifaste* (for *heteueste*), N *vnwrih*, W *wrihe*; among the latter: N *buð*, W *bituhhen*, W *derue*, N, L *ei*, W, N *euch(e)*, W *forwariede*, W *irnene*, W *kinebearn*, W *lasteles*, N, L *me* adv., W *menged*, N, L *imengd*, L *strunden*, N *strundes*, N *studen*, N, L *i-suneged*, W *trin*, L *unwurhð*, L *warpe*, R *weorp* (pt.), W *wealdes*, W, L *wrahte*.

It is therefore clearly evident that the manuscripts herein designated as R, L, N, and W are closely connected, not only in content and style (as has been shown) but linguistically: moreover, that the bond of their relationship is a common AB element which they all share.

In each of these manuscripts, however, there is another element which is not AB; and the separation or identification of this element is rendered more difficult by the fact that in each manuscript, except W, it likewise is of western origin. Moreover, in AB certainly and in these other manuscripts probably, we are dealing, not with 'pure' local dialects, but with cultured and eclectic literary media, of which the regional colouring is less strongly marked and the provenance less rigidly confined. At the present state of our knowledge, therefore, opinions as to the precise localization of these manuscripts must be regarded with caution.

Of them all, R is closest to AB. Although our text is too short to exhibit all R's characteristics, R has been studied elsewhere; and it might almost be regarded, if not as AB strictly, at least as a variant of the same medium, literary Central West Midland of the early thirteenth century. Yet in some ways it is very different (see the above table): in its not infrequent *a* for OE. *æ*, *ær*+cons.

liv *Introduction*

and $\bar{æ}^2$; in its not preserving the *i*-forms of Class II (*a*) weak verbs. Because of these and other divergent features, R is not an exception to the formula (AB+*x*) suggested for the mixed languages of these manuscripts. Both AB and R have with some probability been associated with Herefordshire.[1] The non-AB ingredient in R would probably be well enough accounted for if it had had its origin somewhat north of the centres of AB culture, but in the same county. Miss Serjeantson has suggested 'somewhere between Hereford and Leominster, perhaps in the Bromyard and Bishop's Frome district'.[2]

In L, the AB ingredient is also clearly discernible (see the above table), but the other ingredient presents difficulties. Like R, L most often has *a* < OE. *æ*; like N, *o* < OE. *ā*; like W, a variant *e* < OE. *ēo*. If, as suggested, the *Ureisun* was added to fill up the manuscript, since it is in a different hand, it may have been added some years later; and the lapse of time may help to explain its dialectal composition—e.g. *a* < OE. *æ* and *o* < OE. *ā*. Yet, like the *Lambeth Homilies*, it has both ʒ as a back spirant for OE. medial back *g* and the (earliest) occasional development of this ʒ to *w*.[3] *Laʒamon A* retains this ʒ, and has also, as variants, *e* < OE. *eo* and *er*+cons. < OE. *er*+cons.; but its language may not be that of Ernleʒe.[4] Miss Serjeantson finds *er*+cons. in both thirteenth-century NW. Worcs. and Glos.[5] If Lambeth 487 came from Gloucestershire,[6] Wilson's comment that 'such an origin would fit in very well with what we know of the dialect'[7] could still be right, and apply to the whole MS. including the *Ureisun*. However, except as some possible form of early SW. Midland when the border with Southern ME. was still 'unclear',[8] the non-AB ingredient in L cannot on present evidence be precisely localized.

Although the AB element in N is proportionately smaller, its detection is for general reasons so important that where AB developments are shown only sporadically some recapitulation of evidence may be useful. Thus (see the above table): no. 4

[1] By Tolkien, d'Ardenne, Mack, *et al.*
[2] Serjeantson, p. 324.
[3] Jordan, § 186 and Anm. 1.
[4] Cf. Luick, § 31.
[5] Serjeantson, p. 194.
[6] See p. xi, above.
[7] R. M. Wilson, op. cit., p. 39.
[8] Luick, § 33, Anm. 1.

Dialect, Textual History, and Date

(OE. *ald*) *baldeliche*, no. 5 (OE. *ā*) *bihat*, no. 6 (i) (OE. *ǣ*²) *leafdi*, no. 9 (OE. medial back *g*) *eihen, muhen, stihen*, no. 14 (pr. of Wk. II (*a*) verbs) *wilni* inf., *halsi, sunegi, wilni*, all 1 s. pr. The preponderating other element has a more southern cast. However, since its most characteristic features are *both* southern and midland, it most probably comes from the dialectal borderland between the two. In this borderland some of the most important ME. developments (as *ǭ* < OE. *ā*) first took hold; and in this manuscript (including AR) the developments of *w* < OE. medial back *g*, and of glide vowels between vowels and *h, ht*, though anticipated elsewhere, were first regularly presented.[1] While variant spellings for [ǒ] are probably not, in this case, dialectally significant, they may indicate that the *e*-spelling was the norm in the non-AB ingredient, for the interlining of *o* after originally written *e* is, according to Miss Day,[2] the most frequent correction in the whole manuscript. (That *eo* was to some extent unfamiliar to the writer of *e* might be assumed from such errors as *i-beoren, biheouede, weopinde, steopes, freomede, dere⟨o⟩wurð*.) However, *e* for [ǒ] was a not uncommon variant in this area (and others) in thirteenth-century texts from *Laȝamon A* to Robert of Gloucester's *Chronicle* which rhymes *eo* and *e*. From close affinities of N with L, we might assume that N was of similar provenance—but farther south, in view of its regular *w* < *ȝ*, its glides before *h, ht*, its arbitrary dropping or adding of initial *h* (the dropping sometimes corrected). However, the dialectal borderland is not likely to have coincided exactly with county boundaries. On the first flyleaf of the manuscript are written the names of five men. By identifying four of these as sixteenth-century inhabitants of Gloucester, some five miles as it happens from the learned abbey of Winchcombe, Miss Day has contributed what may be the most valuable evidence thus far, for the actual provenance of MS. N.[3]

The dialectal peculiarities of W—the subject of very divergent opinions in the past[4]—result from the admixture of two ingredients

---

[1] Luick, §§ 369, 402, Anm. 1, 403, Anm. 1.
[2] Day, op. cit. p. xvii.   [3] Ibid., pp. xii f.
[4] For example, Kölbing (*Englische Studien*, xxiii (1897), 306, Anm. 1) called MS. Titus D. xviii 'ältestes mittelenglisches Denkmal des Nordens', Morris (*OE. Hom.*, p. li) listed Midland and especially northern peculiarities in which it differed from 'the oldest MSS. of the *Ancren Riwle*', Mühe

more remote from each other and more fully exhibited concurrently than those found in any other of our texts. One of these ingredients is AB, or a very similar dialect (which may have been closer to original R, or, as it happens, to 'corrected B').[1] This ingredient predominates, at least so far as the phonology is concerned. The other ingredient, though clearly enough definable to have a separate column in the above table, is less conservative and less consistent, especially in its accidence. For it was in the north and east that the OE. inflexional system was earliest dislocated and simplified. Thus, other north-eastern features which predominate in W are: avoidance of the weak pl. of nouns, and of the *e*-ending of nouns after prepositions; use of the pronouns *i* (not coalesced) and *þai*; the verbal endings *es* for 2, 3 s. pr. and 2 s. pt. (weak) and *en* for pr. pl.; the 2 s. pt. (strong) having the same form as the rest of the pt. s. Moreover, there are many forms certainly or most likely of north-eastern provenance (as *heht* pp., *hengedes, mades, reftes, setis*), and also words, not in AB, which occur elsewhere chiefly in northern and eastern texts (as *bekinde, biclaried* (?), *carpe, dunchen, karlische, rattes, sperred*); and, although words from ON. were already widespread in ME. (and numerous in AB), the fair number in W is consistent with its north-eastern ingredient. In the dialect of Lincolnshire, for instance, Scandinavian influence is known to have been strong.

Since W is after all a short (unique) text, it is important to note that Mühe's analysis of phonology and accidence in various excerpts of AR(T) produced closely similar results; that exclusively northern forms are lacking in W;[2] that the north-eastern features listed in the above table and most of the others just added are paralleled (though there may be other variants) in the dialect of Orm. Though the evidence is not conclusive, details such as the 3 s. pr. in *es*, which in Orm is always *eþ*, give W a more northern appearance. Thus, while it is not possible to locate precisely the non-AB ingredient in W, that other language is certainly East

(p. 161) wrote 'daß derselbe ein Gemisch von nordwestmittelländischen und südlichen Dialektformen enthält', and Wyld put the *Wohunge* among his representative southern texts (*A Short History of English*, London, 1914, p. 98).

[1] See Mack, p. xv.
[2] For *setis*, see note to W 504.

Dialect, Textual History, and Date

Midland; and could have had its home in the northern part of that area.

The dialectal composition of the four manuscripts may thus be stated: R is composed of AB and NWM.; L and N of AB and SWM.; W of AB and NEM. It follows that they are all copies. Moreover all, in varying degree, present typical copyist's errors, such as errors which arise from failing to understand certain words in the original (see below), or from anticipating (the spelling of) a word subsequent to the word being transcribed. Fairly certain errors of the second type are W *heali* (for *hali*) *heaued*, N *peors* (for *peos*) *wordes*, W *eorn* pt. s. (for *orn) . . . *eorðe*.

Leaving aside fanciful explanations,[1] the first fact of the textual history of these pieces is that it is not necessary to assume intermediate versions between the originals and the copies at hand. Moreover, since each text is blended of two dialects only, any intermediate version must have been in the dialect of the original or in a similar admixture. In parallel versions of the same piece (as N(U) and L, N(Le) and R), sufficiently frequent instances of better or more correct (and probably closer-to-the-original) readings, now in one version and now in the other, reveal them as independent copies. There is only one clear instance where the same error occurs in parallel passages: *spetnesse* (for *swetnesse*) N(U) 3/L 2, which may point to illegibility of the original.

In any one of these pieces it might be more difficult to determine which of the blended dialects is the original; but, when they are taken together as a group, there is little doubt that the common element AB is the language in which they were first composed. This is evident from their literary connexions, as has been shown. For, despite the ubiquity of the Latin background, they are so similar in subject and phraseology, so closely related to

---

[1] For example, Mühe (regarding AR in T): 'Das lat. Original wurde von zwei Autoren, von dem einen in anglischem, vom andern in südlichem Dialekt übersetzt. Die letztere Uebersetzung liegt Morton's Text zu Grunde. Die angl. Uebersetzung wurde unter Mitbenutzung der südlichen . . . verfertigt und von einem südlichen Schreiber kopiert. Aus dem so gewonnenen Texte entstand durch Abschrift der des ms. Cotton Titus D. XVIII' (op. cit., p. 163). Hall: 'This manuscript stands nearest in dialect to the original; it appears to be a copy of a North-Midland text made by a scribe not long enough resident in the Midland area to have quite forgotten his native Southern speech' (ii, p. 373).

Introduction

other contemporary WM. writings (such as the *Riwle*), and yet so unique in their kind at the time, as to make influence upon one another and proximate composition highly likely.

This conclusion is supported by linguistic evidence. Given ME. methods of transcription from one dialect into another, one will expect the copyist's language at least to predominate over that of the original. This happens in N, L, and R: in W, the scribal dialect is presented at least as clearly as the AB original. Moreover, in all these texts, the scribal dialect is handled with relative firmness. The most significant errors (indicating real confusion rather than mere carelessness) are in transcribing AB forms. Thus: W *girre* (for *gure*), *hetelifaste* (for *heteueste*), *huide* (blending AB *hude* and NE. *hide*); L *eini* (blending AB *ei* and L *eni*), *eafter* (blending AB *efter* and L *after*); N *ȝif* (for *ȝef* pret.), *uuward* (for *uppart*). Some of N's interlined corrections also probably show preliminary unfamiliarity with AB forms, as *hel⟨i⟩unge, ƥorne⟨ne⟩*, and the frequent later insertion of *o* after *e* (see above). Similar errors occur elsewhere in the same manuscript and in other manuscripts containing transcriptions of original AB matter.

So far as can be determined (with differences of locality taken into consideration) the dialects blended in these texts are all more or less contemporary. This indicates that the dates of original composition and of copying cannot have been far apart—a fact with which the orthographical and palaeographical evidence is not at variance. More specific dating depends on the following circumstances: (1) that the original dialect AB was a linguistic phenomenon of short duration;[1] (2) that AB is also the basic language of the *Ancrene Riwle*, the 'Katherine Group', and other related WM. works, all in extant forms (for various reasons) belonging to the early thirteenth century. The AB originals of the 'Wooing Group' are of the same period. The earliest extant manuscript of the *Ancrene Riwle*[2] cannot be earlier than 1225;[3] but it is obviously an enlarged copy, showing traces of earlier language, and for this and other general reasons indicates an original written some years before, perhaps *c*. 1200. If, as is likely but not certain, one or more of the 'Wooing Group' were in-

[1] Tolkien, pp. 120–1.   [2] MS. C.C.C.C. 402.
[3] Because of its reference to the Dominican and Franciscan orders.

Dialect, Textual History, and Date

fluenced by the *Riwle*, it would be reasonable to allow some years after composition of the *Riwle* for it to become known, perhaps through transcribed versions such as those of MSS. T and N. In any case, the extant texts of the 'Wooing Group' must be dated long enough (probably a few years) after their originals to allow for transmission and copying. More precise dating is not possible; and nothing is gained by assuming, as has been done, that at least one of the scribes journeyed to AB 'territory' to copy his text.

We conclude that our six texts are based on four AB originals. These pieces comprise a distinct group; and are further evidence of the flourishing of religious prose in the early thirteenth-century West Midland dialect, circumstantial evidence at least, that this dialect was also the original language of the *Ancrene Riwle*. The popularity of these pieces is attested by their transcription so soon into other dialects, even, in the case of the *Wohunge*, into a dialect of the North-East Midlands—where additional (if later) influence of the West Midland school is seen in the Pepys MS.[1] of the *Ancrene Riwle* and a Latin version[2] of the same work. That their popularity endured is seen in the late fourteenth-century *A Talkyng of þe Loue of God*, based on two of them. By that time, according to M. Salvina Westra, such pieces 'were known by heart by many devout people. They wrote them down, with or without additions of their own, for the edification of others'.[3]

---

[1] MS. Magdalene Coll., Camb., Pepys 2498 (Notts., end 14th cent.). This and the MS. cited in fn. 2 adapt AR for men. AW began the process of wider adaptation.

[2] MS. Cotton Vitellius E. VII (according to Smith's Catalogue, 1696: 'Hunc librum Frater Robertus de Thorneton, quondam prior, dedit claustralibus de Bardenay', i.e. Bardney Abbey in Lincolnshire).

[3] Op. cit., p. xx.

ABBREVIATIONS AND CHIEF REFERENCES

AB   Tolkien's designation for the literary West Midland common to:
       A: MS. Corpus Christi College, Cambridge, 402, containing AW.
       B: MS. Bodley 34, containing HM, J, K, M, and SW.

AR   MS. Cotton Nero A. xiv (MS. N) of the *Ancrene Riwle*, ed. J. Morton (Camden Soc., London, 1853); ed. Mabel Day (E.E.T.S., o.s. 225, 1952). References, unless stated, are to the latter.

AW   *Ancrene Wisse* in MS. Corpus Christi College, Cambridge, 402.

B/T   J. Bosworth and T. N. Toller, *Anglo-Saxon Dictionary* and *Supplement* (Oxford, 1898–1921).

E.D.D.   Joseph Wright, *English Dialect Dictionary* (Oxford, 1898–1905).

HM   *Hali Meidenhad*, ed. F. J. Furnivall and O. Cockayne (E.E.T.S., o.s. 18, 1922); *Hali Meiðhad*, ed. A. F. Colborn (Copenhagen, 1940). Both B and T versions are given in both these editions. Citations are made from the E.E.T.S. edition.

Hall   J. Hall, *Selections from Early Middle English* (Oxford, 1920). Contains excerpts of J (B and R), K (R), AW, AR (N and Caius), and SW (B and R).

Jordan   R. Jordan, *Handbuch der mittelenglischen Grammatik*, I. Teil: *Lautlehre*. 2. Auflage bearbeitet von H. C. Matthes (Heidelberg, 1934).

J(*uliene*)   and d'Ardenne *þe Liflade ant te Passiun of Seinte Iuliene*, ed. S. T. R. O. d'Ardenne (Liége, 1936). Gives B, R, and (from MS. Bodley 285) Latin versions, and an emended text. References to this edition are to the Language sections unless otherwise noted.

K(*atherine*)   *Life of St. Katherine*, with its Latin Original, ed. E. Einenkel (E.E.T.S., o.s. 80, 1884). The English text is K(R).

L   *On Ureisun of ure Louerde*, occurring in MS. Lambeth 487: not the manuscript as a whole unless specifically indicated.

Luick   K. Luick, *Historische Grammatik der englischen Sprache* (Leipzig, 1913–29).

M(*arherete*)   and Mack   *Seinte Marherete, þe Meiden ant Martyr*, ed. F. M. Mack (E.E.T.S., o.s. 193, 1934). Gives both B and R texts.

Morris   *Old English Homilies and Homiletic Treatises of the Twelfth and Thirteenth Centuries*, Series I, Part II, ed. R. Morris (E.E.T.S., o.s. 34, 1868). Contains the only complete

Abbreviations and Chief References lxi

previous edition of the whole 'Wooing Group', of which N(Le) is the only text printed in its entirety elsewhere. See footnote to text. Also contains SW(B).

Morris and Skeat   R. Morris and W. W. Skeat, *Specimens of Early English*, Pt. 1 [ed. Morris], 1150–1300 (Oxford, 1887). Contains an excerpt from W (317–564), pp. 124 ff.

Mühe   T. Mühe, *Über den im MS. Cotton Titus D. XVIII enthaltenen Text der Ancren Riwle* (diss., Göttingen, 1901).

N   MS. Cotton Nero A. XIV with reference usually only to the pieces presented here.

N(U)   *On wel swuðe god ureisun of God Almihti* (MS. Cotton Nero A. XIV).

N(Lo)   *On Lofsong of ure Louerde* (MS. Cotton Nero A. XIV).

N(Le)   *On Lofsong of ure Lefdi* (MS. Cotton Nero A. XIV).

R   MS. Royal 17 A. XXVII, with reference usually only to *þe Oreisun of Seinte Marie* presented here.

S(*awles*) W(*arde*)   The B text was edited by Morris (see above), the B text completed from R by Hall (see above), the B, R, and T texts edited by Wilhelm Wagner (Bonn, 1908), and by R. M. Wilson (Leeds, 1938). Citations are made from Wilson's edition.

Serjeantson   M. S. Serjeantson, 'Dialects of the West Midlands', *R.E.S.*, iii (1927), 54–67, 186–203, 319–31.

S/B   F. H. Stratmann (ed. H. Bradley), *A Middle English Dictionary* (Oxford, 1891).

T   MS. Cotton Titus D. XVIII, and the language thereof. Contains the (unique) MS. of W, and also versions of AR, K, HM, and SW.

Tolkien   J. R. R. Tolkien, 'Ancrene Wisse and Hali Meiðhad', *Essays and Studies by Members of the English Association*, xiv (1929), 104 ff.

VP   *Vespasian Psalter*, i.e. the language of the OE. glosses to the *Vespasian Psalter* and *Hymns*, in *The Oldest English Texts*, ed. H. Sweet (E.E.T.S., o.s. 83, 1885).

W   *þe Wohunge of ure Lauerd*, and the language thereof.

WGr.   'Wooing Group': designation sometimes used for convenience to refer collectively to the texts edited herein.

Wyld   H. C. Wyld, *A Short History of English* (3rd edn., London, 1927).

Other abbreviations are those in common use. Other printed excerpts of the 'Wooing Group' are mentioned in footnotes at the opening of each text.

NOTES ON THE TEXT

THE manuscripts are reproduced in general according to procedures being followed by the Society in printing the manuscripts of the *Ancrene Riwle*, except that the greater brevity of these pieces has permitted preservation of the original line divisions, which seem responsible for numerous verbal irregularities (see p. xiii, fn. 2). There is emendation only in a very few obvious cases of letters lost, as through page-trimming or compression at the end of a line. These are placed in square brackets, [ ]. Alterations made by the original scribe are put in angular brackets, ⟨ ⟩; letters or words expuncted are so printed; alterations by other hands (when other hands can be distinguished) are recorded in the footnotes. Contractions are normally expanded without italics, according to the practice of each manuscript; but þ (for *þet* and *þat*), ⁊ (for *and* and *ant*), and *ɼc* (for *et cetera*) are left unexpanded. Wyn (ƿ) is transcribed as *w*, and the rare occurrences of the letter-form *w* are indicated in the footnotes. The hyphens and punctuation marks are those of the manuscripts. Though none of the manuscripts is written with great care, scribal intentions are normally quite apparent. However, for reasons already given (see pp. xiii, xiv), it is very often impossible to determine indisputably when capitalization and word-division (despite crowding) do or do not occur. In these aspects of spelling, an effort has been made to reproduce all that appears certain or obvious (especially where some principle seems to be applied—though never consistently—such as the coalescence of *pron.* and *verb*, *prep.* and *subst.*, &c., or the separation of prefix from stem, of the elements of compounds, &c.); and, beyond that, to put into text or footnotes enough of the more arbitrary, debatable, and probably most often unintentional abnormalities to indicate the actual state of the manuscripts without attempting to provide a substitute for them. The detection and interpretation of erasures is sometimes fully as difficult. It is only within limitations of this kind that the transcription of these and similar manuscripts of the period can be described as diplomatic.

On ureisun of ure louerde*
[Lambeth MS. 487]

Iesu soð god . godes sone . iesu soð goð . soð mon . Mon
Maidene bern . Iesu min hali loue min sikere spet
nesse . Iesu min heorte . Misel . misaule hele . Iesu
swete . iesu mi leof . mi lif . mi leome . Min halwi .
Min huniter . þu al þ̄ ic hopie . Iesu mi weole mi wun
ne . Min bliþe breostes blisse . Iesu teke þ̄ tu art se
softe . ⁊ se swote . ȝetteṭ to swa leoflic . swo leoflic
and swa lufsum . þ̄ te engles . a . biholdeþ þe . Ne beoþ
heo neuer fulle . forto lokin on þe . Iesu al feir a
ȝein hwam . þe sunne nis boten a schadwe . ase þeo
þ̄ leoseþ here liht . and scomeþ aȝein þi brihte
leor . of hire þesturnesse . þu þ̄ ȝeuest hireliht .
⁊ al þ̄ leome hauest aliht mi þester heorte . ðef
þibur brihtnesse . mi saule þ̄ is suti ȝet . make
hire wurþe to þiswete wunninge . Ontend me
wiþ þe blase . of þi leitinde loue . let me beo ni
leofmon . ⁊ her to loue þe . louie þe louende louerd .
wa þ̄ ic am swa fremede . wiþ þe . Ah ase þu
licomliche iwend iwend me from þe worlde . wend
me . ⁊ heorte liche . ⁊ turnme allunge to þe . wiþ
soþe loue . ⁊ bileue . Ich nabbe no mong . ne felawsci
pe . ne priuete . wiþ þe wor⟨l⟩d . for wel ich þat mi leofmon
dear ich swa clipien . þ̄ flehsliche loue . ⁊ gostliche .
eorþliche louọ ⁊ heouenliche . ne maȝen onone
wise beddin in a breoste . hwa se euer haueð longe
wone of gastliche elne . of heouenliche murhðe

---

* The only previous edition is by R. Morris in *Old English Homilies*, I
(E.E.T.S., o.s. 34, 1868), pp. 183 ff. The title is Morris's.

    1 goð *for* god   2–3 spetnesse *for* swetnesse   4 halwi: w *in the form* w (*not wyn*)   7 ȝetteṭ *for* ȝette   10 schadwe: w *in the form* w   16 ni: *four minims in MS. joined together, the third being subpuncted and stroke denoting* i *over the fourth; context requires* þi   17 her *for* ler?   18 *gap of about seven spaces after* wa   22 wor⟨l⟩d: l *interl.*; þat *for* wat   23 clipien: *first* i *altered from* u *by subpuncting first minim* (N cleopien)   24 louọ *for* loue   26 heouenliche: c *badly formed and subpuncted*

hit is for þi ha haueþ . oþer wilneþ after cunfort
on eorþe . ꝥ is fikel . and fals . ⁊ al imengd wiþ balew
sið . ⁊ wiþ bitternesse . nis nan blisse soþes inan
30 þing ꝥ is utewið . ꝥ ne beo to bitter aboht . ꝥet
huni þer in beoþ liked of þornes . me nis he fol
f. 66 chapmon þe buþ deore awac þing . ⁊ for forsakeþ a deor
wurþe þing . ꝥ me beodeþ him for naut ⁊ bi hat him
þer take mede . forto nimenhit . Min iesu liues louerd
35 þubeodest us þin elming . al wiþ uthen bune . ⁊ þer
after bihastest us wiþ þon ꝥ we neomen hit heouen
liche blissen . ⁊ we wendeþ us þer from . ⁊ buggeþ worl
dles froure . wiþ moni sori teone . ⁊ elne of monnes
speche . a iesu louerd þi griþ . hwi abbe ich ein licung
40 in oþer þing þene in þe . hwi loue ich ein þing boten
þe one . hwi ne bi hold ich hu þu strahstest þe for me
on þe rode . hwine warpe ich me bitweone þe ilke ear
mes . swa swiþe wide to spradde . he openeþ swa þe moder
hire earmes hire leoue child forto cluppen.· ðe soþes
45 ⁊ tu deorwurþe louerd . gostliche to us ⁊ to deorlinges
wiþ þe ilke spredunge gest . asþe moder to hire
child . hua leof.· hwa lif.· hwa deþ him þe bitweonen . .
hwa wule beo bicluppet.· a iesu þin eadmodnesse . and þin
muchele milce . hwi nam ich inþin earmes . In þin ear
50 mes swa istrahte . ⁊ isprad on rode . and weneð ei to
beon bi clupped bitwene þine blisfulle earmes . In heo
uene bute he warpe . er her bitweone þine rewfulle ear
mes on þe rode . Nai soþes . nai . Ne wene hit neuer no
mon . þurh his lahe clupping . me mot come heh to þe ꝥ
55 þe wule bicluppe . þe þear swilc . ase þu art þear louerd of
leome . he mot cluppe þe ear her swilc . ase þu makedest
te her wreche . for us wreches . ꝥ is to suggen hwa se euer
wule habbe lot wiþ þe of þi blisse.· he mot deale wiþ þe of
þine pine on eorþe . Nis na trewe ifere þe nule naut scot
60 tin in þe lure . ase in þe biȝete.· he mot scottin efne after

30 ꝥet *for* þet ? (N ðet tet . . . ne)   32 for: *dittographed in error*
35 elming *for* elning, *or perhaps for* elnung; wiþ uthen *for* wiþ uten
36 bihastest *for* bihatest   41 strahstest *for* strahtest   46 *gap of
two spaces between* gest *and punctum*

his euene . [þ]e wule beo þin felaӡe luuiende louerd . he
mot foleӡi þine steapes þurh sar . ⁊ þurh sorewe to to
wunninge . of weole ⁊ of eche wunne . Ne wene na mon
to stihen wið este to þe steorren . A swete iesu hwi w[ið] ear
mes of luue ne cluppe ich þe swa faste . þ̄ na þing ne þe   65
onne ne maӡe breide min heorte . hwi ne cusse ich þe swete
liche ine gaste wið swote munegunge . of þine god deden.
hwi nis me bitter al þ̄ mi flehs likeð . hwi nis me unwurhþ
elc wurþliche þing . aӡein þe muchel delit of þi swetnesse .
hwi ne fele ich þe in mi breostes swo swote ase þu arṫ . hwi   70
art tu me swo fremede . hwi ne con ich woӡe þe wiþ swete
luue . uor alle þinge swetest . alre þinge leoflucest . ⁊ lu
ue wurðest . wei . wei . þe bitternesse of mine sunnen attri
is þe lettunge . mine sunnen beoþ wal bi tweone me ⁊
þe . Mine sunnen werneþ me al þis swotnesse . Mine   75
sunnen habbeþ grimliche iwreþed me . ⁊ iueed me
towart te luueliche louerd . ⁊ þ̄ is lute wunder . for swa
ich am wiþ hare hori fenliche ifuled . þ̄ ich ne mai ne ne
dear cume lufsum god in þin ehsihþe . A iesu þin
aore hwet deþ þenne þi blod isched on þe rode . hwet   80
deþ þenne þe large broc of þi softe side . þe strunden
þe striken adun of þine deorwurþe fet . ⁊ of þine edi
honden . Nes hit for to waschen sunfulle saulen . . Nes hit
for to sauuin seke inne sunne . hwa is þenne unwaschen
þe haueþ þis halwende wet inwið his heorte . hwa derf   85
beon un sauuet þe haueþ se mihti salue . ase ofte as
he þer to haueþ trewe bileue . min heoueneliche le
che . þ̄ makedest us of þi seolf se mihti medicine . iblesced
beo þu euer as mi trust is þer to . hit beo mi lechunge
hit beo mi bote . Ӡef min uuel is muchel . þe mihte þ̄   90
of is more . as wis ase dieope of þi deorwurþe blod . mahte
waschen a wai alle folkes fulþe . ase wis lifes louerd þe
ilke fif wallen þ̄ of þi blisfulle bodi sprungen . ⁊ strike
dun strondes of blode wasche mine fif wittes of alle bodi

61 [þ]e?: *space for one letter before* e   62 to to *for* to þe?
64 w[ið]: *space for two letters after* w   71 *interl. signs indicate* þe
should precede wiþ swete   90 þ̄ *for* þer   91 dieope *for*
drope

95 sunnen . of al þ ich abbe mis seien mid eȝen . mid min
eren iherd . mid muþ ispekin . oþer ismaht . ⁊ wið
neose ismelled . wiþ eini lim mis ifeled . ⁊ wið flehs isu
neged . þine wunden healen þe wunden of mi saule . þi
deaþ adeadi in me flehces licunge . ⁊ licomliche lustes .
100 ⁊ do me liuien to þe . þer ich maȝe . seggen.' wiþ sein
te pawel þe seiþ . Ic liuie naut ic ac crist lineð in me .
þ is to seggen . Ic liuie ic ilif þ ic leuede . ah crist liueþ
in me þurh his wunende grace . þ acwikeð me wel wes ha
iboren þo mai iesu þis baldeliche segge to þe . þu þ ert
105 eafter him alle helpleses help . ⁊ sunfulles hele þ to þe
habbeþ hope . helpe me englene quene . heoueneliche
leafdi seinte marie moder ⁊ maiden deorwurþ wimmon
forto salui sunne iesu crist bicom þi sone . for ure sake
þu were maked maiden godes moder . Nere þu naut
110 þ tu art edi ouer alle ȝef sunfulle neren for þi aȝen
sunfulle to cleopien to þe baldeliche . for hwam þu hauest
þin edinesse . ⁊ ti muchele heh schipe . maiden moder .
maiden ⁊ hwas moder his hwas dohter þu art . his þat
wrahte . ⁊ walt þat ischapen is . his þ naueþ nouþer
115 ne biginnunge þ is euer ilic wiþ ute truchunge . þ halt
euer anon wiþ ute sturunge . O . muchele menske
to beon moder of swuche sone . mid holscipe of maiden
⁊ hasben him swa abandun . þ he wule þ al þine wil ihwer
beo iforþed . for to schawen us þis he strahte forþ his riht
120 earm ase stod o rode . and bereþ dun towart te his
deorwurþe heaued ase þah he saide . Moder þ þu wult

    95 eȝen: ȝ *on erasure*   100 maȝe: ȝ *on erasure*   102 *a letter
erased before* ah   114 *two letters (probably* al) *erased after* walt (N al);
ende *omitted after* nouþer   118 hasben *for* habben   121 *text ends
abruptly at end of f. 67; f. 67ᵛ is left blank.*

Þis is on wel swuðe god ureisun of God almihti.*
[B.M. Cotton MS. Nero A. xiv]

Iesu soð god ⟨soð⟩ godes sune . Iesu soð god . soð mon .
⁊ soð meidenes bern . Iesu min holi luue . Mi si
kere spetnesse . Iesu min heorte . mine soule
hele . Swete iesu mi leof . mi lif . mi leome . min
healewi . min huni ter . þu ert al þet ich ho 5
pie . Iesu mi weole . mi wunne . mi bliðe breostes
blisse . Iesu teke þet þu ert so softe . ⁊ so swete .
ȝet þerto þu ert so leoflich . so louelich . ⁊
so lufsum . þet te engles euer biholdeð þe .
ne ne beoð heo neuer ful . forto logen on þe . 10
Iesu al feir . a ȝein hwam þe sunne nis buten
ase a scheadewe . ase þeo þet leoseð hire liht.·
⁊ schineð a ȝein þine brihte leore uor hire
þeosternesse . þu þet ȝeouest hire liht . ⁊ al
ðet leome haueð . aliht mine þeostri heorte . 15
ȝif mi bur brithnesse . ⁊ brihtte mine soule
þet is suti . ⁊ make hire wurðe to þine swete
wuninge . Ontend me wið blase . of þine leitinde
luue . Let me beon þi leofmon . ⁊ ler me for to
louien þe liuiinde louerd . woa is me þet ich am 20
so freomede wið þe . auh ase þu al hauest licamliche iwend me from þe worlde.· wend me
ec heortliche . ⁊ turn me allunge to þe . wið
soðe luue . ⁊ mid bi leaue . þet ich nabbe no mong
ne felauhschipe . ne speche . ne priuite wið þe 25
worlde . for ich wot mi leofmon . der ich so cleopien þe . ðet fleschlich luue ⁊ gostlich . eorðlich
luue ⁊ heouenlich.· ne muhen onone wise bedden in one breoste . hwoa so euer haueð longe
wone of gostlich elne . of heouenliche murðe.· 30

* The only previous edition is by Morris in *O.E. Hom.* I, pp. 200 ff. The title is in the MS. in red.
1 Iesu: *seventeen-line capital* I *in red; second* ⟨soð⟩ *interl.*   3 spet-nesse *for* swetnesse   25 felauhschipe: uh *on erasure*

hit is for þi . ðet heo haueð . oðer wilned⸴ efter
cumfort on eorðe . ðet is fikel . ꝛ fals . ꝛ al imengd
wið baluhsið . ꝛ wið bitternesse . Nis no blisse
soðes iþinge ðet is wtewið⸴ ðet ne beo to bitter
35 abowt . ðet tet uni ðer inne . ⟨ne⟩ beo ilicked of þor
nes . Me nis he fol chepmon . ðet buð deore a woc
þing . ⸳ forsakeð a deorwurðe þing . ðet me beot
him for nowt . ꝛ bihat him þer teken mede .
for to nimen hit ? Mi iesu liues louerd . þu
40 beodest þin elning . al wið ute bone . ꝛ þer
efter bi⟨h⟩otest us wið þen ðet we nimen hit .
he-ouenliche blissen ? ꝛ we wendeð us þer
from . ꝛ buggeð worldes froure . wið moni
sor . ꝛ teone . ꝛ elne of monnes speche ? a⸴
45 iesu louerd . þi grið . hwi habbe ich eni li-
licunge . in oðer þinge⸴ þeni þe . hwi luuie ich
ei þing bute þe one ? hwi ne bihold ich hu
þu streihtest þe for me on þe rode ? hwi ne wor
þe ich me bi tweonen þeoilke ermes so swi
50 ðe wiðe to spredde . ꝛ i openeð so þe moder deð
hire ermes . hire leoue child for to bi cluppen ?
ȝe soðes . ꝛ þu deorewurðe louerd gostliche
to us ꝛ to ðine deorelinges . wið þe ilke spre
dunge ȝeiest . ase þe moder to hire childe . hwo
55 leof ? hwo lif ? hwo deð ⟨him⟩ her bitweonen ? hwoa
wule beon bi clupped ? a iesu   þin edmod
nesse . ꝛ þi muchele milce . hwi nam ich iþin
ermes so istreihte . ꝛ ispred on rode ? ꝛ weneð
ei to beon bi clupped bitweonen þine blis
60 fulle ermes in heouene . bute he worpe er
him her⸴ bi tweonen þine rewōful ermes
oðe rode ? Nai soðes nai⸴ ne wene hit neuer
nomon . þuurh þis lowe cluppinge . me mot
come to þe heie⸴ þet wule bi cluppen þe þer

35 ⟨ne⟩ *interl.*   41 bi⟨h⟩otest: h *interl.*   45 li- *anticipates*
licunge *on verso*   50 i openeð *for* i opened ? deð: *in margin in*
darker ink, and probably different hand   55 ⟨him⟩ *interl.*   56 for (?)
erased after iesu   61 rewōful: e *erased after* l

swuch.' ase þu ert þer louerd of leoue . he 65
mot cluppen þe er her . swuch ase þu make
ðest þe her . wrecche.' for us wrecches . ðet is to
seggen . hwoa so euer wule habben lot wið
þe of þine blisse.' he mot delen wið þe.' of
þine pine on eorðe . nis he nout treowe ifere 70
þet nule nout scotten iþe lure.' ase iþe bi
ӡete . he mot scotten efne efter his euene .
þet wule beon þi felawe.' liuiinde louerd .
he mot folewen þine steopes . þuruh sor . ⁊ f. 125
þuruh seoruwe . to ðe wununge of weole.' ⁊ of 75
eche wunne . Ne wene nomon to stihen wið este
to þe steorren . A swete iesu . hwi mid ermes of
luue ne cluppe ich þe so feste . þet no þing þe
onne ne muwe breiden mine heorte ? hwi ne
cusse ich þe sweteliche ine goste . wið swete 80
munegunge of þine goddeden ? hwi nis me
bitter . al þ̄ mi flesch likeð . hwi nis me unwurð
euerich wordlich þing aӡein þe muchele de
lit of þine swetnesse ? hwi ne iuele ich þe imi
ne breoste so swete ase þu ert ? hwi ertu me so 85
freomede ? hwi ne con ich wowen þe . wið swete
luue wordes alre þinge swetest . ⁊ alre þinge
leoflukest ⁊ luue wurðest ? wei wei . þe bitter
nesse of alle mine attri sunnen is þe lettunge .
Mine sunnen beoð wal bi tweonen me . ⁊ þe . 90
Mine sunnen werneð me.' al þis swotnesse .
Mine sunnen habbeð grimliche iwursed me .
⁊ iueied me toward þe lueliche louerd ? ⁊ þ̄
is lutel wunder . forso ich ham wið hore horie
fenliche ifuled.' þ̄ ich ne mei . ne ne der lufsum 95
Godd.' cumen iþine eihsihðe . a.' iesu þin ore .
hwat deih þeonne þi blod ischd oþe rode . hwat deih þeonne þe large broc of þine softe si
de . þe streames þet striden adun of þine deo
rewurðe uet . ⁊ of þine eadie honden . nes hit 100
forto waschen sunifule soulen ? nes hit forto

101 sunifule: *reading doubtful*, sinnfule *or* sumfule *possible*

Ureisun of God Almihti [N(U)]

f. 125ᵛ saluen seke ine sunnen ? hwoa is þe⟨o⟩nne un
weaschen . þet aueð þis halwende wet inwið
his heorte ? hwoa þerf beon unsalued . þet
105 haueð so mihti salue . ase ofte ase he þerto
haueð treoue bileue ? Min heouenliche leche .
ðet makedest us of þi seolf so mihti medicine .
iblesced beo þu euer . a se min trust is þer to.'
hit beo mi lechnunge . hit beo mi bote . ʒif min
110 uuel is muchel.' þe mihte þer of . is more . ase
wis ase a drope of þine deorewurðe blode . muh
te weaschen awei alle folkes fulðe.' ase wis liues
louerd þeo ilke fif wellen of þine blisfule bodie
sprungen ⁊ striken dun strundes of blode . weasch
115 mine fif wittes.' of alle blodie sunnen . of al þ̄
ich habbe misiseien mid eien ⁊ mid min
earen iherd . wið muðe ispeken . oðer i-sma⟨u⟩ht
⁊ wið noese ismelled . wið eni lim mis iueld .
⁊ wið fleschs isuneged . þine wunden helen þe
120 wunden of mine soule . þi deað.' a deadie in
me flesches licunge.' ⁊ licamliche lustes . and
makien me liuien to þe ðet ich muwe seg
gen wið seinte powel ðet seið . Ich liuiee nout
ich.' auh crist liueð in me . ðet is to seggen . ich
125 liuie nout ine liue þet ich liuede . auh crist
liueð in me . þuruh his wuniinde grace.' ðet a
cwikeð me . wel was he ibeoren þet mei iesu
þis baldeliche seggen to þe . : þu ðet ert efter
him . alle helplease help . ⁊ sunfules hele þet to
f. 126 130 þe habbeð hope . help me englene cwene of he
ouene.' heouenliche leafdi . seinte marie . Mo
der ⁊ meiden deorwurðe wimmon . for to saluen
sunfule.' iesu crist bi com þi sune . ⁊ for ure sake

102 þe⟨o⟩nne: o *interl.*   107 medicine: *caroline* d *resembles* cl (*elsewhere insular* d *used*)   109 lechnunge: *first* n *badly rubbed or partially erased*   111 a drope: ad rope   114 weasch: weaschs *with final* s *added in later hand and darker ink*   116 *one letter erased after* misiseien *and after* eien   117 i-sma⟨u⟩ht: u *interl.*   118 *one letter erased after* lim   119 fleschs: *final* s *here in original hand (cf.* weasch⟨s⟩ 114)   128 efter: fter *on erasure*   129 helplease: lease *on erasure*

Ureisun of God Almihti [N(U)]

þu were imaked meiden.' godes moder . Nere þu
nout ðer þu ert . eadi ouer alle.' ȝif sunfule ne 135
ren . for þi owe sunfule . for to cleopien to þe bal
deliche.' for hwam þu ⟨h⟩auest þin eadinesse . ⁊
þine muchele heihschipe . Meiden . ⁊ moder .
Meiden . hwas . moder   dohter þu ert
his þet wrohte ⁊ welt . al þet ischeapen is . his 140
þet naueð nouðer ende.' ne biginnunge . þ
is euer i liche . wið ute sturiunge owe muchele
menske to boen moder of swich sune wið ihol
schipe of meiden . ⁊ habben him so abaundune . ðet he wule ðet þin wille oueral beo i uorðed 145
for to scheawen us þis.' he streccheð þene ritht
erm uorð . ase he stont orode . ⁊ beieð adun to
ward þe . his deorewurðe heaued . ase þauh he
seide . Moder al ⟨þ⟩ þu wult.' al ich wulle . aswete
leafdi . hwi leafdi hwi.' nabe ich euer bi foren 150
mine heorte eihen . þeo ilke þreo stondunges .
þe þi sune was ituht on rode . þurh driuen
fet ⁊ honden . wið dulte neiles . blodi his side .
⁊ þi stondunge leafdi . ⁊ sein iohanes ewange
listes weopinde otwo half wið sorhfule sikes ? 155
hwi ne bi hold ich þis euer in mine heorte . ⁊
þenche ðet hit was for me . ⁊ for oðre sunfule
to aredden of helle . ⁊ forto ȝiuen us heoueriche f. 126ᵛ
blisse ? þis þoht wolde sikerliche ontenden so
soð luue on me . Nere þe heorte so cold . þet ne 160
schulde neuer sunne habben forðer inȝong .
þer þis brune were . a iesu hwuder schal ich fleon
hwon þe deouel hunteð efter me bute to þi
            :   ne rode ?

137 ⟨h⟩auest: h *interl.*   139 ⁊ *erased after* Meiden .; his *erased after* hwas .; *word of four letters erased after* moder, *remaining traces being not inconsistent with* hwas (*cf.* L 113)   141 *a letter erased before* naueð   149 ⟨þ⟩ *added in margin, its position indicated by a guidemark interl. after* al   164 *The sign* (:) *separates the end of* N(U) *from the opening words of* N(Le) *written at the beginning of the same line*

On lofsong of ure louerde*
[B.M. Cotton MS. Nero A. xiv]

f. 128   Iesu crist godes sune soð godd ⁊ soð mon of
þe eadie meiden iboren maria . þet is meiden
⁊ bute make moder . ich of alle sunfulle am on
mest ifuled of sunne ase ich drede . ich bidde
5 ⁊ bi seche þe wið inwarde heorte þurh þin
akennednesse ⟨ine⟩ meidenes licame of þe holi-
Goste . ⁊ þuruh þin iborenesse wið uten bru
che of hire bodie þuruh al ꝥ ðu tawhtest .
⁊ þoledest for sunfule in eorðe . þurh þine
10 vif wunden . ⁊ þe eadie flod þet of ham fled
de . þuruh ðe irene neiles ⁊ þe þornene crune . ⁊
þuruh þe pinen ⁊ þe schomen ⁊ þi deorewurðe
deað oðe rode ⁊ þuruh ðe ilke rode ihalewed of
þine deorewurðe limen . ðet þu on hire milde
15 liche streihtest . ⁊ þine moderes ream ⁊ sein
i[o]hanes soruwe þo þu somnedest ham ase su
ne ⁊ moder . uor rewðe of þine pinen ⁊ þurch
þine blisfule ariste þe þridde dai of deaðe .
⁊ þuruh þine wurðful astiunge in to heouene .
20 þuruh ðe grace ⁊ þe ʒeoue of þe holi goste . ꝥ þu
on hwite sune dai sendest þine deorewurðe
f. 128ᵛ deciples . ⁊ ʒettedest to þeo ꝥ rith luuieð þe
⁊ leued . ⁊ þuruh þine eisfule cume a domesdai
to demen boðe cwike ⁊ deade . ⁊ þuruh þine eadi
25 flesche ⁊ þine iblescede blode i sacred oðe we
ouede . þuruh þe mihte of fuluht . þuruh alle þe oðre
sacremens . ꝥ holi chirche ileueð . þuruh þine mu
chele milce ⁊ merci þet is more þen al ꝥ is

---

* The only previous edition is by Morris in *O.E. Hom.* I, pp. 209 ff. The title is Morris's.

1 Iesu: *eleven-line capital* I *in red with guide-letter* i *in margin*   6 ⟨ine⟩ *interl.*   7, 8 þuruh : uh *on erasure*   11, 12 *here and most often in* N(Lo) ꝥ *is written for* þuruh   13 ⁊ þuruh . . . of *on erasure*   16 i[o]hanes : *space for one letter between* i *and* h

Lofsong of ure Louerde [N(Lo)]

inempned wið ute þe grace of þe oli goste .
þet is efne wið þe ⁊ wið þin eadi feder . Godd 30
of alle godd ful . haue merci of me ⁊ iher
mine bonen . þuruh þe selie bonen of þine
milde moder ⁊ seint iohanes ewangeliste . ⁊
alle þine halewen . for ȝif me mine sun
nen þet ateliche beoð ⁊ grisliche i þine eih 35
sihðe . louerd ich i seo ham wið muchel ugge
of þin eie . ne bihold þu ham nout leste þu
wreoke ham on me iwodschipe of þine
þredðe . louerd þin apostel seið þus . ȝif
we ne fordemden us seoluen ne schulde we 40
nout beon elles hwar for demed . milde mer
ciable godd ich deme to þe⸱ efter þine milce þet
is ⟨[m]ore þen al min [uu]el is ? ase wis [as]e a drope of⟩
þine de⟨o⟩rewurðe blode þ tu o rode scheddest
were inouh to weaschen alle folkes fulðe . þeo 45
sterke stremes ⁊ þet flod þet fle⟨a⟩w of þine
wunden . moncun uor to helen⸱ clense ⁊ pe
asch mine sunfule soule þuruh þine fif wun
den iopened o rode . wið neiles uor driuene
⁊ seoruh fulliche fordutte . hel me uor-wunded 50
þuruh mine fif wittes wið deadliche sunnen . ⁊ ope f. 129
ne ham heouenli⟨che⟩ king to⟨u⟩ward he⟨o⟩uenliche þin
ges . ⁊ turn to þe worlde þi wurðfule rode þ þu
spreddest þe on . beo mi scheld ⁊ mi warant on
euche half⸱ aȝein þes feondes flon þ he sche- 55
ot to me on euche halue þe swikc . þi passiun
acwenche þe passiun of sunnen þet wunieð
wið inne me . þine pinen buruwen me from
þe pinen of helle . ⁊ þi dereowurðe deað from þe-

---

39 þredðe *for* wreððe   42 þet *added in margin in darker ink and probably later hand*   43 *after* is *an interl. sign indicates a marginal addition partly lost through trimming the page. It is here placed in* ⟨ ⟩, *with reconstructions (after Morris) in* [ ]. *MS. line 43 then continues with what is here placed in line* 44   44 de⟨o⟩rewurðe : o *interl.*   46 fle⟨a⟩w : a *interl.*   47–48 pe (*prob. for* pe) *crossed out by a later hand, which also added* p *in margin before* asch, *and* s *after* asch, *giving* paschs, *an unsatisfactory form*   52 heouenli⟨che⟩, to⟨u⟩ward, he⟨o⟩uenliche : che, u, o *interl.*   59 helle *on erasure*

ne deað ðet neuer ne deieð . ꝧ ði deað adeadie þe deaðliche lustes of mine licame . ⁊ te lawen of mine limen beo ðe world to me . and me to þe
worlde . þuruh þine ariste louerd to liue.' bute deaðe .
of soule deaðe arer me . ⁊ ʒif me lif in ðe . ꝧ
65 ich iþisse worlde ne luuie nout bute þe liuinde
louerd . ⁊ hwat so god is uor þe . ꝧ ich' to þe world
beo dead . ⁊ euer liuie to þe . ꝧ ich muwe siggen
wið seinte powel þet seið . ich liuie nout ich.'
auh crist liueð in me . louerd þi merci ase ich
70 ham heie iclumben wið þis ilke bone . þet
ligge so lowe . ⁊ uor eorðliche luren so muche
mislicunge habbe in mine heorte . Milde godd
þi milce . for her-þurh ich deie þet spec er of
swuche þinge . ⁊ deaðliche sunegi . heie helin-
75 de godd help me . ⁊ hel herof mine heorte . leo
ue louerd iesu crist loke toward me ase ich
ligge lowe . ⁊ mone to ðe of þinge ðet me der
ueð mest nuðe efter mine sunnen . heie heli-
f. 129ᵛ nde beih þe to me . ⁊ buh to mine bonen . Nabbich
80 nowðer in me wisdom ne wurschipe ⁊ am redleas nab ich
⟨[h]waremide le[de]n mi lif iþis[se] worlde ⁊ am⟩
helples . ich habbe on monie wise ~~wise~~ misli-
~~habbe~~ cunge of þonke ⁊ heorte sec of sorwe .
⁊ nabbe hwoa me froure . Deorewurðe drihten
85 ase þu ert redlease red · red me ꝧ am helples
⁊ redles . hu ich schule leden me ⁊ liuien on
eorðe wið meidhod ⁊ ine clennesse of soule .
⁊ of bodie boðe . ase þu ert neodfulles help
bihold heie louerd hu monnes help tru
90 keð me . þin help beo me þe ʒarewere forto
þe one ich chulle trusten ⁊ hopien euer bu
ten ende . hefdich ʒare so idon me stode betere
þen me deð ich hit wot to soðe . uor þeo hwi

60 ꝧ . . . deað- *on erasure;* deað- *extends into margin*   63 þuruh
(MS. þ) *on erasure*   67 liuie: *one too many minims in MS.*   79
f. 129ᵛ *wrongly numbered* 130   80 nab ich *extends into margin*   81
whole line in margin and partly trimmed away

Lofsong of ure Louerde [N(Lo)]

le ðet ich truste uppo mon þu seidest . hold
þe to ham ⁊ lettest me al iwurden wið þeo þet
ich truste uppon . ⁊ heo beoð me itrukede heouenlich louerd . ich ileue for mine selhðe
ich herie þe ⁊ þonke . þu ham hauest bi nu
me me . uor þu ⟨i⟩seihe . þ̄ te hope of ham bi
swoc me ⁊ wult þ̄ ich hopie ⁊ truste to þe
one for to schewen hu þis hope to þin ones
help schal gon me betere ut . þen dude er þe
oðres . þu hauest binume me fulst of monne.⸴
uor þu wult þin ȝeouen me . Iblesced beo
þet þus went lure to bi-ȝeate . sikerliche al
mi woa on eorðe schal turnen me to ioie . ȝif
ich Godd luuie mid treowe bileaue . louerd
ich ileue hit ⁊ luuie ⁊ wulle luuien þe more lo
uerd þurh þis wondred þen er in al mine
weole . uor ich wot to soðe hit wolde habben
al bi swike me . ȝif þe help nere louerd of
þine grace . louerd ich bisech(e) ðe wið inwar
de heorte ne ȝif þu me nouðer to muchel ne
to lutel . uor þuruh eiðer moni mon suneggeð i
lome . auh leue me ðet ich mote soðliche seg
gen wið ðe meiden þet of þe seið þeors wor
des . Mi leofmonnes luft erm halt up min hea
ued heo seið . ⁊ his riht erm schal bi-clupen
me abuten . let me beo þi leouemon ⁊ siggen
ase heo seið . leof wið þi luft erm . þ̄ is . wið þi
ne worldliche ȝeouen hold up min heawed
ðet ich þuruh to muche wone ne falle i fulðe of
sunne . ⁊ leof wið þin riht erm . þ̄ is in heue
ne wið endelea⟨se⟩ blissen biclupe me abuten . al
schal beon þ̄ ich wulle þe-onne forð swete
milde louerd bidde oðer wilni ich bidde ðe
ðet ich mote under uon in obedience boðe
wone ⁊ weole þe ine cwemnesse . þau⟨h⟩ ich nabbe

95 þet *extends into margin, in darker ink and probably later hand* 99
⟨i⟩seihe : i *interl.*   124 endelea⟨se⟩ : se *interl., and preceding* a *crowded*
128 þau⟨h⟩ : h *interl.*

14 Lofsong of ure Louerde [N(Lo)]

nout one al ðet me bi-heo-uede ne me ne cu
130 me nowt ase sone ase ich wolde . ich ne misho
pie þe nout auh am al siker of ðet þu wult
binime me ðet me wolde herm don . ⁊ ʒife me
þ̄ me is bi⟨h⟩eue swete milzfule louerd . auh þu
þ̄ alle þing isihst ðet abidest histime . Nu ich
135 habbe uorloren almoncunne froure ich wot
f. 130ᵛ þ̄ þu wult senden me þene holi gost to elnen
me . ⁊ reden me ⁊ helpen me ⁊ froure me betere
þen alle þeo ilke muhten þ̄ ich on truste . uor
þus seið þe salmwruhte dauið iþe sawter . þe
140 world haueð for let me . ⁊ godd haweð underfo
me . eft elles hwar he seið . haue þi licung ine
godd ⁊ he wule ʒiuen þe bonen of þine heor
te . vnwrih him þene wei þ̄ is þi wilnunge . ⁊ he
wule hit forðen . þu wost hwat ich wilni al wel-
145 dinde Godd . auh of þ̄ ase of helles hwat.⸴ iwur
ðe þi wille euer . uor þu wult inouhreðe don
betere bi me þen is þ̄ ich wilni . ⁊ ich buhsumli
che bisechi þe louerd þuru⟨h⟩ non of seruunge
to ðe . auh þuruh þis hope . ⁊ i þis trust to þine mu
150 chele milce . ðet þu beo mi red nu . Min help ⁊
min elne . auh þe ich chulle luuien nu . uor
ham þ̄ ich luuede er ⟨⁊⟩ truste to ⁊ ⟨h⟩opede . uor nu
ich understonde hu soð hit is ðet seint austin
seið in his boc . uniseli is ðet is wið luue to e
155 ni eorðlich þing iteied . uor euer bið ðet swe
te.⸴ abouht mid twofold of bittre . auh me ne
hit under-ʒit nout er þen me hit leose .
⁊ to lure hit bi kumeð of hwuche half so hit
~~wurð~~ falleð.⸴ er me lest wene .
160 Swete softe iesu iseli beoð ðet þe luuieð ⁊
þine siker swetnesse . þ̄ no mon ne mai
leosen bute he þe treulac of þine luue lete

131 al siker of : alsikerof   133 bi⟨h⟩eue : h *interl.*   148 þuru⟨h⟩ :
h *interl.*   152 ⟨⁊⟩ . . . ⟨h⟩opede : ⁊ *and* h *interl.*   157 *space
left before* under-ʒit *to avoid a letter showing through from recto*   160
swete : *two-line capital* S *in red, beginning new section*

Lofsong of ure Louerde [N(Lo)]

auh wið uten þine ȝeoue he mai þe non
luuien . wið þe lai louerd of þe holigost . þ is þi fe
der luue ⁊ þin . tend mine heorte ⁊ uorbern al þat
is baluful . þer inne ⁊ fed hit so forðward . þ hit
ontende me euere iþine bileaue ⁊ in þine luue .
so lengre so more . Mi luue ⁊ mi red al min help
⁊ mi froure fulst me euer to gode ⁊ cher me from
sunne . ⁊ ȝif ⟨me⟩ wil ⁊ mihte ⁊ wit to leten euch uuel ⁊
wel uorto wurchen . deorwurðe drithen þu nowest
none mon nowitht þuruh his of seruunge auh dest
us al þ þu dest þuruh þine swete grace al unofserued
cuið in me hwat is milce ⁊ þ grace is grace nout
hure werkes auh do so bi me . þ mine fon grenn
en ⁊ gode gladien ⁊ blescien þine nome . ⁊ herien
buten hende . hwat mote ich milzfule louerd to
þe þ alle þing meiht . ⁊ const . ⁊ wult wel don . ⁊ wult
al þ god is . al þ me euer is neod . ich biseche þe
godd of alle godd ful wið þeos þreo wordes . ase
þu meiht . ⁊ const . ⁊ wult . Milzfule louerd haue
merci of me ⁊ of alle cristene men . amen.

170 me *interl.*

On lofsong of ure lefdi*
[B.M. Cotton MS. Nero A. xiv]

f. 126ᵛ Swete leafdi seinte
marie meiden ouer alle meidnes . þ-
bere ðet blisfule bern . þet aredde al moncun
up . þet was adun afallen . ðet þuruð adames
5 sunne . ⁊ ðet þuruh his holi passiun werp þe
ne deouel adun . ⁊ heriede helle . ich on sori sunfule þing.' bidde þin ore . ðet tu beo mi motild
aȝeines mine soule fon . þ heo hire ne mu
wen bitellen . auh were me . ⁊ help me milz
10 fule meiden.' in alle mine neoden . Mine wi
derwines habbeð biset me on euche half
abuten.' ⁊ secheð mine soule deað . luðre men
and deoflen . heo habbeð monie wunden on
me ifestned.' þet acwelleð mine soule . bute
15 þu beo mi leche . ich habbe ofte ibuw-en to al
le mine þreo ifon . to þe feond . ⁊ to þe world .
and to mine flesches sunne . ich icnowe me
gulti . ⁊ creie þe leafdi merci . for ich habbe i-
maked ȝetes of alle mine fif wittes . to sun-
20 fule unþeawes . mis i loked Mis ihercned .
Mis ifeled . mis ispeken . ⟨iloued⟩ swote smelles . prude
⁊ wilnunge of pris.' me habbeð sore iwunded .
f. 127 ase wre⟨ð⟩ðe . ⁊ onde . lesunge . mi⟨s⟩sware . vuele ihol
den treouðe . cursunge . bacbitunge . ⁊ fikelunge.'
25 summe tide . ich habbe iheued of oðer monnes
mid woh . ⁊ mid unriht iȝeuen mis . ⁊ inumen
mis . ⁊ mis etholden ofte . tovel.' spac . ⁊ slow.' to

---

* Previous editions: Morris in *O.E. Hom.* I, pp. 205 ff., G. Sampson, *Cambridge Book of Prose and Verse* (1924), pp. 196 ff. The title is Morris's 1 Swete: *two-line capital S in red with guide-letter* s *in margin* 2 mark (hyphen?) *after* þ   3 aredde *for* arerde (R arerde)   4 adun: *one letter* (b?, 1?) *erased after* n   5 þuruh: h *on erasure*   20 le unþeawes. mis i *on erasure*   21 iloued *interl.*; swote smelles: swotes melles   23 wre⟨ð⟩ðe . . . mi⟨s⟩sware: ð *and* s *interl.*   26 unriht: ht *on erasure*

Lofsong of ure Lefdi [N(Le)]

Godd . ȝemeleas.' ⁊ unlusti . sumehwile to pleiful.' to drupi oðer hwiles . ich habbe isuneged
ine mete . ⁊ ine drunche boðe . ⁊ mid wiꝛ̃ fles   30
ches fulðe ifuled me . þus ich am lodliche i
hurt ine licame . ⁊ ine soule.' wið alle cunnes
sunnen . for þauh þet werc nere i þe bodie.' þe
wil was in þe heorte . al þis ich i cnouelechie
þe swete leafdi seinte marie . heiest alre ha   35
lewen . Nim mot for me ⁊ were me . for ich am
pine wurðe . bi sech for me þine seli sune.'
Milce . ⁊ merci . ⁊ ore . for nout ne mai he wer
ne þe.' maiden þe hine bere of alle þine bi
socnen . Ich bide þe ⁊ biseche þe ⁊ halsi ȝif   40
me howeð hit.' bi his flech founge of þine e
adie bodie . bi his iborenesse . bi his eadi festunge iþe wildernesse . bi þe herde hurtes ⁊ þe
unwurðe wowes ðet he for us sunfule willeliche
þolede . bi his deað-fule grure . ⁊ bi his blodie   45
swote . bi his eadi beoden in hulles him one .
bi his nimunge . ⁊ bin-dunge . bi his ledunge
forð . bi al ꝥ me him demde . bi his cloðes wrix
lunge . Nu red . nu hwit . him on hokerunge . bi
his scornunge . ⁊ bi his spotlunge . ⁊ bufettunge .   50
⁊ his hel⟨i⟩unge . bi þe þorne⟨ne⟩ crunununge . bi ðe ki-   f. 127ᵛ
neȝerde of rode . him of scornunge . bi his
owune rode . on his softe schuldres . so herde
druggunge . bi þe dulte neiles . bi þe sore
wunden.' bi þe holie rode . bihis side openun-   55
ge . bi his blodi Rune þet ron inne monie
studen . In umbe keoruunge . in his blod spe
tunge . in his pine þornene crunun-

---

31 h *erased before* am   35–39 *mended strip in MS. separates* leaf/di
35, m/ot 36, bi/sech 37, ⁊/ore 38, maiden/þe 39   42 bi his: bihis
46 beoden: n *erased after* beo   49 *scribe joins* on to hokerunge *with a
hyphen*   51 hel⟨i⟩unge . . . þorne⟨ne⟩: i *and* ne *interl.*   52 ne
not at edge of margin to avoid ge *of* fikelunge 24 *which has come through
from the recto*   55 bi his: bihis   56 Rune: R *altered from* k; *a letter*
(r?) *erased and expuncted after* R   57–58 spetunge *for* swetunge;
after spetunge, sco[rn?]unge *erased*

ge . erest in his one hond ⁊ seoððen in his
60 oðer . olast in his side þurlunge wið ute so
re wunde . ʒet ase halewen weneð . þet to-ðe
blod-rune . was in his erest⟨e⟩ . nimunge in þe
feste bindunge . þet tet blod wrong ut et
his eadie neiles . ich halsi þe þ ðu bise
65 che him bi his schome . bi his sor . bi his
de⟨a⟩ð on rode . bi al þ he seide wrohte ⁊ þolede
in eorðe . bi þe holi sacrement of his flech ⁊
of his blod þ ðe preost sacreð . þuruh þe grace of
fuluht . þuruh alle þe oðre sacremenz . þet holi
70 chirche foluweð ⁊ useð . þuruh alle ich bi seche þe
godes deore wurðe moder þ heore mihte hel
pe me . ⁊ hore strencðe go forð . þer min offrin
ge wonteð . for min bileue is þ ich schal þuruh ham beon iboreuwen . iesu þi sune ⁊
75 Godes sune . ʒif us al him suluen ⁊ al is ure
þ he spec ⁊ wrohte ⁊ þolede in orðe . his pine
on rode ⁊ his deað acwellen Mine sunnen .
⁊ his ariste arere me in lif holinesse . ⁊ his
f. 128 up ariste dome stepen uwward inheie ⁊ holi
80 þeawes . from heih ⁊ toherre euer ðet ich iseo
in syon þe heie tur of heouene.' þene louerd
of leome . þ te engles euer biholdeð . ⁊ euer
so lengrre so heo ʒirneð hit . ⟨more⟩ for iþ seli song
is al þ me secheð . leafdi þurh þin erndin
85 ge tu-ðe me mine bone to þine eadi sune amen .

59 *small space left before* one   62 erest⟨e⟩ : *last* e *interl.*   63–
66 *mended strip in MS. separates* blod / wrong 63, halsi / þe 64, *second*
bi / his 65, seide / wrohte 66   66 de⟨a⟩ð : a *interl.*   79 do me :
dome   83 ⟨more⟩ *interl.*   85 tu-ðe *for* cuðe ?

Her cumseð þe oreisun of seinte Marie.*

[B.M. Royal MS. 17 A. xxvii]

Swete lefdi seinte marie meiden ouer meid
nes þu bere þ̄ blisfule bern . þe arerde mon
cun þ̄ wes adun ifallet þurh adames sun
nen . ant þurh his hali passiun weorp þen deouel adun
⁊ herehede helle . Ich a sari sunful þing bidde þin are . þ̄   5
tu beo mi motild aȝeines mine sawle fan . þ̄ ha hire ne
bitellen . ah were me ant help me milzfule meiden . in
alle mine neoden . ha habbeð monie wunden o me nunan
ifestnet . þe acwelleð mi sawle bute þu beo mi leche .
ich habbe ofte ibuhen to alle mine þreo fan . to þe feont .   10
ant te þeo world . ⁊ to mi flesches sunne . ich cnawe me schul
di . ⁊ crie lefdi merci . for ich habbe imaket ȝeten of alle mi   f. 70ᵛ
ne fif wittes to sunfule unþeawe . Misloket . Mishercnet .
Misispeken . Misifelet . Misiliket swote smelles . prude
ant wilnunge of pris me habbeð sare iwundet . alswa wreð   15
ðe . ⁊ onde . leasunsunge . Missware . uuele halden treowðe .
cursunge . bacbitunge . ⁊ fikelunge summe tide . ich hab
be ihaued of oðer monnes mid woh . ⁊ wið unrihte . iȝeue
mis . iunne mis . ⁊ ethalden ofte . spac to uuel . ⁊ slaw to
god . ȝemeles ant unlusti . sum time to pleiful to drupi   20
oderhwiles . ich habbe isuneget in mete ant idrunch baðe
wið flesches fulðe ifulet þ̄ ich am ladliche ihurt ilicome ant
isawle wið allescunes pinen of sunnen sor þah þe werc nere in
þe bodi þe wil wes in þe heorte . al þis ich cnawlechi to þe swete
lefdi seinte marie . hehest alre halehen . Nim mot for me   25
⁊ were me . for ich am þine wurðe . bisech for me þi milde sune
Milce . Merci . are . for nawt ne mei he wernen þe: moder þ̄
him bere . of alle þine bisocnen . ich bidde ⁊ biseche þe . ⁊ halsi
ȝef me haheð hit . bi his flesch founge of þin edi bodi . bi his
ibornesse . bi his edi uestunge iþe wildernesse . bi þe harde hur   30
tes . ant te unwurðe wohes þ̄ he for us sunfule willeliche
[þolede].

* The only previous edition is by Morris in *O.E. Hom.* I, p. 305. Title
written in red perhaps by a different hand.
  1 Swete: *five-line capital* S *in red*   16 leasunsunge *for* leasunge
23 sor *for* for   29, 30 bi his: bihis   30 bi þe: biþe   32
[þolede]: *from* N

Her biginnes þe wohunge of ure lauer[d]*
[B.M. Cotton MS. Titus D. xviii]

Iesu swete iesu . mi druð . mi derling . mi drihtin . mi healend
mi huniter . mi haliwei . Swet
ter is munegunge of þe þen
mildeu o muðe . Hwa ne mei
luue þi luueli leor ? Hwat her
te is swa hard þ ne mei to mel
te iþe munegunge of þe ? Ah
hwa ne mej luue þe luueliche iesu ? for inwið þe ane arn
alle þe þinges igedered þ eauer
muhen maken ani mon lu-
uewurði to oðer . feirnesse ⁊
lufsum neb . flesch hwit under
schrud makes moni mon beo
luued te raðer . ⁊ te mare . Summe gold ⁊ Gersum ⁊ ahte of
þis werlde makes luued ⁊ heried . Sume.' fredom ⁊ largesce
þ leuer is menskli to ʒiuen
þen cwedli to wið halde . Summe.'
wit ⁊ wisdom ⁊ ʒapschipe of
werlde . Summe.' maht ⁊ strengðe to beo kid ⁊ kene ifiht his
riht for to halde . Summe.' noblesce . ⁊ hehnesse of burðe .
Summe.' þeaw . ⁊ hendeleic ⁊ lastelese lates . Summe.' menske ⁊

---

* The only complete text previously printed is in Morris, *O.E. Hom.* I,
pp. 269 ff.; ll. 317–564 are in Morris and Skeat, *Specimens*, i. 124 ff.;
534–97 in Zupitza–Schipper, *Alt- und mittelenglisches Übungsbuch* (Leipzig,
1928), pp. 117 f. Title in upper margin in red; **d** of **lauer[d]** probably
cut off in trimming page.

1 Iesu: *eighteen-line capital* I *in red and green*   18 werlde: *first* e
indistinct, could be worlde

Wohunge of ure Lauerd [W]

mildeschipe ⁊ debonairte of
herte ⁊ dede . And ȝette ouer al
þis./ kinde makes sibbe frend
euchan to luuen oðer . Nu mi
derewurðe druð . mi luue . mi
lif . mi leof . mi luueleuest
mi heorte haliwej . mi sawle
swetnesse . Þu art lufsum on
leor . þu art al schene . al engles lif is ti neb to bihalden .
for þi leor is swa unimete lufsum
⁊ lusti on to loken./ ꝥ ȝif þe forwariede ꝥ wallen in helle mihten
hit echeliche seon./ al ꝥ pinende
pik . ne ꝥ walde ham þunche bote a softe bekinde bað . for ȝif
hit swa mihte beon./ leuere ham were eauer mare in wa for to welle
⁊ o ꝥ welefule wlite eauer mar
to loken./ þen in alle blisse beon ⁊
for gan þi sihðe . Þu art swa schene ⁊ swa hwit./ ꝥ te sunne were
dosk ȝif hit to þi blisfule bleo
mihte beo euenet . Þa ȝif ꝥ
iwile animon for feirnesse luue./ luue iwile þe mi leue lif
moder sune feirest . A iesu mi
swete iesu leue ꝥ te luue of
þe beo almi likinge . Bote
nu iwile for ahte lefmon chese
for aihwer wið chatel mon
mai luue cheape . Ah is ani
ricchere þen þu mi leof ꝥ rixles in heuene . þu art kid keiser
ꝥ al þis werld wrahtes . for as
te hali prophete dauid cwiddes .
drihtines is te eorðe . ⁊ al ꝥ

43 ꝥ *expuncted*

hit fulles werld ⁊ al þ trin
wuneð. Heuene wið þe murhðes ⁊ ta unimete blisses. Al
is tin mi sweting. ⁊ al þu wilt
ȝiue me ȝif i þe riht luuie
Ne mai i naman ȝiue mi
luue to swettere biȝete.
Halde iwile þa to þe mi leof
for þe self luue þeseluen. ⁊
for þi luue leten alle oðre þinges þ min herte fram þi luue
mihte drahe ⁊ turnen. A Iesu
swete iesu leoue þ te luue
of þe beo al mi likinge. Bote
hwat is ahte ⁊ weorldes wele wurð
wið uten fredom? And hwa is frerre þen þu? for first þu mades al
þis werld ⁊ dides hit under mine fet. ⁊ makedes me lauedi
ouer alle þine schaftes þ tu schop
on eorðe. Bote Ich hit rewli for
dide þurh hut mine sunnes. Ah
lest ine al forlesede þu ȝef þeseluen for me to lese me fra pine
Þenne ȝif i ani wile for largesce
luue.· luue iwile þe iesu crist largest ouer oðre. For oðre largemen
ȝiuen þise uttre þinges. bute
þu swete iesu for me ȝef þeseluen. þ tin ahne heorte blod
ne cuðes tu wið halde. Derre
druri ne ȝef neauer na lefmon
to oðer. And tu þ erst me ȝef
al þe seluen.· þu hafdes me heht
mi lefmon to þe ȝiue al me
seluen. to rixlen o þi rihthond
crunet wið þeseluen. Hwa is

88 al forlesede: alforlesede

Wohunge of ure Lauerd [W]

col. 2

ta largere þen þu . Hwa for largesce is betere wurð to beo luued
þen þu mi luue lif . A iesu swe-   105
te iesu leue ꝥ te luue of þe beo
al mi likinge . Bote largesce is lutel wurð þer wisdom
wontes . And ȝif ꝥ iwile animon
luue for wisdom.' nis nan wisere   110
þen þu ꝥ art wisedom cald of þi
fader in heuene . For he þurh þe
ꝥ wisdom art al þis world wrahte
⁊ dihteð hit ⁊ dealeð as hit
best semeð . Inwið þe mi leue   115
lif is hord of alle wisedom hid
as te bok witnesses . A iesu swete iesu leue ꝥ te luue of þe
beo al mi likinge . Bote mo-
ni man þurh his strengðe ⁊   120
hardischipe ek makes him
luued ⁊ ȝerned . And is ani
swa hardi swa ar tu ? Nai . for
þu þe ane dreddes nawt wið þin
anre deore bodi to fihte aȝai-   125
nes alle þe ahefulle deueles
of helle . ꝥ hwuch of ham swa is
lest laðeliche ⁊ grureful . mihte he swuch as he is to monkin
him scheawe.' al þe world were   130
offeard him ane to bihalde
for ne mihte na mon him seo ⁊
in his wit wunie . bute ȝif þe grace
⁊ te strengðe of crist baldede   f. 128ᵛ
his heorte . þu art ȝette   135
her wið swa unimete mihti
ꝥ wið þi deorewurðe hond nailet on rode.' þu band ta helle dogges . ⁊ reftes ham hare

125 anre *for* ahne?

140 praie þat tai hefden grediliche gripen ⁊ helden hit
faste for adames sunne . þu
kene kidde kempe robbedes
helle hus . lesedes tine prisuns
145 ⁊ riddes ham ut of cwalm hus
⁊ leddes ham wið þe self to
þi ʒimmede bur . bold of eche
blisse . for þi of þe mi lefmon
was soðliche quiddet . Drihti[n]
150 is mahti strong ⁊ kene ifihte . And for þi ʒif me likes stalewurðe lefmon.· luue iwile þe
iesu strongest ouer alle . þat þi
maht felle mine starke saw-
155 le fan . ⁊ te strengðe of þe helpe
mi muchele wacnesse . ⁊ har
dischipe of þe balde min herte . A iesu swete iesu leue ꝑ te
luue of þe beo al mi likinge .
160 Ah noble men ⁊ gentile ⁊ of
heh burðe ofte winnen luue   col. 2
lihtliche cheape . for ofte mo
ni wummon letes hire mensket þurh þe luue of wepmon
165 ꝑ is of heh burðe . þenne swete
iesu up o hwat herre mon
mai i mi luue sette . hwer
mai i gentiller mon chese
þen þe ꝑ art te kinges sune
170 þat tis world wealdes . ⁊ king
⁊ euene wið þi fader . king ouer
kinges lauerd ouer lauerdes
And ʒette onont ti mon
had born þu wes of marie
175 meiden mildest o mod . ki-
ne bearn of burðe . of dauið-

149 Drihti[n]: Drihti

Wohunge of ure Lauerd [W]

es kin þe king . of Abrahames streone . Hehere burðe
þen þis nis nan under sunne.
Luue iwile þe þa swete iesu 180
as te gentileste lif þ eauer
liuede on eorðe . alswa for in
al þi lif neauer na leaste nes
ifunden . mi deore lefmon
lasteles . ꝛ tat com þe of bur- 185
ðe . ꝛ of foster alswa . þu þat
eauer wunedest i þe hurd of heouene . A mi deorewurðe druð f 129
swa gentile ꝛ swa hende . ne þole me neauer mi luue nohwer 190
to sette o karlische þinges . ne
eorðli þing ne fleschli aʒaines
te ʒerne ne luue aʒain þi
wille . A iesu swete iesu leue þat
te luue of þe beo al mi likinge . 195
Meknesse ꝛ mildschipe makes
mon eihwer luued . ꝛ tu mi leue iesu for þi mikle meknesse
to lamb was euenet . For aʒaines al þe woh ꝛ te schome þ tu 200
þoledest . ꝛ aʒaines al þe wa ꝛ te
pinfule wundes.· neauer neh
opnedes ti muð to grucchen
aʒaines . ꝛ ʒette þe schome
ꝛ te woh þ te sunefule of þe world 205
euch dai don þe.· mildeliche
þu þolest hit . ne wrekes tu
þe nawt sone after ure Gultes
Bote longe abides bote þurh
ut ti milce . Þenne þi deboneir 210
schipe mai make þe eihwer
luued . ꝛ for þi is riht þ i luue
þe . ꝛ leaue alle oðre for þe . for

202 neh *for* ne

muchel þu haues ti milce
toward me scheawed . A iesu
swete iesu leue þ̄ te luue of þe
beo al mi likinge . Bote for þi
þ̄ sibbe frend kindeliche euchan luues oðer.' þu schruddes
te wið ure flesch . nam of hire
flesch mon born of wummon
þi flesch nam of hire flesch wið
uten meane of wepmon . nam wið
þ̄ ilke flesch fulliche monnes
cunde to þolen al þ̄ mon mai
þole . Don al þ̄ mon deð wiðuten
sunne ane . for sunne ⁊ unwit
schipe ne hafdes tu nowðer .
Þenne aȝaines kinde Gað hwa
þat swuche kinsemon ne luueð
⁊ leueð . And for þi þ̄ trewere
luue ah beo imong breðre
þu monnes broðer bicom of an
fader wið alle þoa þ̄ cleneliche
singen . Pater noster . Bute þu
þurhut kinde . ⁊ we þurhut
grace . ⁊ mon of þ̄ ilke flesch þ̄
we beren on eorðe . A . hwam mai
he luue treweliche hwa ne lu
ues his broðer . Þenne hwase þe
ne luues.' he is mon unwreastest
Nu mi swete iesu . leaued haue i for þi luue flesches sibnesse
⁊ ȝette borne breðre hauen
me forwurpen . bote ne recches me na þing hwils þ̄ iþe halde . for iþe ane mai ich alle frend
finden . þu art me mare þen fader . mare þen moder . Broðer
suster . oðre frend narn nawiht

col. 2

244 f. 129ᵛ *wrongly numbered* 130

aȝaines te to tellen . A iesu swete iesu leue þ̄ te . ⁊c . Þenne
þu wið þi fairnesse . þu wið ri
chesce . þu wið ~~richesce~~ largesce . þu wið wit ⁊ wisdom . þu wið   255
maht ⁊ strengðe . þu wið nobles
ce ⁊ hendeleic . þu wið meknes
se ⁊ mildeschipe ⁊ mikel debo
nairte . þu wið sibnesse . þu wið
alle þe þinges þ̄ man mai lu-   260
ue wið bugge.' haues mi luue
chepet . Ah ouer alle oðre þinges
makes te luuewurði to me þa
harde ~~harde~~ ⟨atele⟩ hurtes . þa schomeliche wohes þ̄ tu þoledes   265
for me . þi bittre pine ⁊ passiun . þi derue deað o rode . telles
riht in al mi luue . calenges
al mi heorte . Iesu mi liues luue . min herte swetnesse . þre   270
fan fihten aȝaines me . ⁊ ȝet-
mai ich sare for hare duntes

col. 2   drede . ⁊ bihoues þurh þi grace
ȝapliche to wite me . þe werld
mi flesch . þe deouel . þe world   275
to make me þewe . Mi fles.' to
make me hore . þe deuel þurh
ut þise twa to drahe me to
helle . Arh ich was meself ⁊ wah
⁊ neh dune fallen . ⁊ mine fan   280
derue . swa bucchede ⁊ swa kene
þ̄ hwen þai sehen me swa wak ⁊
swa forhuhande ⁊ buhande
toward ham . þei swiðre sohten uppo me . ⁊ wenden of me wrecche   285
haue maked al hare ahen ⁊

264 atele *in margin to replace crossed-out repetition of* harde

hefden forsoðe maked . nere helpe
nere þe nerre . Þai grennede
for gladschipe euchan toward
oðer as wode wulues þ̄ fainen
of hare praie . Bote þer þurh
understonde i þ̄ tu wult hauei
me to lefmon ⁊ to spuse . þ̄ tu
ne þoledes ham noht fulli fai
nen of me . ⁊ alle gate haue
wurpen me in schome ⁊ in sinne
⁊ ter after in to pine . Bote þer
þe bale was alre meast . swa was
te bote nehest . Þu biheld al
þis ⁊ tu allegate seh þ̄ ine
mihte stonde aȝain hare
wilfulle crokes þurh wit oðer strengðe þ̄ wes in me seluen . Bot neh
hefde i fulliche buhed til alle
mine þre fan . þu com me to
helpe . feng to fihte for me . ⁊
riddes me fram deaðes hus sorhe
⁊ pine of helle . Þu biddes me
bihalde hu þu faht for me . þ̄ i
pouerte of worlde ne schome of
wicke monnes muð for uten
mine Gulte . ne secnesse of mi
bodi . ne flesches pine drede . hwen
þ̄ i bihalde hu þu was poure for
me . hu þu was schent ⁊ schomet
for me.' ⁊ atte laste wið pineful
deað henged orode . Iesu mi
liues luue riche ar tu as lauerd
in heuene ⁊ in eorðe . ⁊ tah þoure
þi bicom for me . westi ⁊ wrecched
Poure þu born was of þe meiden
þi moder . for þenne iþi burð tid

287 helpe : pe *blurred*   292 hauei *for* haue   319 þoure *for* poure
320 þi *for* þu

in al þe burh of belleem ne fant
tu hus lewe þer þine nesche childes limes inne mihte reste . Bot 325
in a waheles hus imiddes þe strete . Poure þu wunden was irattes ⁊ i clutes ⁊ caldeliche dennet in a beastes cribbe . Bote
swa þu eldere wex. swa þu poure- 330
re was . For i þi childhad hafdes
tu þe pappe to þi fode . ⁊ ti moder readi hwen þu pappe ȝern-
des . Bote hwen þu eldere was .
þu þ̃ fuhel ofluht . fisch iflod 335
folc on eorðe fedes. þoledes for
wone of mete moni hat hungre as clerkes witerliche in godspel reden . ⁊ tu þ̃ heuene ⁊ eorðe ⁊ al þis werld wrahtes . naue- 340
des in al þis werld hwer þu o þin
ahen þi heaued mihtes reste .
Bot⟨e⟩ baðe ȝung ⁊ eldre alle
Gate þu hafdes hwer þu mihtes
wrihe þine banes . Ah atte laste 345
of þi lif hwen þu for me swa
rewliche hengedes on rode . ne
hafdes in al þis world hwer wið
þ̃ blisfule blodi bodi þu mihtes
hule ⁊ huide . ⁊ swa nu swete lef- 350
mon poure þu þe self was . ⁊ te
þoure þu raðeste cheas . pouerte þu luuedes . pouerte þu tah
tes . ⁊ ȝiuen þu haues echeliche þin endelese blisse . til alle 355
þ̃ clenli for þi luue mesaise ⁊
pouerte wilfulliche þolien . A
hu schulde i beo riche . ⁊ tu mi

343 Bot⟨e⟩: e *interl. above subpuncted* o   352 þoure *for* poure
358 *small hole over* t *in* tu

leof swa poure ? for þi swete
iesu crist wile i beo poure for þe.
as tu was for þe luue of me.
for to beo riche wið þe i þin eche
blisse. for wið pouerte ⁊ wið wa
schal mon wele buggen. A iesu
swete iesu leue þ̄ te ⁊c. Bote
pouerte wið menske is eað for
to þolien. Ah þu mi lef for mi
luue wið al þi pouerte was schomeliche heaned. for hu mon
þe ofte seide schomeliche wordes ⁊ haðfule hokeres. long
weren hit al to tellen. Bote
muche schome þu þoledes. hwen
þu þ̄ neauer sunne dides. was taken as untreowe. Broht biforen sinfule men þa heaðene
hundes of ham to beo demet. þ̄
demere art of werlde. þer þu
bote of mon kin schomeliche
was demed. ⁊ te monquellere
fra deðes dom was lesed. For
as i þe godspel is writen. alle
þai crieden o wode wulues wise
Heng heng þ̄ treitur iesus on
rode. Heng him o rode. ⁊ lese
us Baraban. was tat barabas
a þeof þ̄ wið tresun i þe burh
hafde a mon cwelled. bote mare
schome þu þoledes hwen þ̄ te
sunefule men iþi neb spitted
A iesu hwa mihte mare þo-
len cristen oðer heaðen. þen
mon him for schendlac i þe
beard spitted. And tu iþi welefulle wlite. i þ̄ lufsume leor

386 *small hole after* us

Wohunge of ure Lauerd [W]

swuche schome þoledes . And al
þe menske þuhte for þe luue of me . þ tu mihtes wið
þ spatel þ swa biclaried ti
leor wasche mi sawle . ⁊ make   400
hit hwit ⁊ schene ⁊ semlike
iþi sihte . ⁊ for þi þu biddes me
her up on þenche . Scito quoniam
propter te sustinui opprobrium
operuit confusio faciem meam . Vnderstond   405
þu seist ⁊ herteliche þenke
þat i for þe luue of þe þolede
schome ⁊ bismere . ⁊ schomeliche spateling of unwurði
ribauz þa heaðene hundes   410
hilede mi neb for þe . As tah
he seide . ne dred tu nawt for þe
m⟨i⟩e of me to þole schome
of worlde wið ute þine Gulte .
Bote schome ouer schomes   415
þoledes tu hwen þu wes hen-   f. 131
ged bituhhe twa þeofes . As
hwase seie . He þis is mare
þen þeof . And for þi as hare
meister he henges ham bi-   420
tuhhen . A iesu mi liues luue hwat herte ne mai to breke hwen ha herof þenches
hu þu þ menske art of al
monkin . of alle bales bo-   425
te . mon for to menske swuch
schome þoledes . Mon spekes
ofte of wundres ⁊ of selcuðes
þ misliche ⁊ monifald ha
uen bifallen . bote þis was te mea-   430
ste wunder þ eauer bifel on
eorðe . ʒa wunder ouer wundres

416-58 (approx.) f. 131ʳ rubbed, but legible

Wohunge of ure Lauerd [W]

435
þ tat kidde keiser cruned
in heuene . schuppere of
alle schaftes . for to mensken hise fan . walde henge
bituhhe twa þeoues . A iesu
swete iesu þat tu wes schent
for mi luue leue þ te luue

440
of þe ʐc . Inoh were pouerte
ʒ schome wið uten oðre pi
nes bote ne þuhte þe neauer
mi liues luue þ tu mihtes
fulliche mi frendschipe

445
buggen hwilf þe lif þe lasted
A . deore cheap hefdes tu on
me . ne was neauer unwurði
þing chepet swa deore . Al þi
lif on eorðe wes iswink for

450
me swa lengre swa mare
Ah bifore þin ending swa unimeteliche þu swanc ʒ swa
sare þ reade blod þu swattes
for as . seint luk seið i þe god

455
spel . þu was i swa strong a
swing þ te swat as blodes
dropes eorn dune to þe eor
ðe . Bute hwat tunʒe mai
hit telle . hwat heorte mai

460
hit þenche for sorhe ʒ for reowðe of alle þa buffetes ʒ ta
bali duntes þ tu þoledest
i þin earst niminge hwen
þ iudas scharioth brohte

465
þa helle bearnes þe to taken ʒ bringen biforen hare
princes . hu ha þe bunden swa
hetelifaste þ te blod wrang ut at
tine finger neiles as halhes

col. 2

f. 131ᵛ

445 hwilf *for* hwils   455 strong *indistinct, could be* strang

Wohunge of ure Lauerd [W]

bileuen ⁊ bunden ledden rewli ⁊
dintede unrideli o rug ⁊ o schul
dres . ⁊ bifore þe princes buffeted ⁊
beten . Siðen bifore pilat hu þu
was naket bunden faste to þe pi
ler . þ̶ tu ne mihtes nowhwider
wrenche fra þa duntes . þer þu wes
for mi luue wið cnotti swepes swungen swa þ̶ ti luueliche lich mih
te beo to torn ⁊ to rent . ⁊ al þi
blisfule bodi streamed on a Girre
blod . Siðen o þin heaued wes set
te crune of scharpe þornes .
þ̶ wið eauriche þorn wrang ut
te reade blod of þin heali heaued . Siðen ȝette buffetet ⁊ to
dunet i þe heaued wið þe red ȝer-
de þ̶ te was ear in honde ȝiuen
þe on hokerringe . A hwat schal
i nu don ? Nu min herte mai to
breke . min ehne flowen al o wa
ter . A nu is mi lefmon demd for
to deien . A nu mon ledes him forð
to munte caluarie to þe cwalm
stowe . A lo he beres his rode up
on his bare schuldres . ⁊ lef þa
duntes drepen me þ̶ tai þe dunchen ⁊ þrasten þe forðward swiðe toward ti dom . A lefmon hu
mon folhes te . þine frend sariliche wið reming ⁊ sorhe . þine
fend hokerliche to schome ⁊
wundren up o þe . A nu haue þai
broht him þider . A nu raise
þai up þe rode . Setis up þe warh
treo . A nu nacnes mon mi lef
A . nu driuen ha him up wið
swepes ⁊ wið schurges . A hu li-

ue i for reowðe þ seo mi mi lef
mon up o rode . ⁊ swa to drahen
hise limes þ i mai in his bodi
euch ban tellen . A hu þ ha nu
driuen irnene neiles þurh þine feire hondes in to hard rode
þurh þine freoliche fet . A nu
of þa honden ⁊ of þa fet swa luueli . streames te blod swa rewli . A nu beden ha mi leof þ seið
þ him þristes. aisille surest alre ~~þinge~~ drinch menged wið
galle þ is þing bittrest . Ewa
Bale drinch iblodleting swa
sur ⁊ swa bittre . bote ne drinkes
he hit noht . A nu swete iesu . ȝet
up on al þi wa ha eken schome
⁊ bismer . lahhen þe to hokere
þer þu o rode hengest . þu mi
lueliche lef þer þu wið strahte
earmes henges o rode. was reowðe
to rihtwise . lahter to þe luðere
And tu þ al þe world fore mihte drede ⁊ diuere. was unwreste folk
of world to hoker lahter . A þ
luuelike bodi þ henges swa rewli
swa blodi ⁊ swa kalde . A hu schal
i nu liue for nu deies mi lef for
me up o þe deore rode ? Henges
dun his heaued ⁊ sendes his sawle
. Bote ne þinche ham nawt ȝet
þ he is ful pinet . ne þ rewfule deade bodi nulen ha nawt friðie .
Bringen forð longis wið þ brade scharpe spere . he þurles his side
cleues tat herte . ⁊ cumes flowinde ut of þ wide wunde . þe

520 Ewa *for* Twa   541 *small hole after* Bringen

Wohunge of ure Lauerd [W]

þlod þ bohte . þe water þ te world 545
wesch of sake ⁊ of sunne . A swe
te iesu þu oppnes me þin herte
for to cnawe witerliche ⁊ in to reden trewe luue lettres . for þer
i mai openlich seo hu muchel 550
þu me luuedes . Wið wrange schuldi þe min heorte wearnen
siðen þ tu bohtes herte for herte .
Lauedi moder ⁊ meiden þu stod
here ful neh ⁊ seh al þis sorhe 555
vpo þi deorewurðe sune . was wið
inne martird iþi moderliche her
te . þ seh to cleue his heorte wið
þe speres ord . Bote lafdi for þe Ioie
þ tu hefdes of his ariste þe þridde 560
dai þer after. leue me vnderstonde
þi dol ⁊ herteli to felen sum hwat
of þe sorhe þ tu þa hefdes ⁊ helpe þe to wepe . þ i wið him ⁊ wið þhi
þe muhe imin ariste o domes 565
dai gladien ⁊ wið ʒu beon iblis-
se þ he me swa bitterliche wið
his blod boþhte . Iesu swete iesu
þus tu faht for me aʒaines
mine sawle fan . þu me deren- 570
nedes wið like . ⁊ makedes of me
wrecche þi leofmon ⁊ spuse . Broht
tu haues me fra þe world to bur
of þi burðe . steked me i chaum
bre . I mai þer þe swa sweteli kissen 575
⁊ cluppen . ⁊ of þi luue haue gast
li likinge . A swete iesu mi liues
luue wið þi blod þu haues me
boht . ⁊ fram þe world þu haues me
broht . Bote nu mai i seggen wið 580
þe salmewrihte . Quid retribuam

545 þlod *for* blod   568 boþhte *for* bohte

domino pro omnibus quæ retribuit mihi. Lauerd hwat
mai i ʒelde þe for al þ tu haues
ʒiuen me. Hwat mai þole for þe
585 for al þ tu þoledes for me? Ah me
f. 132ᵛ bihoueð þ tu beo eað to paie.
a wrecche bodi ⁊ a wac bere
ich ouer eorðe. ⁊ tat swuch as
hit is haue ʒiuen ⁊ ʒiue wile
590 to þi seruise. Mi bodi henge
wið þi bodi neiled o rode. sperred querfaste wið inne fowr
wahes ⁊ henge i wile wið þe
⁊ neauer mare of mi rode cu
595 me til þ i deie. For þenne schal i lepen fra rode in to reste.
fra wa to wele ⁊ to eche blisse
A. iesu swa swet hit is wið þe
to henge. forhwen þ iseo o þe
600 þ henges me biside.· þe muchele swetnesse of þe.· reaues me fele of pine. Bote
swete iesu hwat mai mi bodi
aʒaines tin. For ʒif ich m-
605 ihte a þusand fald ʒiue þe
me seluen nere hit nowt
onont te þ ʒef þe seluen
forme. And ʒet ich haue
an heorte unwrest ⁊ un
610 wurði ⁊ westi ⁊ poure of
alle gode þeawes ⁊ tat swuch
as hit is.· tac hit to þe nu
leue lif wið treowe luuenes   col. 2
se. ⁊ ne þole me neauer nan o-
615 ðer þing aʒain þi wille luuie
for ne mai ich nowhwer

586–639: *parts of f. 132ᵛ rubbed, but legible*   600–1 mu-chele: ele *indistinct*   603 mai: m *indistinct*   605 fald: f *indistinct*   610 wurð: ð *indistinct*   611 swuch: c *indistinct*

mi luue bettre sette þen o
þe iesu crist þ̄ bohtes hit swa
dere . nis nan swa wurði
to beo luued as tu swete 620
iesu þ̄ in þe haues alle þing
hwer fore mon ah beo luuewurði to oðer . þu art best
wurð mi luue þ̄ for mi
luue deidest . ȝette 625
ȝif þ̄ imi luue bede for to
selle . ⁊ sette feor þer upon
swa hehe swa ich eauer wile.'
ȝette þu wult hit habbe
⁊ teken al þ̄ tu haues ȝi- 630
uen.' wil tu eke mare . ⁊
ȝif i þe riht luuie . wilt me
crune in heuene wið þe self
to rixlen werld in to werlde
A iesu swete iesu mi luue . mi 635
lef . mi lif . mi luue leuest
þ̄ swa muchel luuedes me
þ̄ tu deides for luue of me
⁊ fra þe world haues broht
me . ⁊ ti spuse haues ma 640 f. 133
ked me . ⁊ al þi blisse haues heht me.' leue þ̄
te luue of þe beo al mi
likinge .

Prei for me mi leue 645
suster . þis haue i writen
þe for þi þ̄ wordes ofte
quemen þe heorte to
þenken on ure lauerd

624 *small hole before* þ̄   625 *gap of about seven spaces before*
ȝette *and MS. surface uneven*   640 *The folio number replaces cancelled*
134. *Some readings on f. 133 rubbed, but almost all legible*   645 *Following a clear space of one line,* Prei, *with two-line capital* P, *begins a new
section;* P *is ornamented in green.* Prei: ei *crowded*

650 And for þi hwen þu
art on eise carpe to-
ward iesu ⁊ seie þise
wordes . ⁊ þenc as tah
he heng biside þe blo-
655 di up o rode . And he
þurh his grace opn[e]
þin heorte to his luue
⁊ to reowðe of his pine.

    651 carpe: r *indistinct*   655 he: h *indistinct*   656 opn[e]: e *illegible*   657 luue: uu *indistinct*.
The Wohunge *ends about six lines from the bottom of the first column. Nothing is written on the rest of f. 133ʳ*

NOTES

On Ureisun of ure Louerde [L]

1 soð god. godes sune ... soð mon: cf. N(Lo) 1. These three aspects of Christ are the theme of Katherine's longest discourse.

5 For *art* omitted after *þu,* cf. N(U) 5.

8–9 þ te engles ... fulle: cf. SW 255 f.: *þet te engles ne beoð neauer ful on him to bihalden;* cf. also HM 57/598 f.

14 þi: for *mi*? Cf. N(U) 16. But *þi bur* may refer to *mi saule ... þi swete wunninge.*

16 ni: for *þi,* cf. N(U) 19.

17 her: the parallel passage in N(U) 19 has *ler,* the reading expected here.

18 wa: the missing words are probably *is me*; cf. N(U) 20.

19 The first *iwend* is pp. with auxil. omitted; cf. N(U) 21–22.

24–25 ne maʒen ... breoste: cf. HM 59/638: *ne muhen ha nanes weis bedden in a breoste.*

30–31 Parallel N(U) 35 has *ðet tet uni ... ne beo.* L *þet* [sic] is probably due to misreading *þ tet* in the original.

þet huni ... þornes: cf. HM 11/98: *ha lickeð huni of þornes.*

31–32 me nis ... buþ: cf. AR 92/18 f: *nis he fol chepmon þet hwon he wule buggen* (&c.).

42–44 þe ilke earmes ... cluppen: cf. AR 103/6 f.: *ase ðe moder mid hire gunge deorlinge ... mid i spredde ermes leapeð lauhwinde uorð ⁊ cluppeð.*

47 hua leof ...: possibly 'what loved one, what living creature, who puts himself between those arms?' (reading *þe bitweonen* as *þer-bitweonen* 'there-between'); cf. N(U) 55. That alliterating *leof* and *lif* frequently go together in the language of love is apparent from N(U) 4, L 4, W 34, 636.

50 ei: see d'Ardenne, Etym. Appendix, p. 151.

52 him (refl.) is omitted after *warpe;* cf. N(U) 61.

55 One *þe* is redundant (possibly the second *þe* as an anticipation of the next word *þear*); but cf. N(U) 64. In *þear* the *ea* may be due to shortening.

57–60 hwa se euer ... biʒete: cf. AR 157/20 f.: *vor ase seinte powel seið. Si compatimur.' et conregnabimus. ase ʒe schotteð mid him of his pine on eorðe.' also ʒe schulen scotten mid him of his blisse ine heouene;* AR 163/24 f.: *nis he neuer god feolawe. ne treowe.' þet nule scotten iðe lure.' ase eft iðe biʒeate.*

59 scottin: ME. formation probably < ON. *skot*' contribution ', cognate with OE. *gesceot* 'a shot (from a weapon, &c.)', but possibly influenced by OF. *escot;* cf. AR 157/21 *schotteð,* 157/22 *scotten.*

62–63 to to wunninge: the parallel passage (N(U) 75 has *to ðe wununge*.

63–64 Ne wene ... steorren: cf. AR 165/26: *ne wene non mid este: stien to þe steorren*.

65–66 ne þeonne: the *ne* is an error; cf. N(U) 78–79.

67 ine: d'Ardenne (p. 105) explains this form as either a reduction of *inne* adv. in prepositional use, or the partial assimilation of *in* to *inne*.

69 See note to N(U) 83.

73 mine sunnen attri: position of adj. probably an error; cf. N(U) 89.

76 iueed may be a correct or archaic form, or it may be a miswriting of *iueied*, as N(U) 93. Both seem to be derivatives of OE. *fāh* 'hostile, at enmity' (pointing to OE. **fǣhjan*); but the development of these verbs with original medial *hj* in OE. is obscure, and medial front *g* (= [j]) seems to have been developed in infinitive forms; cf. **fǣhjan* 'to paint'.

79–80 A iesu þin aore: cf. AR 11/27, 35/1.

81 broc: cf. AR 115/28: *brokes of ful brode ⁊ deope wunden*.

strunden: see note to N(U) 114.

85 derf: for *ðerf*; see Orthography, p. xiv.

94 A preposition (*in*?) is probably omitted before *strondes*, and before *strundes* in (parallel) N(U) 114.

bodi: for *blodi*? Cf. N(U) 115. Cf. also N(Lo) 43–51, and AR 11/28 f.: *uor þeo ilke uif wunden ... hel mine blodi soule of alle þe wunden þ heo mide [is] iwunded þuruh mine uif wittes*.

95–97 mis seien ... mis ifeled: cf. N(Le) 20–21, R 13–14, and AR 39/35 f. The senses are referred to in similar order in L, N, R, and AR.

98–99 þi deaþ ... lustes: cf. N(Lo) 60–61.

101 Cf. Galatians ii. 20; see N(U) 123–4, N(Lo) 68–69, and AR 159/17 f.

102 *naut* is omitted after *liuie*; cf. N(U) 125.

103–4 See note to N(U) 127–8.

114 *al* is omitted after *walt*, and *ende* is omitted after *nouþer*; cf. N(U) 140–1.

115 truchunge: probably an error for *trukunge* (see *trukeð* < OE. *trucað* in Glossary); but the spelling and sense (?) might be influenced by OF *trichier* 'to trick or deceive'. O.E.D. s.v. *Troke* 'fail' cites *truches* 2 s. pr. from *Alexander* (a. 1400–50), 1. 1988.

118–19 al þine wil ... iforþed: cf. AR 186/27: *þi word beo iuorðed*.

119–21 he strahte ... heaued: *he* is probably omitted before *stod*; cf. N(U) 147. Cf. also AR 183/15 f.: *(He) þet tospret so touward ou his ermes and buhð ase uorto beoden cos:' a duneward his heaued*.

Notes

On Ureisun of God Almihti [N(U)]

10 Repetition of *ne* is an error.

13 **schineð**: L has *scomeþ* (11), a better reading.

17 **suti**: probably a new adj. from the stem of OE. *besūtian* 'to make foul or sordid' (see B/T Suppl.); cf. HM 53/561.

33 **baluhsið**: may be erroneous, but the intrusive *h* may be compared with that of *selhðe*, &c.; see Phonology under OE. *g*. L has *balewsið*.

36 **Me** conj. 'but, however' (an AB introductory word), not < OF. *meis*, of similar sense, but probably points to a special sense development of VP. *mæ*.

54 **ȝeiest**: either from OE. **gēgan* cognate with ON. *geyja* 'bark', or a new formation replacing OE. *cēgan* 'call' with [ȝ] from other yell-words, as OE. *gellan*, ME. *ȝuren*, and possibly influenced by ON. *geyja* (d'Ardenne, p. 155).

83 **wordlich**: probably for *worldlich*, which may suit the context better than *wurpliche* L 69, in the parallel passage.

114 **strundes**: cf. *strondes* L 94, *strunden* L 81. The *u*-forms, which are probably < OE. **strynd* cognate with *strand*, are found (only?) in Western texts in the thirteenth century (see *O.E.D.* under *Strand²*, *Strind²*).

122 **makien**: an error for *makie*, 3 s. pr. subj.

127-8 **wel was he ibeoren ...**: the sense is improved if *þis* 128 is omitted. The parallel passage in L (103-4), where *ha* is probably miswritten for *he*, makes better sense, but awkwardly.

139 See L 113 for the omissions. The first words expand the previous phrase *Meiden. ϡ moder* 138—thus 'maiden and whose mother?' —which suggests oral rhetoric.

142 **owe** does not make sense. Parallel L 116 has *O*, interj.

151 **þeo ilke þreo stondunges**: literally 'those same three standing ones', or, more freely, 'those same three standing there'; cf. *stondunge* 154. The reference is to John xix. 26, 27; cf. N(Lo) 15 f., 29 f., AR 46/25. He who *stont orode* in N(U) 147 is the third *stondung*—a piece of realism derived from the footrest, fixed to the cross, which gave necessary support to one crucified. This is seen in many representations of the cross.

153 Supply *his* before *fet*.

dulte: 'blunt'. This is a ME. formation, and is perhaps a blend of *dul* (< OE. **dyl*, related to OE. *dol* 'shortwitted, foolish') and *stunt* (< OE. *stunt* of similar meaning). The development of other senses, as 'stunted, short and thick', is possibly influenced by the cognate ON. *stuttr* (< **stuntr*). *Dulte neiles* occurs in AR 131/32, 132/1-2, and *dult wit* in K 1262.

On Lofsong of ure Louerde [N(Lo)]

3–4 **on mest**: the most ? the one most ?

10 **fledde**: possibly influenced by *flod* (same line), or < OE. **flēdan* 'to flood or overflow' implied in OE. *flēding* 'inundation'. See note to N(Lo) 46.

22 ʒettedest: possibly < LOE. *gēatan* 'assent, say yes, grant' < ON. *játa*; but OE. *gēotan* 'pour out' fits the context better (so Morris).

þeo þ rith luuieð þe: cf. K 950 f., AR 1/8.

33 **ewangeliste**: in these texts spelt with *wyn* (see N(U) 154), but in AB with *w* and *uu*.

46 **fleaw**: probably an error for *fleow*; but it may be an AB form influenced by alliterating OE. *flēotan, flēat*, of related meaning.

47 **clense**, pr. subj., probably takes its sg. number from *flod*, the nearest subject. Such was probably intended for *waschs* [sic] 48; see footnote to text.

60–64 Cf. Romans vii, especially vv. 5, 6, 23.

62 The reading is defective. Morris stops the sentence after *limen*, and supplies *dead* after *world*.

101 **ones**: 'singular, unique, unaided'?

103 **oðres**: g. pl. '(the help of) others'.

105 **þus went lure to bi-ʒeate**: cf. HM 55/580: *eihwer passeð ... te lure ouer al, al þe biʒeate*.

117–19 Song of Solomon ii. 6 (viii. 4).

136 **elnen** < OE. *elnian* (< *ellen* n.) where it usually meant 'emulate'. The new sense of 'comfort, &c.' (for verb and noun), is first common in WM. texts. See AR 4/27, 48/4, 80/14, HM 37/384, &c.

153–6 **hu soð ... bittre**: cf. HM 39/406 f.: *forþi, as seint Austin seið, þat is wið to muche luue to eni eorðliche þing iteiet, for eauer beð þat swete aboht wið twa dale of bittre*. Cf. also HM 11/98 f.

On Lofsong of ure Lefdi [N(Le)]

1–2 **Swete leafdi seinte marie**: this phrase begins each of the five orisons to the Virgin, AR 16/14–17/21.

3–6 Cf. the tighter sentence structure in (parallel) R 2–4.

3 **aredde** 'delivered, rescued' makes sense; but with *up* adv. in the context (4), parallel *arerde* (R 2) 'raised' is better.

4 **ðet**: probably an error; cf. R 3.

10–13 **Mine widerwines ... deoflen**: not in R.

21 Interlined *iloued* breaks the alliterating parallelism, and is thus less satisfactory than (parallel) *Misiliket* R 14.

25 **summe**: the doubling of *m* in inflected forms is regular in AB.

27 **tovel? spac**: cf. R 19.

28 ʒemeleas: cf. AR 92/36 f.: *þeonne is hit gemeleste under accidie? et ich cleopede slouhðe*.

Notes

36 mot: derived from OE. *gemōt* 'meeting, conflict', with sense influenced by OE. *mōtian* 'converse', and possibly by ON. *mót*; cf. K 1316.

40 bide: for *bidde*.

41 howeð (R *haheð*; see note to R 29): probably an error, and possibly due to the influence of *bihouin* (OE. *behōfian*) which in ME. at this time meant 'to befit, be proper'.

49–51 hokerunge ... crununge: cf. AR 83/11 f.: *hokeres. buffetes. spotlunge. blindfellunge. pornene crununge.*

51 heliunge '(face) covering, blindfolding'. See Mark xiv. 65, Luke xxii. 64; AR 46/29–30, and W 410 f.: *pa heaðene hundes hilede mi neb for þe.*

54 druggunge: probably < OE. **drycgan*, related to OE. *drēogan*. If the *gg* represents [gg] the development may be parallel with that seen in MnE. *drag, tug, wag.*

58 *and* is probably omitted after *pine*.

59 i.e. (*his blod swetunge*) *erest in his one hond* ..., &c.

61–64 ȝet ase ... neiles: cf. W 468–70; M 47/4: *bunden hire þat tet blod barst ut et te neiles*; J (B) 446 f.: (*ha*) *bond bihinden his rug ba twa his honden. Þ him wrong euch neil ȝ blakede of þe blode.*

75 suluen: (non-AB) < WS. type *sylf*.

81 syon þe heie tur of heouene: cf. HM 5/27, 35–36.

Þe Oreisun of seinte Marie [R]

5 herehede: OE. *her(e)gode* 'harried', in which *g* though deriving from original [j] appears to have become a back spirant; cf. forms like *murhðe* (Phonology under OE. *g*), and see M (R) 23/31, J (B) 610, K 336.

19 iunne makes sense, but could be an error for *inumen*, as in (parallel) N(Le) 26.

29 haheð: AB **hahien* < ON. *haga* 'to suit, be suitable' (*hagligr* 'fit, proper'); cf. OE. *anhagian* 'to be within one's power or means, to afford'. See note to N(Le) 41, and cf. *O.E.D.* s.v. *Hagheli*.

Þe Wohunge of ure Lauerd [W]

1 druð: AN. *drud*, already found (once only) in LOE.

3 N and AB *healewi* 'balm, balsam' points to OE. **hǣlewǣg*, **hālwǣg* from *hǣl, hǣlu* 'health' and *wǣg* 'water', possibly with some influence of *hāl* 'healthy', *hālig* 'holy'. The vowels in W *haliwei*, L *halwi*, and R (M 33/13) *halewi* may be due to shortening. Cf. ON. *heilivágr*, MHG. *heilwǣge*.

3–5 Swetter is munegunge of þe þen mildeu o muðe: derived from the Latin hymn *Dulcis Iesu Memoria*, the extensive influence of which is treated by Miss Allen (op. cit.); see F. J. Mone, *Lat. Hymnen des Mittelalters*, i (Freiburg, 1853–5), p. 329, No. 258, ll. 1–4.

4 munegunge: see d'Ardenne, Etym. Appendix, p. 166, under *Sunegin*.

21 **cwedli**: ME. formation, with more generalized sense, from OE. *cwēad* 'filth, dung'. In this instance *cwedli* is used in contrast to *menskli* 20, whence Morris gives 'niggardly', Stratmann-Bradley 'sparingly'. *O.E.D.* cites *E.E. Psalter*, xvii. 22 (Harl. MS., c. 1300) as the first use of *quedly*.

28 **lates**: if from OE. *lǣt* is influenced by oblique cases like *lātum*, but it may be from ON. *lát*.

menske: 'kindness, humanity, honour'. From ON. *mennska* 'kindness, humanity, human nature', with semantic development in ME. to senses of the descendant of OE. *ār*. See note to 163, and *mensken, menskli* in Glossary.

40 **forwariede**: characteristic AB form pointing to OE. (or OAB) **wærigan* (*wergan*); cf. *awariet* J 350. AB spellings of this word are *war-, wear-*. Orm has *forrwarrʒedd* 8048.

42-44 **al þ pinende pik ... bað**: cf. J (B) 673-80: (*he*) *het fecchen aueat. ꝫ wið pich fullen ... hit colede anan. ꝫ warð hire ase wunsum as þah hit were a wlech beað*.

43 **þ**: although expuncted, it was probably in the original, with some noun (parallel to *pik*) after it.

44 **bekinde**: see *O.E.D.* s.v. *Beek*, and also Jamieson, *Etymological Dictionary of the Scottish Language*.

46 **welle**: from OE. (non-WS.) *wællan, wellan* (WS. *wiellan, wyllan*) a causative verb beside OE. *weallan* (see *wallen* in Glossary).

50-51 **te sunne were dosk**: cf. SW 26/246 f.: *for aʒein þe brihtnesse ꝫ te liht of his leor. þe sunne gleam is dosc*.

51 **dosk**: a characteristic AB word; see d'Ardenne, Etym. Appendix, p. 147, under *dorc*.

55 **moder sune**: apparently the first instance preserved of the quasi-compound *moder-sune* (so *O.E.D.*).

A: prob. from AN. *a*, but OE. *ǣ*, ON. *æ, ai* are cognate. *O.E.D.* gives first use of *A* interj. as *c*. 1280.

63 **wrahtes**: in the parallel passage *A Talkyng* (Westra, p. 30) has *weldeþ*, a better reading.   65-67 Cf. Ps. xxiv. 1.

66 **trin** = *terin(þerin)*, with characteristic AB contraction before a following vowel.

78 **leoue**: error for *leue*, as in other repetitions of the refrain.

82-85 **þu mades ... schaftes**: cf. AR 176/23 f.: *al ðet is iðe worlde. he werp under ure uet*; HM(T) 43 f.: *godes spuse ... of all þe world lauedi, as he is of al lauerd*.

82 **mades**: a north-east Midland form, interesting because one of the earliest contracted preterites of this verb. *O.E.D.* gives *mad*, pp. from *Gen. and Exod.* (*c*. 1250) as its earliest example.

96-99 **Derre druri ... seluen**: cf. AR 176/30 f.: *he ʒef us nout one of his. auh dude al him suluen. So heih ʒeoue! nes neuer i ʒiuen to so louwe wrecches*.

99 **heht**: earliest instance of northern and eastern use of *heht* as pp.

Notes 45

(not in *O.E.D.*); cf. *Cursor Mundi* 1276 *me was hight*. The original version probably had *hattes*, pt., as regularly in AB, which may explain *hafdes* ... *heht* 99, where *haues* ... *heht* would fit the context better.

111–12 þu þ ... heuene: cf. AR 125/30: *iesu crist. ðet is his feder wisdom*; J(B) 327: *Ihesu ... þ art þi feader wisdom*.

115 semeð < OE. *sēman* 'reconcile, put right': but the ME. senses derive more from the cognate ON. *sóma* 'beseem, befit' (pt. subj. *sømdi*) and from the related ME. adj. *seme, semelich* (ON. *sømr, sømiligr*).

131 offeard: for *ea* in words containing OE. *ǣ*[1], see d'Ardenne, Phonol. § 19. This reduction of *offeared, offearet* is characteristic of T.

139 reftes: probably due to the analogy of preterites like *leftes(t)*. This is another easternism. Cf. *O.E.D.* s.v. *Reft*, sb[1].

151 stalewurðe: OE. *stælwyrðe* probably had *ǣ* shortened before *lw*, but since short *æ* was not raised to *e* before *l* in WM., it retains [æ], spelt *ea*, in AB, which in other dialects > *a*. Later an obscure vowel was developed between *l* and *w*.

157 balde: probably from OE. *bældan*, though the *a* here must be due to influence of the unaltered adjective *bald*.

163 mensket 'honour, virginity'. The semantic development here is due to senses represented by AN. *honor* 'honour, repute, beauty'.

173 onont: a characteristic AB word probably resulting from a blending of OE. *on efen, on emn* with an earlier form of classical ON. *á iamt*.

183 leaste: the irregular vowel *ea* is typical of AB and is probably also seen in AB *keasten*. See d'Ardenne, Etym. Appendix, p. 159, under *keasten*.

187 hurd points to a rare OE. *hȳred* beside more common OE. *hīred* (VP *heored*). Influence of ON. *hirð* would account for loss of *e*.

191 karlische þinges: apparently a pejorative expression for earthly husbands; cf. OE. *ceorl* 'man, husband', *ceorlian* 'to take a husband', and HM(T) 570: *ʒ te cheorl chideð* which has the AB spelling.

213 leaue: OE. *lǣfan*, with sense influenced by OE. *lǣtan* through ME. *leten*.

244–5 Cf. M 19/33, J(B) 277 f.

245 forwurpen: see Glossary under *warpe*, and d'Ardenne, Etym. Appendix, p. 169, under *warpen*.

258 mikel: the existence here of both *k* and *ch* forms illustrates the dialectal admixture; see Phonology, p. xl. The *ch* is AB; the *k* probably shows influence of OE. oblique cases (*miclum*, &c.), where [k] was preserved, and possibly also of ON. *mikill*. See Glossary under *muchel*.

267 derue: OE. *dearf* with sense probably influenced by OE. *gedeorf* 'hardship' and *derfan* 'to labour'; cf. ON. *djarfr* 'bold, daring'.

279 **arh**: OE. *earg*, cognate with ON. *argr*. The sense here is prob. similar to *wrah* (see following).

wah: most probably an error for *wak* 'weak' owing to the similarity (monosyllables ending in *h*) and grammatical parallelism of neighbouring words, *arh* 279 and *neh* 280: but possibly *wah* may represent either (i) *wrāh*, of which the basic meaning is 'twisted, perverse' (perhaps related to OE. *wrīgian* 'to turn, twist'), but with the meaning possibly developed here to 'wayward, headstrong, slothful', i.e. in a state of 'irritation . . . that anguish of a troubled heart, or *anxietas sive tædium cordis*', which was one form of Accidie among the Seven Deadly Sins; cf. *ne wrah ne mispaiet*, AR (C) (Morton 416 n.), which is good evidence for AB, and *wrouehede*, *O & N* 1400; and the form *wrah* points to OE. *wrǣg* cognate with Sw. *vrd*; see Stratmann–Bradley and Atkins's note to *O & N* 1400; or (ii) *wa, wai* (adj. from OE. *wā*) 'woeful, sorrowful'; cf. *himm wass wagg*, Orm 11904, and *then wes he wa*, Barb. i. 348. If this is the source of the form in W, the final *h* (and the final *gg* of Orm's word) might be due to emphatic pronunciation.

281 **bucchede**: probably 'cursed, vile, fierce'. Of obscure origin: *O.E.D.* associates it with equally obscure *bunch* (see note on *dunchen* 496, below). More probably *bucchede* is to be compared with *bicched* 'execrable' (the etymology of which is uncertain) which has been connected with OE. *bicce* 'bitch'. The form in this text is, however, against this etymology unless the *u* is an error. See Skeat's note on *bicchede bones* in *Pard. T.* 656 (*Oxford Chaucer*, v. 285) and *O.E.D.* s.v. *Bicched*.

283 **forhuhande**: probably 'self-despising, ready to give up', and a genuine form pointing to OE. **forhūgian*. This word appears in Ælfric (*De Consuetudine Monachorum* 441, 1085), the early (c. 1160) *Hatton Gospels* (Matt. xxiii. 10), and elsewhere in Titus and other (mainly northern) ME. texts. The vowel appears to be long, and thus it is unlikely to be a variant of OE. *forhogian*, though the vowel may have been influenced by OE. *būgan, forbūgan*, especially in view of the association of *forhuhande* and *buhande* in the present line. HM(T) 238 has *forhuh* where HM(B) has *forbuh*.

288 **nere**: probably erroneous repetition of *nere* in prec. line.

307 **deaðes hus sorhe**: 'sorrow of death's house, pain of death'. Uninflected *hus* is probably genitival in function, illustrating avoidance of the repetition of the *es* inflexion in consecutive words; cf. *deðes dom* 'sentence of death' 381.

311 **wicke**: see *Wick* adj. in *O.E.D.*, which cites Orm 6185, *Bestiary* 593, and AR(T) 104 as the earliest examples.

324 **hus lewe**: OE. *hūs-hlēow* 'houseroom', &c. Here the sense of *hlēow* 'shelter, protection' may be modified by contact with AN. *liu* 'place, space'.

328 **dennet**: ME. formation from OE. *denn* n. 'den, habitation of

a wild beast'; cf. *Bestiary* (Lion) 36–37: *Ne wu he dennede him in ðat defte meiden*, and the modern *denny* 'provided with a den'.

329 beastes: from AN. *beste*. See d'Ardenne, Glossary under *beast*, where she suggests that loss of final *e* may be due to assimilation in gender to native *dēor*; but final *e* appears to be lost in other words after *st*, as ME. *host* < OF. (*h*)*oste*.

329–32 Bote ... fode: cf. AR 116/4 f.: *de poure lefdi of heouene uostrede ⁊ fedde hine mid hire lutle milke.' ... þis was muchel pouerte. auh more com per efter*.

338 witerliche: see *Witterly* adv. in *O.E.D.*

339–42 tu þ heuene ... reste: cf. AR 115/36 f.: *ðe þet wrouhte ðe eorðe. he ne uond nout on eorðe so muche place ase his luttle licome muhte beon i leid on*; AR 116/9 f.: *seoðen ... nefde he hwar he muhte resten his heaued* [Matt. viii. 20].

343–50 Bote...huide: probably, as Morris suggests (*Spec.* i. 324), a reference to the seamless coat of which Jesus was deprived at the crucifixion.

344 The context here requires a negative (perhaps *nafdes* for *hafdes*); but the original may not. See Konrath, op. cit., p. 91; and cf. *A Talkyng*, Westra, p. 42.

369 heaned: see *O.E.D.* under *Hean, Hene*; cf. *heaneð* HM(T) 154.

393 for schendlac 'to give insult, put to shame', &c. From OE. *scendan* 'to put to shame' and suffixal *lāc*, which is used in AB to make a few nouns expressing verbal action, as *fearlac*. To form nouns of quality AB used *lec*, as in *godlec* 'goodness', *freolec* 'nobility', &c. In other dialects the more regularly developed *-leic, -laik* < ON. *-leikr* are used in both functions. *Schendlac* occurs in other AB texts, as K 1278, SW 134.

399 biclaried: 'besmeared'? *O.E.D.* cites Morris's emendation to *biclarted* 'besmeared' under MnE. (Nth. and Scot. dial.) *clart*, but *clart, clarty* is also of unknown origin and is not recorded early. The MS. has *-ied*: if this reading is retained, the absence of mutation shows *i* must be an adjectival ending and this verb a formation from **clāri* 'muddy' (cf. *biblōdgin* < *blōdi, forwariede*, &c.). As to the etymology of **clār, *clāri*, it is either (i) an old variant of *clām* 'mud' with different suffix; or (ii) a new ME. development made out of OE. *clām*, OE. *lām* 'clay', and ON. *leir*, ME. *laire* 'mud'.

403–5 Scito quoniam ...: Ps. lxviii. 8 (Vulg.); lxix. 7 (A.V.).

412–13 ne dred tu nawt: should possibly continue *forþi for me to pole schome* 'therefore dread thee not at all to suffer shame for me'; but *A Talkyng* (and original W?) has *ffor þe loue of me* (Westra, p. 44).

429 misliche ⁊ monifald: in this instance, *misliche* probably preserves the meaning of OE. *mislic* 'various', &c. But Stratmann–Bradley give 'badly' (adv.) for this reference, *O.E.D.* gives 'wrongly' for *misliche*, O & N 1773, and d'Ardenne gives 'unpleasantly, little to your liking' for *misliche* J(R) 124. These latter senses indicate unexplained semantic change from OE. *mislic* or a new formation from the OE. pejorative prefix *mis*. Both the original and the later meanings of *misliche* are found in AB.

434 schuppere: see d'Ardenne, Etym. Appendix, p. 164, under *Schuppen*.

454–7 for as ... eorðe: cf. AR 48/33 ff.: *þet ilke ned* (= *red* ?) *swot ... puhte read blod ... te streames vrnen adun to ðer eorðe*; AR 132/15 f.: *þo he swette ase blodes swotes dropen ðet urnen adun to ðer eorðe*. Cf. also AR 83/13.

462 bali: Stratmann–Bradley connect *bali* with *bale* adj. (q.v.); but the alternative spelling, *beali*, in B (as in J 699, and AW 77^v, 81^r) makes this impossible. *Bali* is more probably from OE. *bælg*, here in the derived sense of 'belly'. Hence *bali duntes* would be a loose compound construable as 'body-blows'.

duntes: see note to W 496.

468 hetelifaste: probably a corrupt form of characteristic AB *heteueste* 'excessively tight', under influence of OE. *hetelice* 'excessively, violently'.

471 dintede: 3 pl. pt. of *dinten*, a ME. formation from OE. *dynt* 'blow, dint'. Cf. Icel. *dynta*, Sw. (dial.) *dunta* 'strike'. See note to W 496.

472–3 'and before the princes (thou wast) buffeted and beaten.'

480–1 on a Girre blod: good evidence for the AB basis of W, since this expression is found elsewhere only in AB, and was probably rare. *Girre* is probably a misspelling for AB *gure* (as in *al o gure-blod* J(B) 241) due to scribal bungling of an unfamiliar word (cf. AR 132/35: *al o grure blod*). However, the stem vowel *i* may result from northern and eastern development of OE. **gyru*, n. and adj., both preserved in oblique cases only, *gyrwe*, &c., and related to OE. *gor* 'filthy moisture, slime'. In the loose compound *girre-blod*, it is impossible to say whether *girre-* is n. or adj. See B/T and d'Ardenne, Glossary, under *gure-blode*.

485 todunet: from OE. *dynian* 'resound, make a din', through ME. *dunien*, with sense extended through influence of words similar in form (see *dinten*, *dunchen*, *duntes*), and perhaps through word-play. *O.E.D.* gives *dun* v. 'thunder', and (possibly derived from this) post-1600 *dun* v. 'pester, assail constantly'; cf. ON. *dynja*, MLG. *dunian*. See note to W 496.

492 f. On depiction of the crucifixion in WGr, see Konrath, op. cit. p. 92; Westra, op. cit. p. xix; Morgan, *R.E.S.*, N.S. iii (1952), p. 103.

495 lef: most probably imper. 'grant', as in J(B) 112, 244, M(R) 13/26, 15/16, &c., but it might be pron. (= *leof*) 'beloved', especially in this text.

496 dunchen: pr. 3 pl. (Morris translates as preterite). In respect of form, it belongs to a group of similar ME. words (*dunchen, bunchen, punchen*, and the familiar AW *schunchen*, &c.) which are new forma-

Notes

tions, as appears from the absence of mutation before *nch*. *Punchen*, certainly, and *schunchen*, possibly, come from OE. *punian* and *scunian* respectively. *Dunchen* and *bunchen* may therefore point to OE. *dunian and *bunian. Further evidence for the existence of *dunian* is seen in the rhyming of *wunest* (OE. *wunian*) with *adunest*, *O & N* 337–8 (cf. also *tobuneð*, *O & N* 1166, and Atkins's note). *Dunchen, bunchen, punchen* all have the general sense of striking or punching, with *nch* possibly due to the emphatic or onomatopoeic variation of earlier and simpler forms. Moreover, they may be influenced by, or variants of, each other—forming a group to which new words might be added by similar emphatic and onomatopoeic efforts; cf. MnE. *crunch, scrunch*. *Dunchen* has considerable authority, however, showing possible influence (through ME. derivatives) of OE. *dynian* 'resound, make a din', OE. *dūnian 'stun, deafen', and OE. *dynt* 'blow'; cf. *dintede, duntes, todunet*. In ME., *dunchen* is a northernism, and in MnE. it is still found in Nth. and Scot. dialects. It is also to be connected with OSw. *dunsa* 'push or jog with fist or elbow', and (modern) Sw. *dunka*, Dan. *dunke*, of similar meaning, and with OHG. *donsen*. This is the earliest instance of *dunchen* given in *O.E.D.* (See d'Ardenne, Etym. Appendix, p. 164, under *schunche*.)

501–2 **to schome ꝫ wundren**: possibly requires some inf. (*don*? *bringen*?) after *to*; cf. Morris, p. 282; but both *schome* and *wundren* may be verbs.

504 **Setis** has the appearance of a northern plural. The contrast of *haue þai broht, nu raise þai*, with *setis* (without pronoun) would be in accordance with northern syntax (where the pl. and 1 s. have *es* only when the personal pronoun is not present); but *setis* here probably stands for, or is an error for, *setis mon*, and is thus 3 s. It is immediately followed by *nu nacnes mon* 505. The *is* inflexion has no relation to AB *i*-forms, but is an early example of the northern and eastern tendency to turn final *es* into *is*. There is nothing else like it in W.

508 **mi mi**: for *nu mi*?

518–20 **aisille ... bittrest**: cf. AR 184/18: *eisil of sur nið and galle of bitter onde*.

520–2 **Twa Bale drinch ... bittre**: cf. AR 49/31 f.: *his diete þet dei i ðen ilke blodletunge. so baluhful. ꝫ so bitter*.

531 **diuere**: of uncertain etymology, but probably connected with Icel. *dyja* 'shake', Scot. *daver*, LG. *dæveren* (cf. *dither*). ME. *diueren* is frequentative; see K 622, M(R) 39/24.

532 **to hoker lahter**: 'as a laughing-stock'.

541 **longis**: St. Longinus, the centurion who pierced the side of the Saviour, according to the *Golden Legend*; cf. *Piers Plowman B*, xviii, 79. 'The name was no doubt invented with reference to the λόγχη or lance, which the centurion used.' (Morris, *Spec.* i. 324.)

545 Zupitza–Schipper (op. cit.) supply *me* after first *þ*.

547–51 þu oppnes ... luuedes: cf. AR 179/12 f.: *(He) ... lette openen his side. uorte scheawen hire his heorte. and forto scheawen hire openliche. hwu inwardliche he luuede hire.*

555 here: see d'Ardenne, Glossary, under *here*.

559–60 Bote lafdi ... ariste: cf. AR 17/1 f.: *Swete lefdi seinte marie vor þe ilke muchele blisse þ tu hefdest þo þu iseie þine deorewurðe sune ... arisen.*

570 derennedes: shows the weakening of OF. *ei* in medial syllables, or it may be from AN. *deresnier* with a change of *esn* to *enn*, as in ME. *rennable* from AN. *resnable*; or the first *n* may be due to scribal error, the writing of an extra stroke after *ei*.

572–4 Brohte ... burðe: cf. Song of Solomon iii. 4.

574 steked: from OE. *stecan 'pierce', with sense influenced by cognate OE. *stician* (intrans.) 'be placed, remain fixed'. ME. confused *steke* and *stike* from these two sources. Cf. LG. *stecan*, and also *O.E.D.* s.v. *Steek*, v.

581–2 Quid retribuam domino ...: Ps. cxv. 12 (Vulg.); cxvi. 12 (A.V.); and also in the (priest's) communion of the Mass.

584 Zupitza–Schipper supply *i* after *mai*.

587 wrecche: adjectival or quasi-genitival use of *wrecche* n. <OE. *wrecca*; cf. *wrecched* W 320.

590–1 (et seq. to 602; also 653–5): cf. AR 160/12 f.: *rihte ancren ne beoð nout one pilegrimes ... vor al hore blisse is. uorte beon an honged soriliche ʒ scheomeliche mid iesu ! on his rode.*

591–3 sperred ... wahes: cf. AR 172/10 f.: *ʒe beoð ibunden wiðinnen uour large wowes*; AR 75/7 f.: *ʒ bibarred ase he was oðe deore rode.* Cf. 76/22 f. (The cloistered life is alluded to.)

591 sperred: possibly an adaptation of MDu. *sperren* (so *O.E.D.*), but cf. OE. *gesparrian, besparrian* 'shut, bar', and modern Nthb. *speer* of similar meaning.

602 fele: probably adv. '(very) much' (OE. *feola*). Here, however, Morris translates as adj., 'of many pains', Stratmann–Bradley as n., 'feeling' (OE. *gefēle*, OFris. *fēle*).

603–4 'what is my body worth compared with thine?'

645–7 Prei for me ... þis haue i writen þe: despite my own conclusions (p. xxiv, above) and Einenkel's vigorous denial (op. cit., p. 281, Anm. 1), it must remain possible that either the whole *Wohunge* was composed by a man for a *leue suster* or that the envoy was composed by a scribe.

646–52 þis ... iesu: cf. AR 196/3: *O þisse boc redeð eueriche deie: hwon ʒe beoð eise*, and also *A Luue Ron* 201–10.

GLOSSARY

ALL the forms are listed (except those in Morris's titles); and, unless the usual grammatical order would be disturbed, AB forms are shown first. In the interest of conciseness, glossing and cross-reference have been kept as simple as possible. In the main, annotation is avoided here, but some lexical matters are dealt with in the Notes.

Other things being equal, line references are given in the order of the texts according to their size, viz. W, N, L, R. The method followed is to give the line reference for the first occurrence of a form, and thereafter, in parentheses (round brackets), not the line references, but the *frequencies of occurrence*. However, if a form occurs only once in a manuscript, the line reference, rather than a frequency of (1), is given. Thus, W 38(2), N(2), L(3), R 17 means that the form concerned occurs first in W at line 38, appears twice (in all) in W, twice in N (any of the N texts), thrice in L, and once in R at line 17. Although some frequencies are not as useful as others, it has been thought best to follow the method consistently, except that, in some special cases, more line references are given.

The customary abbreviations are used; and the others are repeated below for the sake of convenience. The letter forms used represent those of the manuscripts, except that þ is regularly used initially, ð medially and finally (see Orthography). The sign / separates two variant forms which occur in parallel positions in two versions of the same work.

Abbreviations

L   *Ureisun of ure Louerde*, p. 1
N   MS. Cotton Nero A. xiv as presented here, viz:
      N(Le)   *Lofsong of ure Lefdi*, p. 16
      N(Lo)   *Lofsong of ure Louerde*, p. 10
      N(U)   *Ureisun of God Almihti*, p. 5
R   *Oreisun of Seinte Marie*, p. 19
W   *Wohunge of ure Lauerd*, p. 20

a *adv.* ever, always L 8.
a *prep.* at, on N(Lo) 23.
a *interj.* ah! oh! W 55(35), N(6), L(2). Varies in force from vague introductory word to strong interj. See **ah, o**.
a, an *art.*: a (before cons., except *h*) W 44(11), N(4), R 5; **an** (before *h*) W 609; **on** (before *w*) N(U) title; **an** *num. adj.* one W 233; **one** (after *prep.*) N(U) 29, N(Le) 59; **ones** *gen. s.* N(Lo) 101. See **ane, on** *advs.*

abandun *adj.* at (your) command L 118/**abaundune** N(U) 144.
abidest *v. 2 s. pr.* abidest N(Lo) 134; **abides** W 209.
aboht *pp.* bought L 30/**abowt** N(U) 35; **abouht** N(Lo) 156.
abuten *adv.* about N(Lo) 119(2), N(Le) 12.
acwelleð *v. 3 pl. pr.* destroy N(Le) 14, R 9; **acwellen** *3 pl. pr. subj.* N(Le) 77.
acwenche *v. 3 s. pr. subj.* quench N(Lo) 57.

acwikeð v. 3 s. pr. quickens, gives life (to) N(U) 126, L 103.
adeadie v. 3 s. pr. subj. deaden, quell N(Lo) 60, N(U) 120/**adeadi** L 99.
adun adv. down L 82, N(4), R(2).
afallen pp. fallen N(Le) 4.
aȝain prep. against, in opposition to, in comparison with W 193(3); **aȝein** L 9(3), N(4); **aȝaines** W 125(9); ~ te in thy despite W 192; **aȝeines** N(Le) 8, R 6.
aȝaines adv. in response, back W 204.
ah v. 3 s. pr. ought W 232(2); **aȝen** 3 pl. pr. L 110/**owe** N(U) 136. Neg. form: **nowest** 2 s. pr. owest not N(Lo) 171. See **ahen**.
ah conj. but W 60(8), L(2), R 7; ac L 101; **auh** N(15). Often a mere introductory word with little force as conj., and sense sometimes influenced by a interj.; **ah** wherefore W 8.
ahefulle adj. pl. awful W 126.
ahen adj. & pron. own W 286(2); **ahne** wk. W 95(2) and prob. 125 (MS. anre); **owune** N(Le) 53.
ahte n. possessions W 17(3).
aisille n. vinegar W 518.
akennednesse n. conception N(Lo) 6.
al adj. all, every, whole W 30(35), N(10), L(3), R 24; **alle** (after prep.) W 48(2), N(2); **alles** gen. s.: ~ cunes of every kind R 23; **alle** pl. W 11(16), N(16), L(4), R(4); **alre** gen. pl. (and with superls.): W 298, N 518, N(3), L 72, R 25; **alle** gen. pl. L 92, N(3).
al pron. all, everything W 65(12), N(15), L(3); **alle** pl. all (men, people) W 153(2), L 110.
al adv. entirely W 37(3), N(11), L(3).
aliht v. s. imper. illumine N(U) 15, L 13.
alle ȝate adv. always, by all means, altogether W 295(3).
allunge adv. entirely N(U) 23, ·L 20.

almihti adj. almighty N(U) title.
alswa adv. also W 182(2), R 15/**ase** N(Le) 23.
alweldinde adj. all-ruling, omnipotent N(Lo) 144.
amen interj. Amen N(Lo) 182, N(Le) 85.
and (R **ant**) conj. (usually written ȝ) and W 30(191), N(185), L(41), R(19); ȝc et cetera W 252(3).
ane adv. alone, only W 10(5); one N(5), L 41.
anon adv.: euer ~ ever the same, forever L 116.
apostel n. apostle N(Lo) 39.
are n. mercy, grace R 5(2); **ore** N(U) 96, N(Le)(2); **aore** L 80.
aredden v. inf. rescue, save N(U) 158; **aredde** 3 s. pt. N(Le) 3. See **riddes**.
arere v. 3 s. pr. subj. raise up N(Le) 78; **arer** 2 s. imper. N(Lo) 64; **arerde** 3 s. pt. R 2.
arh adj. craven, cowardly, sluggish W 279.
ariste n. resurrection W 560(2), N(3).
ase, as rel. adv. & conj. as, just as, even as W 114(2), N(13), L(5); having force of pron. with whole clause as antecedent: W 63(6), N(2), L 89; as pah (tah) as if W 411(2), N(U) 148, L 121; swuch as(e) such as, even as W 129(3), N(2); swilc ase L 55(2); in correlative constructions: W 619(2), N(9), L(5); with one correlative missing: W 318(2), N(U) 71, L 60; with prepositional force, expressing identity: W 181(5), N(2).
astiunge n. ascension N(Lo) 19.
atele adj. pl. horrible, cruel W 264.
ateliche adj. pl. horrible, dreadful N(Lo) 35.
attri adj. pl. venomous N(U) 89, L 73.
awei adv. away N(U) 112/**awai** L 92.

Glossary

bacbitunge *n.* backbiting N(Le) 24, R 17.
balde *v. 3 s. pr. subj.* make bold W 157; **baldede** *3 s. pt. subj.* W 134.
baldeliche *adv.* boldly N(U) 128(2), L(2).
bale *n.* danger, evil, woe W 298; **bales** *pl.* W 425.
bale *adj. pl.* baleful, deadly W 521.
balewsið *n.* affliction, grief L 28/ **baluhsið** N(U) 33.
bali *adj. pl.* grievous, deadly W 462.
baluful *adj.* baleful, hurtful N(Lo) 166.
ban *n.* bone W 511; **banes** *pl.* W 345.
band *v. 2 s. pt.* didst bind W 138: **bunden** *3 pl. pt.* W 467; **bunden** *pp.* W 470(2).
bare *adj. pl.* bare, naked W 495.
bað *n.* bath W 44.
baðe *adj. & adv.* both W 343; **boðe** N(4).
beard *n.* beard W 394.
bearn *n.* child W 176; **bern** L 2, N(2), R 2; **bearnes** *pl.* W 465.
beastes *n. gen. s.* beast's W 329.
beddin *v. inf.* be embedded, repose L 25/**bedden** N(U) 28.
beieð *v. 3 s. pr.* bows, bends N(U) 147; **beih** *2 s. imper.* N(Lo) 79.
bekinde *pr. p.* warm, fomenting W 44.
beoden *n. pl.* prayers N(Le) 46.
beodest *v. 2 s. pr.* offerest N(U) 40, L 35; **beodeð** *3 s. pr.* L 33/**beot** N(U) 37; **bede** *1 s. pr. subj.* W 629; **beden** *3 pl. pr.* W 517.
beon *v. inf.* be W 45(3), N(8), L(2); **beo** W(12), N 119, L(3); **boen** N(U) 143; **am** *1 s. pr.* L 18(2), N(7), R(2); **ham** N(U) 94, N(Lo) 70; **art** *2 s. pr.* W 36(13), L(6); **ert** N(10), L 104; *artu* art thou W(2), *ertu* N(U) 85; **is** *3 s. pr.* W 4(30), N(40), L(11); **bið** (consuetud.) N(Lo) 155; **beoð** (consuetud.) L 31; **beoð** *3 pl. pr.* L 8(2), N(5) **arn** W 10; **beo** *1 s. pr. subj.* N(Lo) 67; **beo** *2 s. pr. subj.* W 586, N(4), L 89, R(2); **beo** *3 s. pr. subj.* W 57(8), N(6), L(3); **beo** (consuetud.) L 30, N(2); **beo** *s. imper.* N(Lo) 54; **wes** *2 s. pt.* W 174(4); **was** W(16); **were** L 109; **wes** *3 s. pt.* W 303(3), L 103, R(2); **was** W(9), N(5); **were** N(U) 134(2); **were** *3 s. pt. subj.* W 45(4), N(Lo) 45, **weren** (for *were*) W 372. Negative forms: **nam** am not N(U) 57, L 49; **nis** is not W 110(3), N(6), L(5); **nes** W 183, N(U)(2), L(2); **narn** are not W 250; **nere** *2 s.* wert not N(U) 134, L 109; **nere** *3 s.* were not W 287(3), N(3), R 23; **neren** *3 pl.* were not N(U) 135, L 115.
bere *v. 1 s. pr.* bear W 587; **bereð** *3 s. pr.* L 120; **beres** W 494; **beren** *1 pl. pr.* W 238; **bere** *2 s. pt.* N(Le) 3(2), R(2); **born** *pp.* W 174(3); **iboren** N(Lo) 2, L 104/ **ibeoren** N(U) 127; **borne** *pp. pl.* W 244.
beten *pp.* beaten W 473.
bi *prep.* by, for, with respect to R 29(4), N(27).
biclaried *v. 3 s. pt.* soiled? besmirched? W 399.
bicluppen *v. inf.* embrace N(U) 51(2); **bicluppe** L 55; **biclupen** N(Lo) 118; **biclupe** *s. imper.* N(Lo) 124; **bicluppeð** *pp.* N(U) 56(2), L 51; **biclupet** L 48.
bidde *v. inf.* pray, ask, command N(Lo) 126; **bidde** *1 s. pr.* R 5(2), N(2); **bide** N(Le) 40; **biddes** *2 s. pr.* W 308(2).
bifel *v. 3 s. pt.* befell W 431; **bifallen** *pp.* W 430.
biforen *prep.* before, in the presence of W 375(2), L 150; **bifore** W 472(2); before, previous to W 451.
biginnes *v. 3 s. pr.* begins W title.
biginnunge *n.* beginning N(U) 141, L 115.
biȝeate *n.* gain, acquisition N(Lo) 105; **biȝete** W 72, N(U) 71, L 60.
bihalden *v. inf.* behold W 38; **bihalde** W 131(2); **bihalde** *1 s. pr.* W 314; **bihold** (pron.

following) N(U) 47(2), L 41; **biholdeð** *3 pl. pr.* L 8, N(2);
bihold *s. imper.* N(Lo) 37(2);
biheld *2 s. pt.* W 299.
biheue *adj.* needful N(Lo) 133.
bihotest *v. 2 s. pr.* promisest N(U) 41/**bihatest** (MS. *bihastest*) L 36;
bihat *3 s. pr.* N(U) 38, L 33.
bihoueð *v. 3 s. pr.* behoves, is needful W 586; **bihoues** W 273;
biheouede *3 s. pt.* N(Lo) 129.
bikumeð *v. 3 s. pr.* becomes N(Lo) 158; **bicom** *2 s. pt.* W 233(2);
3 s. pt. N(U) 133, L 108.
bileaue *n.* belief, faith N(U) 24, N(Lo) 107(2); **bileue** L 21(2), N(2).
bileuen *v. 3 pl. pr.* believe W 470.
bindunge *n.* binding N(Le) 47(2).
binime *v. inf.* take, deprive N(Lo) 132; **binume** *pp.* N (Lo) 98(2).
biseche *v. 1 s. pr.* beseech R 28, N(6); **biseche** *2 s. pr. subj.* N(Le) 64; **bisech** *s. imper.* N(Le) 37, R 26.
biset *pp.* beset N(Le) 11.
biside *prep.* beside W 600(2).
bismer *n.* mockery, scorn W 525;
bismere W 408.
bisocnen *n. pl.* requests N(Le) 39, R 28.
biswoc *v. 3 s. pt.* deceived N(Lo) 99;
biswike *pp.* N(Lo) 111.
bitellen *v. inf.* accuse N(Le) 9, R 7.
bitter *adj.* bitter, unpleasant N(U) 82, L 68; **bittre** *wk.* W 266; as *n.* after *prep.*: N(Lo) 156; **bittre** *pl.* W 522; **bittrest** *superl.* W 520.
bitter *adv.* bitterly, dearly N(U) 34, L 30.
bitterliche *adv.* bitterly, painfully W 567.
bitternesse *n.* bitterness N(U) 33(2), L(2).
bituhhen *prep.* between W 420;
bituhhe W(2).
bitweonen *prep.* between N(U) 49(4); **bitweone** L(3); **bitwene** L 51.
blase *n.* blaze, flame N(U) 18, L 16.

bleo *n.* appearance, form, complexion W 51.
blescien *v. 3 pl. pr. subj.* bless N(Lo) 176; **iblesced** *pp.* L 88, N(2);
iblescede *wk.* N(Lo) 25.
blisfule *adj. wk.* blissful, blessed W 51(3), N(2), R 2; **blisfulle** L 93;
blisfulle *pl.* N(U) 59, L 51.
blisse *n.* bliss, blessing W 48(7), N(4); **blissen** *pl.* L 37, N(2);
blisses W 68.
bliðe *adj.* blithe N(U) 6, L 6.
blod *n.* blood W 95(8), N(4), L(2);
blodes *gen. s.* W 456; **blode** (after *prep.*) L 94, N(3).
blodi *adj.* bloody W 349(3), N(2);
blodie *s.' wk.* N(Le) 45; **blodie** *pl.* N(U) 115.
blodleting *n.* blood-letting W 521.
blod-rune *n.* stream of blood N(Le) 62.
boc *n.* book N(Lo) 154; **bok** W 117.
bodi *n.* body W 125(11), L(2), R(2);
bodie (after *prep.*) N(5).
bold *n.* abode, dwelling-place W 147.
bone *n.* prayer, petition N(Lo) 70, N(Le) 85, N(U) 40/**bune** L 35;
bonen *pl.* N(Lo) 32(4).
bote *n.* remedy, cure, redress W 209(4), N(U) 109, L 90.
brade *adj. wk.* broad W 541.
breiden *v. inf.* draw away N(U) 79;
breide L 66.
breostes *n. gen. s.* breast's (or *pl.*?) N(U) 6, L 6; **breoste** (after *prep.*) L 25, N(2); **breostes** *pl.* L 70.
brihte *adj. wk.* bright N(U) 13, L 11.
brihtnesse *n.* brightness L 14;
brithnesse N(U) 16.
brihtte *v. s. imper.* brighten, illumine N(U) 16.
bringen *v. inf.* bring, take, lead W 466; **bringen** *3 pl. pr.* W 541;
brohte *3 s. pt.* W 464; **broht** *pp.* W 375(5).
broc *n.* brook, stream N(U) 98, L 81.
broðer *n.* brother W 233(3);
breðre *pl.* W 232(2).
bruche *n.* breach N(Lo) 7.

Glossary

brune *n.* burning N(U) 162.
bucchede *adj.* cursed ? vile ? fierce ? W 281.
bufettunge *n.* beating N(Le) 50.
buffeted *pp.* dealt blows W 472; **buffetet** W 485.
buffetes *n. pl.* blows W 461.
buggen *v. inf.* buy, redeem W 364(2); **bugge** W 261; **buŏ** *3 s. pr.* N(U) 36, L 32; **buggeŏ** *1 pl. pr.* N(U) 43, L 37; **bohtes** *2 s. pt.* W 553(2); **bohte** *3 s. pt.* W 545(2); **boht** *pp.* W 579.
buh *v. s. imper.* bow, yield N(Lo) 79; **buhande** *pr. p.* as *adj.* W 283; **ibuhen** *pp.* R 10; **ibuwen** N(Le) 15.
buhsumliche *adv.* submissively N(Lo) 147.
bur *n.* bower, dwelling, chamber W 147(2), N(U) 16, L 14.
burh *n.* town, city W 323(2).
burŏe *n.* birth, nativity W 26(7).
burŏ-tid *n.* natal day W 322.
buruwen *v. 3 pl. pr. subj.* save, protect N(Lo) 58; **iboreuwen** *pp.* N(Le) 74.
bute(n) *prep.* but, except, without N(U) 47(2), N(Lo)(5); **boten** L 40; **bot** W 325: *co-ord. conj.* but, however W 93(2); **bote** W 86(8); **bot** W 303(2); in W, frequently an introductory word indicating little co-ordination or contrast: **bute** W 458; **bote** W 57(15); *subord. conj.* unless N(U) 60, L 52, N(Lo) 162, N(Le) 14, R 9; **bute ʒif** unless W 133; *adv.* but, only N(U) 11; **boten** L 10; **bote** W 44.

cald *pp.* called W 111.
caldeliche *adv.* coldly W 328.
calenges *v. 3 s. pr.* challenges, claims W 268.
carpe *v. s. imper.* speak W 651.
chapmon *n.* merchant L 32/**chepmon** N(U) 36.
chatel *n.* chattels, worldly possessions W 59.
chaumbre *n.* chamber W 574.

cheap *n.* bargain, purchase W 446; **cheape**: *lihtliche* ~ at little cost W 162.
cheape *v. inf.* purchase, buy W 60; **chepet** *pp.* W 262(2).
cher *v. s. imper.* turn N(Lo) 169.
chese *v. inf.* choose W 58(2); **cheas** *2 s. pt.* W 252.
child *n.* child N(U) 51, L(2); **childes** *gen. s.* W 324; **childe** (after *prep.*) N(U) 54.
childhad *n.* childhood W 331.
chirche *n.* church N(Lo) 27, N(Le) 70.
cleneliche *adv.* cleanly, with pure hearts W 234.
clenli *adv.* entirely W 356.
clennesse *n.* purity N(Lo) 87.
clense *v. 3 s. pr. subj.* cleanse N(Lo) 47.
cleopien *v. inf.* to call (upon) L 111, N(2); **clipien** L 23.
clerkes *n. pl.* scholars W 338.
cleues *v. 3 s. pr.* cleaves, cuts W 543.
cloŏes *n. pl.* clothes N(Le) 48.
cluppen *v. inf.* clasp, embrace W 576, N(U) 66, L 44; **cluppe** L 56; **cluppe** *1 s. pr.* N(U) 78, L 65.
cluppinge *n.* embracing N(U) 63/**clupping** L 54.
clutes *n. pl.* clouts, rags W 328.
cnawe *v. inf.* know W 548; **cnawe** *1 s. pr.* confess R 11: see **icnowe**.
cnawlechi *v. 1 s. pr.* acknowledge, confess R 24/see **icnoulechie**.
cnotti *adj.* knotted W 477.
cold *adj.* cold N(U) 160; **kalde** W 534.
con *v. 1 s. pr.* can, be able N(U) 86, L 71; **const** *2 s. pr.* N(Lo) 178(2); **cuŏes** *2 s. pt.* W 96.
creie *v. 1 s. pr.* cry, cry out N(Le) 18, R 12; **crieden** *3 pl. pt.* W 383.
cribbe *n.* crib W 329.
cristen *adj.* christian W 392; **cristene** *pl.* N(Lo) 182.
crokes *n. pl.* wiles, deceptions W 302.
crune *n.* crown W 482, N(Lo) 11.
crune *v. inf.* crown W 633; **cruned** *pp.* W 433; **crunet** W 102.

crununge *n.* crowning N(Le) 51(2).
cuið *v. s. imper.* make known N(Lo) 174; **cuðe** ? (MS. *tuðe*) N(Le) 85; **kid** *pp.* renowned W 24(2); **kidde** *wk.* W 143(2).
cume *n.* coming N(Lo) 23.
cumen *v. inf.* come N(U) 96; **cume** W 594, L 79; **come** N(U) 64, L 54; **cumes** *3 s. pr.* W 543; **cume** *2 s. pr. subj.* N(Lo) 129; **com** *2 s. pt.* W 305; **com** *3 s. pt.* W 185.
cumseð *v. 3 s. pr.* commences R (title).
cunde *n.* (human) nature W 225; **kinde** W 31(3).
cunes *n. gen. s.*: *alles* ~ of every kind R23/**cunnes** *pl.* ?: *alle* ~ N(Le) 32.
cunfort *n.* comfort L 27/**cumfort** N(U) 32.
cursunge *n.* cursing N(Le) 24, R 17.
cwalm *n.*: ~ *hus* abode of torment W 145; ~ *stowe* place of execution W 493.
cwedli *adv.* basely, meanly W 21.
cwelled *pp.* killed W 388.
cwemnesse *n.* pleasure, contentment N(Lo) 128.
cwene *n.* queen N(U) 130/**quene** L 106.
cwiddes *v. 2 s. pr.* sayest W 64; **quiddet** *pp.* W 149.
cwike *adj. pl.* as *n.* (the) quick N(Lo) 24.

dai *n.* day W 206(2).
dead *adj.* dead N(Lo) 67; **deade** *wk.* W 539; *pl.* as *n.* N(Lo) 24.
deadliche *adj. pl.* deadly N(Lo) 51.
deale *v. inf.* deal (with), bestow L 58/**delen** N(U) 69; **dealeð** *3 s. pr.* W 114.
dear *v. 1 s. pr.* dare L 23(2)/**der** N(U) 26(2).
deað *n.* death W 267(2), N(9), L 99; **deaðes** *gen. s.* W 307; **deðes** W 381; **deaðe** (after *prep.*) N(Lo) 18(3).
deaðfule *adj. wk.* deadly N(Le) 45.

deaðliche *adj. pl.* deadly N(Lo) 60; *adv.* N(Lo) 74.
debonairte *n.* gentleness, mildness W 29(2).
deboneirschipe *n.* gentleness, mildness W 210.
deciples *n. pl.* disciples N(Lo) 22.
dede *n.* deed, act W 30; **deden** *pl.* N(U) 81, L 67.
deien *v. inf.* die W 492; **deie** *1 s. pr.* W 595, N(Lo) 73; **deieð** *3 s. pr.* N(Lo) 60; **deies** W 535; **deidest** *2 s. pt.* W 625; **deides** W 638.
deih *v. 3 s. pr.* avails N(U) 97, 98.
delit *n.* delight N(U) 83, L 69.
demen *v. inf.* adjudge, condemn N(Lo) 24; **deme** *1 s. pr.* N(Lo) 42; **demde** *3 s. pt.* N(Le) 48; **demed** *pp.* W 380; **demd** W 491; **demet** W 377.
demere *n.* judge W 378.
dennet *pp.* lodged W 328.
deore *adj.* dear, precious W 125(4); **derre** *compar.* W 96.
deore *adv.* dearly, at great cost N(U) 36, L 32; **dere** W 448(2).
deorewurðe *adj.* precious, dear W 137(3), N(7); **deorwurðe** L 32(5), N(6); **deorwurð** L 107; **derewurðe** W 33; **dereowurðe** N(Lo) 59.
deouel *n.* devil R 4, N(2); *dat.* (after *wite*) W 275; **deuel** W 277; **deueles** *pl.* W 126; **deoflen** N(Le) 13.
derennedes *v. 2 s. pt.* didst defend (a cause), didst vindicate W 571.
derf see **þerf**.
derling *n.* darling W 1; **deorelinges** *pl.* N(U) 53/**deorlinges** L 45.
derue *adj. wk.* grievous, long-suffering W 267; **derue** *pl.* bold 281.
derueð *v. 3 s. pr.* troubles, belabours N(Lo) 77.
dihteð *v. 3 s. pr.* disposes, sets in order W 114.
dintede *v. 3 pl. pt.* struck, struck blows W 471.
diuere *v. inf.* tremble, quake W 531.

Glossary 57

dogges *n. pl.* dogs W 139.
dohter *n.* daughter N(U) 139, L 113.
dol *n.* grief W 562.
dom *n.* doom, decree W 381(2).
domes-dai *n.* Doomsday W 565, N(Lo) 23.
don *v. inf.* do W 226(2), N(3); **dest** *2 s. pr.* N(Lo) 172(2); **deð** *3 s. pr.* W 226, N(3), L(3); **don** *3 pl. pr.* W 206; **do** *3 s. pr. subj.* L 100, N(Le) 79; **dides** *2 s. pt.* put W 83(2); **dude** *3 s. pt.* N(Lo) 102; **idon** *pp.* N(Lo) 92.
dosk *adj.* dim, dark W 51.
drahe *v. inf.* draw, drag W 77(2).
drede *v. inf.* dread W 273(2); **drede** *1 s. pr.* N(Lo) 4; **drede** *1 s. pr. subj.* W 313; **dred** *s. imper.* W 412; **dreddes** *3 s. pt.* W 124.
drepen *v. 3 pl. pr. subj.* strike W 496.
drihtin *n.* lord W 2(2), N(Lo) 84; **drithen** N(Lo) 171; **drihtines** *gen. s.* W 65.
drinkes *v. 3 s. pr.* drinks W 522.
driuen *v. 3 pl. pr.* drive W 506(2); **driuen** *pp.* L 152.
drope *n.* drop L 91 (MS. *dieope*), N(2); **dropes** *pl.* W 457.
druggunge *n.* drudging, toiling N(Le) 54.
drunch *n.* drink : **idrunch** = (*in* + *drunch*) R 21/**drunche** N(Le) 30; **drinch** *pl.* W 519(2).
drupi *adj.* moody, downcast N(Le) 29, R 20.
druri *n.* love-token W 97.
druð *n.* darling W 1(3).
dulte *adj. pl.* blunt N(U) 153, N(Le) 54.
dun *adv.* down W 537, N(U) 114, L(2); **dune** W 457; ∼ *fallen pp.* W 280.
dunchen *v. 3 pl. pr.* beat, batter, thump W 496.
duntes *n. pl.* blows W 272(4).

eadi *adj.* blessed N(Lo) 30(2), N(Le) (2), N(U) 135/**edi** L 110, R(2); **eadie** *wk.* N(Le) 41, N(Lo) (2); **eadi** *pl.* N(Le) 46, **eadie** N(Le) 64, N(U) 100/**edi** L 82.

eadinesse *n.* blessedness N(U) 137/ **edinesse** L 112.
eadmodnesse *n.* humility L 48/ **edmodnesse** N(U) 56.
ear *adv.* previously W 487, L 56; **er** L 52, N(6); **er** *conj.* before N(Lo) 157(2); **erest** *adv. superl.* first N(Le) 59; **erst** W 98.
earen *n. pl.* ears N(U) 117/**eren** L 96.
earm *n.* arm L 120/**erm** N(U) 147, N(Lo)(5); **earmes** W 528, L(7)/ **ermes** N(6).
earst *adj.* first W 463; **ereste** *wk.* N(Le) 62.
eað *adj.* easy W 366(2).
eauer *adv.* ever, always W 11(5); **euer** L 25(4), N(13).
eauermare *adv.* evermore W 46; **euermar** W 47.
eauriche see **eueriche**.
ec *adv.* also N(U) 23; **ek** W 121.
eche *adj.* eternal W 147(3), N(U) 76, L 63.
echeliche *adv.* eternally W 42(2).
efne *adj.* equal N(Lo) 30; **euene** W 171, N(U) 72, L 61.
efne *adv.* equally N(U) 72, L 60.
eft *adv.* again, in turn N(Lo) 141.
efter *prep.* after N(U) 31(4), N(Lo) (2); **after** W 208, L(2); **eafter** L 105.
ehne *n. pl.* eyes W 490; **eihen** N(U) 151; **eien** N(U) 116/**eȝen** L 95.
ehsihðe *n.* sight L 79/**eihsihðe** N(U) 96, N(Lo) 35.
ei *adj. & pron.* any L 50, N(2); **ein** *acc.* L 39(2) (or error for *eni*; but cf. ON. *einn*).
eie *n.* anger N(Lo) 37.
eihwer *adv.* everywhere W 197(2); **aihwer** W 59.
eise *n.* ease W 651.
eisfule *adj. wk.* wrathful, awful N(Lo) 23.
eiðer *pron.* either N(Lo) 114.
eke *v. inf.* add W 631; **eken** *3 pl. pr.* W 524.
elc *adj.* each L 69.
eldere *adj. compar.* W 330(2); **eldre** W 343.

Glossary

elles-hwar *adv.* elsewhere N(Lo) 41(2).
elles-hwat *pron.* whatever else N(Lo) 145 (MS. *helles hwat*).
elne *n.* grace, favour L 26(2), N(3).
elnen *v. inf.* strengthen, encourage N(Lo) 136.
elning *n.* grace, favour N(U) 40, L 35 (MS. *elming*).
ende *n.* end N(U) 141, N(Lo) 92, 177 (MS. *hende*).
endelese *adj. wk.* everlasting W 355; **endelease** *pl.* N(Lo) 124.
ending *n.* end, death W 451.
engles *n. pl.* angels L 8, N(2); **engles** *gen. s.* or *pl.* W 37; **englene** *gen. pl.* N(U) 130, L 106.
eni *adj. & pron.* any N(U) 45, N (2); **eini** L 97; **ani** W 60(3); ∼ *mon* anyone W 12(3). See **ei**.
eorn: see **ron**.
eorðe *n.* earth W 65(11), N(5), L(2); **orðe** N(Le) 76.
eorðli *adj.* earthly W 192.
eorðlich *adj.* earthly N(Lo) 155, N(U) 27/**eorðliche** L 24; **eorðliche** *pl.* N(Lo) 71.
erndinge *n.* intercession N(Le) 84.
este *n.*: *wið* ∼ pleasantly N(U) 76, L 64.
et *prep.* at N(Le) 63; at W 468; **atte** at the W 316(2). See **a** *prep.*
ethalden *pp.* held back, withheld R 19.
euch *adj.* each, every W 206(2), N(Lo) 170; ∼ *an*, *pron.* W 32(3); **euche** (after *prep.*) N(Lo) 56(2), N(Le) 11.
euenet *pp.* compared, likened W 52(2).
eueriche *adj.* every N(U) 83; **eauriche** W 483.
ewangeliste *n.* evangelist N(Lo) 33; **ewangelistes** *gen. s.* N(U) 154.

fainen *v. inf.* rejoice W 294; **fainen** *3 pl. pr.* W 290.
falleð *v. 3 s. pr.* falls N(Lo) 159; **falle** *1 s. pr. subj.* N(Lo) 122; **fallen** *pp.* W 280; **ifallet** *pp.* R 3.

fals *adj.* false N(U) 32, L 28.
fan *n. pl.* foes W 155(6), R 10; **fon** N(Lo) 175, N(Le) 8.
feder *n.* father N(Lo) 30(2); **fader** W 112(4).
fedes *v. 2 s. pr.* feedest W 336; **fed** *s. imper.* N(Lo) 166.
feir *adj.* fair N(U) 11, L 9; **feire** *wk.* W 513; **feirest** *superl.* W 55.
feirnesse *n.* fairness, beauty W 13(2); **fairnesse** W 253.
felaʒe *n.* fellow L 61/**felawe** N(U) 73.
felauhschipe *n.* fellowship N(U) 25/ **felawscipe** L 21.
fele *adv.* very much W 602.
felen *v. inf.* feel W 562; **fele** *1 s. pr.* L 70.
felle *v. 3 s. pr. subj.* fell W 154.
feng *v. 2 s. pt.* (with *to*+inf.) didst undertake W 306.
fenliche *adv.* filthily N(U) 95, L 78.
feond *n.* fiend, enemy N(Le) 16; **feont** R 10; **feondes** *gen. s.* N(Lo) 55; **fend** *pl.* W 501.
feor *n.* value, price W 627.
feste *adj. wk.* fast, firm N(Le) 63.
feste *adv.* fast, firmly N(U) 78/ **faste** L 65, W(2).
festunge *n.* (after *prep.*) fasting N(Le) 42/**uestunge** R 30.
fet *n. pl.* feet W 84(3), N(U) 153, L 82/**uet** N(U) 100.
fif *num.* five L 93(2), N(5), R 13; **vif** N(Lo) 10.
fiht *n.* fight W 24; **fihte** (after *prep.*) W 150.
fihte *v. inf.* fight W 125(2); **fihten** *3 pl. pr.* W 271; **faht** *2 s. pt.* W 309(2).
fikel *adj.* fickle N(U) 32, L 28.
fikelunge *n.* flattery N(Le) 24, R 17.
finden *v. inf.* find W 248; **fant** *2 s. pt.* W 323; **ifunden** *pp.* W 184.
finger *n.* finger W 469.
first *adv.* first W 82.
fisch *n.* fish W 335.
fledde *v. 3 s. pt.* flowed, overflowed N(Lo) 10.
fleon *v. inf.* flee N(U) 162.

Glossary

flesch *n.* flesh W 14(7), N(U) 82/ **flehs** L 68(2); **flech** N(Le) 67; **fles** W 276; **flesches** *gen. s.* W 243(2), N(3), R(2); **flehces** L 99; **flesch** *dat.* W 275; **flesche** (after *prep.*) N(Lo) 25; **fleschs** N(U) 119.

flesch-founge *n.* (after *prep.*) conception R 29/**flech-founge** N(Le) 41.

fleschli *adj.* fleshly W 192.

fleschlich *adj.* fleshly N(U) 27/ **flehsliche** L 23.

flod *n.* flood, sea W 335, N(2).

flon *n. pl.* arrows N(Lo) 55.

flowen *v. 3 pl. pr.* flow, shed W 490; **flowinde** *pr. p.* W 543; **fleaw** *3 s. pt.* N(Lo) 46.

fluht *n.* flight W 335.

fode *n.* food W 332.

fol *adj.* foolish N(U) 36, L 31.

folc *n.* folk W 336; **folk** *dat.* W 531; **folkes** *gen. pl.* L 92, N(2).

foleʒi *v. inf.* follow L 62/**folewen** N(U) 74; **folhes** *3 s. pr.* W 499; **foluweð** N(Le) 70.

for *prep.* for, because of, on account of, for the sake of W 53(49), N(11), L(3), R 31; **uor** L 72, N(4); **for to** (introd. inf.) W 25(9), N(10), L(7); **uor to** N(Lo) 47(2).

for *conj.* for, because, since W 10(28), N(7), L(2), R(2); **uor** N(Lo) 94(7).

fordemden *v. 3 pl. pt.* condemned N(Lo) 40; **fordemed** *pp.* N(Lo) 41.

fordide *v. 1 s. pt.* brought to naught, ruined W 86.

fordutte *pp. pl.* as *adj.* stopped up, filled up N(Lo) 50.

fore *adv.* before W 530.

forgan *v. inf.* forgo, be deprived of W 49.

forʒif *s. imper.* forgive N(Lo) 34.

forhuhande *pr. p.* as *adj.* self-despising ?, ready to give up ? W 283.

forlesede *v. 1 s. pt. subj.* should lose W 88.

forlet *pp.* forsaken N(Lo) 140.

forsakeð *v. 3 s. pr.* gives up, eschews N(U) 37, L 32.

forsoðe *adv.* indeed, truly W 287.

forð *adv.* forth, on W 492(2), N(3), L 119/**uorð** N(U) 147.

forðen *v. inf.* further, bring about N(Lo) 144; **iforðed** *pp.* L 119/ **iuorðed** N(U) 145.

forðer *adj.* further N(U) 161.

forði *adv.* therefore, for which reason W 151(7), N(2), L(2); ~ *is riht* it is therefore right W 212; (similarly) W 148; *for þe* W 412 prob. = *forþi*; **forði þ** *conj.* because, inasmuch as W 217(3).

forðward *adv.* forth, onward W 497, N(Lo) 166.

foruten *prep.* without W 311.

forwariede *pp. pl.* as *n.* accurst, condemned W 40.

forwurpen *pp.* cast aside, renounced W 245.

foster *n.* nurture, upbringing W 186.

fowr *num.* four W 592.

fra *prep.* from W 89(6).

fredom *n.* generosity, liberality W 19(2).

fremede *adj.* strange, estranged L 18(2)/**freomede** N(U) 21(2).

frend *n. pl.* friends W 31(4).

frendschipe *n.* friendship W 444.

freoliche *adj. s. wk.* noble, gracious W 514.

frerre *adj. compar.* more gracious W 81.

friðie *v. inf.* leave in peace, spare W 540.

from *prep.* from L 19, N(5); **fram** W 76(3).

froure *n.* comfort, support L 38, N(3).

froure *v. inf.* comfort, solace N(Lo) 84(2).

fuhel *n.* bird W 335.

ful *adj.* full, satisfied N(U) 10, N(Lo) 180; **fulle** *pl.* L 9.

ful *adv.* fully, sufficiently, very W 539(2).

fulles *3 s. pr.* fills W 66.

fulli *adv.* fully W 294.

fulliche *adv.* fully, altogether, utterly W 224(3).

fulst *n.* aid, succour N(Lo) 103.

Glossary

fulst v. s. imper. help, succour N(Lo) 169.
fulðe n. filth L 92, N(4), R 22.
fuluht n. baptism N(Lo) 26, N(Le) 69.

galle n. gall W 520.
gaste n. spirit L 67/**goste** N(U) 80, N(Lo)(5).
gastli adj. spiritual W 576.
gentile adj. noble, of gentle stock W 160(2); **gentiller** compar. W 168; **gentileste** superl. W 181.
gersum n. riches, costly gifts W 17.
girre-blod n. bloody stream W 480.
gladien v. inf. rejoice W 566; **gladien** pl. pr. subj. N(Lo) 176.
gladschipe n. gladness W 289.
god n. God N(U) title (3), L(3); **godd** N(11); **godes** gen. s. L 1(2), N(5).
god adj. & n. good N(U) title, N(Lo) 179, R 20; **godd** N(Lo) 31(2), N(Le) 28; **gode** n. (after prep.) N(Lo) 169; **gode** pl. W 611, N(Lo) 176; **best** superl. best W 115.
god-deden n. pl. good deeds N(U) 81, L 67.
godspel n. gospel W 338(3).
gold n. gold W 17.
gon v. inf. go N(Lo) 102; **gest** 2 s. pr. L 46; **gað** 3 s. pr. W 229; **go** 3 s. pr. subj. N(Le) 72.
gostlich adj. spiritual N(U) 27(2); **gostliche** L 23.
grace n. grace W 237(3), N(8), L 103.
grediliche adv. greedily W 140.
grennen v. pl. pr. subj. grin, smile N(Lo) 175; **grennede** 3 pl. pt. W 288.
grimliche adv. fiercely N(U) 92, L 76.
gripen pp. grasped W 141.
grisliche adj. pl. horrible N(Lo) 35.
grið n. protection N(U) 45, L 39.
grucchen v. inf. grumble W 203.
grure n. terror, terrible suffering N(Le) 45.
grureful adj. horrible W 128.

gulte n. (after prep.) guilt W 312(2); **gultes** pl. W 208.
gulti adj. guilty N(Le) 18.

ӡa adv. yea W 432; **ӡe** N(U) 52, L 44.
ӡapliche adv. cleverly W 274.
ӡapschipe n. prudence W 22.
ӡare adv. of yore, formerly N(Lo) 92.
ӡarewere adj. compar. readier N(Lo) 90.
ӡef conj. if R 29, L(2); **ӡif** W 40(8), N(6); **ӡif þ** W 52(3); **bute ӡif** unless W 133.
ӡeiest v. 2 s. pr. criest, callest N(U) 54.
ӡelde v. inf. repay W 583.
ӡemeleas adj. negligent N(Le) 28/ **ӡemeles** R 20.
ӡeoue n. gift N(Lo) 20; **ӡeouen** pl. N(Lo) 121.
ӡeouen v. inf. give N(Lo) 104; **ӡiuen** W 20(2), N(2); **ӡiue** W(4); **ӡife** N(Lo) 132; **ӡeouest** 2 s. pr. N(U) 14/**ӡeuest** L 12; **ӡiuen** 3 pl. pr. W 93; **ӡef** s. imper. L 13/**ӡif** N(U) 16, N(Lo)(3); **ӡef** 2 s. pt. W 88(4); **ӡef** 3 s. pt. W 96; **ӡif** N(Le) 75; **iӡeuen** pp. N(Le) 26/ **iӡeue** R 18; **ӡiuen** W(5).
ӡerde n. rod, sceptre W 486. See **kineӡerde**.
ӡerne v. inf. desire W 193; **ӡirneð** 3 pl. pr. N(Le) 83; **ӡerndes** 2 s. pt. W 333; **ӡerned** pp. W 122.
ӡet adv. yet, moreover, furthermore W 271(3), L 14; ~upon in addition to W 523; **ӡette** W 135(6), L 7; **ӡet** conj. yet, but at the same time N(U) 8, N(Le) 61; **ӡette** W 625.
ӡeten n. pl. gates R 12/**ӡetes** N(Le) 19.
ӡettedest v. 2 s. pt. didst grant? N(Lo) 22.
ӡimmede pp. s. wk. bejewelled W 147.
ӡu pers. pron. 2 pl. acc. you W 566.
ӡung adj. young W 343.

ha pron. f. s. she W 423, L 103; **heo** N(Lo) 118(2); **hire** acc., after prep., & dat. her, (to) her L 12(2),

Glossary

N(4), R 6; hire *poss. adj.* W 163(3), N(5), L(4); here L 11.
ha *pron. 3 pl.* they W 467(6), L 27, R(2); heo L 9, N(6); ham *acc.*, after *prep.*, & *dat.* them, (to, for) them W 43(11), N(11); hare *poss. adj.* W 139(6), L 78; hore N(2); heore N(Le) 71.
habben *v. inf.* have L 118, N(4); habbe W 629, L 58; haue W 286(4); habbe *1 s. pr.* R 10(4), N(9); abbe L 39(2); haue W 242(4); hauest *2 s. pr.* L 13(2), N(4); haues W 214(12); haueð *3 s. pr.* L 25(4), N(3); aueð N(U) 103; haweð N(Lo) 140; habbeð *pl. pr.* L 76(2), N(5), R(2); haueð L 27, N(3); hauen W 244(2); haue W 502; haue *s. imper.* N(Lo) 31(3); hefde *1 s. pt.* W 304; hefdich (=*hefde ich*) N(Lo) 92; hafdes *2 s. pt.* W 99(5); hefdes W 446(3); hafde *3 s. pt.* W 388; hefden *pl. pt.* W 140(2); ihaued *pp.* R 18/iheued N(Le) 25. Negative forms: nabbe *1 s. pr.* have not L 21; nabe N(U) 150; nabbich (= *nabbe ich*) N(Lo) 81; nab ich N(Lo) 82; naueð *3 s. pr.* N(U) 141, L 114; nauedes *2 s. pt.* W 340.
haheð *v. 3 s. pr.* is fitting R 29/howeð N(Le) 41.
halde *v. inf.* hold, keep W 25, 73; halde *1 s. pr.* W 246; halt *3 s. pr.* L 115, N(Lo) 117; hold *s. imper.* N(Lo) 94, 121; halden *pp.* as *adj.* R 16/iholden N(Le) 23; helden *pp.* W 141.
half *n.* side N(U) 155, N(4); halue (after *prep.*) N(Lo) 56.
halhes *n. pl.* saints W 469; halehen R 25; halewen N(3).
hali *adj.* hqly W 64, R 4, L 2; heali W 484; holi N(5); oli N(Lo) 29; holie *wk.* N(Le) 55.
haliwei *n.* balm W 3, 35; halwi L 4/healewi N(U) 5.
halsi *v. 1 s. pr.* entreat R 28, N(2).
halwende *adj.* healing L 85, N(U) 103.
hard *adj.* hard, severe W 7, 513;

herde N(Le) 53; harde *pl.* W 264, R 30/herde N(Le) 43.
hardi *adj.* brave, bold W 123.
hardischipe *n.* bravery W 121(2).
hat *adj.* sharp, intense W 337.
haðfule *adj. pl.* hateful W 371.
he *pron. m. s.* he W 112(14), N(17), L(8), R(2); ~ *pis* he, this very man W 418; hine *acc.* N(Le) 39; him W 131(6), N(3), L 118, R 28; (after *prep.*) W 564, N(U) 129, L 105; *dat.* (to, on, &c.) him W 393, L 33, N(5); in impers. constr. W 518; him *reflex.* himself W 121(2), L 47, N(2); ~ *one* by himself alone N(Le) 48; ~ *suluen* himself, N(Le) 75; his *poss. adj.* W 24(16), N(41), L(9), R(4); hise *pl.* W 436(2); his *poss. pron.* N(U) 140(2), L(2).
healend *n.* saviour W 2.
heaned *pp.* mistreated W 369.
heaðen *adj.* heathen W 392; heaðene *pl.* W 376(2).
heaued *n.* head W 342(5), L 121, N(Lo) 117; heawed N(Lo) 121.
heh *adj.* high W 161(2), L 54; hehe W 628; heie N(7); hehere *compar.* W 178; herre W 166, N(Le) 80; hehest *superl.* R 25; heiest N(Le) 35.
hehnesse *n.* highness W 26.
hehschipe *n.* exaltation L 112; heihschipe N(U) 183.
heht *pp.* commanded, promised W 99, 642.
heie *adv.* high N(Lo) 70.
hele *n.* health L 3(2), N(2).
helen *inf.* heal N(Lo) 47; helen *pl. pr. subj.* N(U) 119/healen L 98(2); hel *s. imper.* N(Lo) 50(2); helinde *pr. p.* as *adj.* N(Lo) 74, as *n.* Saviour N(Lo) 78.
heliunge *n.* blindfolding N(Le) 51.
helle *n.* hell W 41(7), R 5, N(3).
help *n.* help L 105, N(8); helpe W 287.
helpen *v. inf.* help N(Lo) 137; helpe W 306(2); helpe *3 s. pr. subj.* W 155, N(Le) 71; help *s. imper.* R 7, N(3); helpe L 106.

Glossary

helpies *adj.* helpless N(Lo) 82(2); **helplease** *pl.* as *n.* N(U) 129/ **helpleses** L 105.
hende *adj.* gracious W 189. See **ende**.
hendeleic *n.* courtesy, graciousness W 27(3).
henge *v. inf.* hang W 436(3); **hengest** *2 s. pr.* W 526; **henges** W(2); **henges** *3 s. pr.* W 420(3); **henge** *3 s. pr. subj.* W 590; **heng** (or *pt.* of *hon*) W 654; **heng** *s. imper.* W 384(3); **hengedes** *2 s. pt.* W 347; **henged** *pp.* W 317(2).
heorte *n.* heart W 135(9), L(4), N(13), R 24; **herte** W(12).
heortliche *adv.* with the heart, earnestly N(U) 23/**heorteliche** L 20; **herteliche** W 406.
heouene *n.* heaven W 67(2); **heouene** (after *prep.*) W 187, N(4), L 51; **heuene** W 62(5), N(Lo) 123.
heouenlich *adj.* heavenly N(U) 28, N(Lo) 96; **heouenliche** L 24(3), N(4); **heoueneliche** L 87; **heouenliche** *pl.* N(U) 42, L 36.
heoueriche *n.* kingdom of heaven N(U) 158.
her *adv.* here L 52(3), N(3), R title; **here** W 555. See **ha** *pron. f. s.*
her-bitweonen *adv.* between these (arms) N(U) 55.
herie *v. 1 s. pr.* praise N(Lo) 98; **herien** *pl. pr. subj.* N(Lo) 176; **heriede** *3 s. pt.* N(Le) 6; **herehede** R 5; **heried** *pp.* W 18.
herm *n.* harm N(Lo) 132.
herof *adv.* hereof W 423, N(Lo) 75.
herteli *adv.* with the heart, earnestly W 562.
her-þurh *adv.* here through N(Lo) 73.
herupon *adv.* hereupon W 403.
herwiđ *adv.* herewith W 136.
hetelifaste *adv.* cruelly tight W 468.
hit *pron. nt. s.* it W 45(23), N(19), L(8), R 29.
hoker *n.* scorn W 532; **hokere** W 525; **hokeres** *pl.* W 371.

hokerliche *adv.* scornfully W 501.
hokerunge *n.* mockery N(Le) 49; **hokerringe** W 488.
holi-gost *n.* Holy Ghost N(Lo) 136(2); **holi-goste** (after *prep.*) N(Lo) 6(2); **oli-goste** N(Lo) 29.
holinesse *n.* holiness N(Le) 78.
holscipe *n.* chastity L 117.
hond *n.* hand W 101(2), N(Le) 59; **honde** W 487; **honden** *pl.* W 515, L 83, N(2); **hondes** W 513.
hope *n.* hope L 106, N(4).
hopien *v. inf.* hope N(Lo) 91; **hopie** *1 s. pr.* L 5, N(2); **hopede** *1 s. pt.* N(Lo) 152.
hord *n.* hoard, treasure W 116.
hore *n.* whore W 277.
hori *n.* pollution, filth L 78/**horie** N(U) 94.
hu *adv.* how W 358(13), L 41, N(4).
huide *v. inf.* hide W 350; **hid** *pp.* W 116.
hule *v. inf.* cover, conceal W 350; **hilede** *3 pl. pt.* W 411.
hulles *n. pl.* hills N(Le) 46.
hundes *n. pl.* hounds W 377(2).
hungre *n.* hunger W 337.
huni *n.* honey L 31/**uni** N(U) 35.
huniter *n.* honey-drop W 3, N(U) 5, L 5.
hunteđ *v. 3 s. pr.* hunts N(U) 163.
hurd *n.* court W 187.
hurtes *n. pl.* hurts, injuries W 264, N(Le) 43, R 30.
hus *n.* house W 144(4). See **lewe**.
hwa *pron. inter.* who W 8(6), L(2); **hwo** N(U) 55; **hwoa** N(U) 55(3); (see **lif**); **hwas** *gen.* L 113, N(U) 139?; **hwam** *acc.* W 238; **hwa** *rel.* W 239; **hwas** *gen.* L 113; **hwam** *acc.* N(U) 11(2), L(2); **hwa** *indef.* whoever, he who W 229, L 47; **hua** L 47; **hwo** N(U) 54(2); **hwoa** N(Lo) 84.
hwaremide *pron.* wherewith N(Lo) 81.
hwa-se *pron. indef.* whosoever W 240(2), L 25(2); **hwoa so euer** N(U) 29(2).

Glossary

hwen *adv. rel.* when W 282(8); **hwon** N(U) 163; **hwen þ** W 313(4).
hwer *adv. inter.* where W 167; **hwer** *rel.* (as *pron.*) anywhere W 341; wherewith W 344; ~ *wið* W 348; ~ *fore* W 622.
hwet *pron. inter.* what L 80(2); **hwat** W 80(5), N(6); **hwat** *adj. inter.* W 6(5); **hwat-so** whatsoever N(Lo) 66.
hwi *adv.* why N(U) 45(13), L(12).
hwile *n.* time N(Lo) 93; **hwiles** N(Le) 29, R 21.
hwils *adv. rel.*: ~ *þ* W 246(2); ~ *pe* (prob. = *hwils þ*) W 445.
hwit *adj.* white W 14(3), N(Le) 49; **hwite** (after *prep.*): ~ *sune dai* Whitsunday N(Lo) 21.
hwuch *pron.*: ~ . . . *swa* whichsoever W 127; **hwuche** (after *prep.*) . . . **so** N(Lo) 158.
hwuder *adv.* whither N(U) 162.

iborenesse *n.* birth N(Lo) 7, N(Le) 42/**ibornesse** R 30.
ich *pron. 1 s.* I W 86(9), N(78), L(15), R(10); **ic** L 5(4); **i** W 70(34). The reduced form **i** usually comes next to its verb, but not always. It coalesces in *iwile*, *schuldi* and *ine* (= *ich*+*ne*). **me** *acc.*, after *prep.*, & *dat.*, me, (to, for, &c.) me W 70(70), N(71), L 14, R(8); **me** *reflex.* & *emph.* (usually followed by *self*, *seluen*) W 100, 274(5); **mi** *poss. adj. s.* (before cons.) my W 1(78), N(23), L(16), R(2); *mi mi* W 508 = *nu mi*?; **min** (before vowel or *h*, rarely other cons.) W 75(4), N(15), L(10); **mine** *s. acc.* & after *prep.* W 312, N(15); **mine** *s. gen.* N(U) 3, N(Le) 12, 17?; **mine** *pl.* W 83(6), N(18), L(5), R(4); **min**: ~ *ehne* W 49; **mi**: *in* ~ *breostes* L 70.
iclumben *pp.* climbed N(Lo) 70.
icnoulechie *v. 1 s. pr.* acknowledge, confess N(Le) 34/ see **cnawlechi**.
icnowe *v. 1 s. pr.* confess N(Le) 17/ see **cnawe**.

ifere *n.* companion N(U) 70, L 59.
ifestnet *pp.* fastened R 9/**ifestned** N(Le) 14.
ifon *n. pl.* foes N(Le) 16.
ifulet *pp.* befouled, besmirched R 22; **ifuled** L 78, N(3).
igedered *pp.* gathered, united W 11.
ihalewed *pp.* as *adj.* hallowed, sanctified N(Lo)13.
iher *v. s. imper.* hear N(Lo) 31; **iherd** *pp.* N(U) 117, L 96.
iholschipe *n.* virginity N(U) 143.
ihurt *pp.* hurt N(Le) 31, R 22.
ihwer *adv.* everywhere L 118.
ileue *v. 1 s. pr.* believe N(Lo) 97(2); **ileueð** *3 s. pr.* N(Lo) 27.
iliche *adj.* alike, the same N(U) 142/**ilic** L 115.
ilicked *pp.* licked N(U) 35.
ilke *adj.* same, very W 224(2), N(7), L(3).
ilome *adv.* often N(Lo) 114.
imengd *pp.* mingled, mixed N(U) 32, L 28.
imiddes *prep.* in the middle of W 326.
imong *prep.* among W 232.
in *prep.* (before vowels and cons.) in, into, &c. W 41(23), N(27), L(10), R(3). **i** (before cons. only, and frequently joined to following word, viz. *drunch*, *fihte*, *flod*, *licome*, *lif*, *mine*, *nan*, *rattes*, *sawle*, *swink*, *þe*, *pinge*, *pis*(*se*), *pi*(*ne*), *wodschipe*) W 8(27), N(12), L 84, R(4); **ine** L 67, N(12).
in *adv.* within, therein W 548.
inempned *pp.* named, called N(Lo) 29.
inȝong *n.* entrance N(U) 161.
inne *prep.* in, into N(Le) 56.
inne *adv.* in, within W 325.
inoh *adj.* enough W 440; **inouh** N(Lo) 45.
inouhreðe *adv.* soon enough N(Lo) 146.
into *prep.* into W 297(4), N(Lo) 19.
inwarde *adj.* (after *prep.*) inward N(Lo) 5(2).

Glossary

inwið *prep.* within, in W 10(2), N(U) 103, L 85.
ioie *n.* joy W 559, N(Lo) 106.
irene *adj. pl.* iron N(Lo) 11; **irnene** W 512.
iseli *adj.* blessed N(Lo) 160.
iseo *v. 1 s. pr.* see N(Lo) 36; **isihst** *2 s. pr.* N(Lo) 134; **iseo** *1 s. pr. subj.* N(Le) 80; **iseihe** *2 s. pt.* N(Lo) 99.
ismaht *pp.* tasted L 96/**ismauht** N(U) 117.
ismelled *pp.* smelt N(U) 118, L 97.
iteied *pp.* tied N(Lo) 155.
ituht *pp.* stretched N(U) 152.
iueed *pp.* made hostile L 76/ **iueied** N(U) 93.
iuele *v. 1 s. pr.* feel N(U) 84.
iunne *pp.* granted, bestowed R 19.
iwreðed *pp.* made wroth, enraged L 76.
iwundet *pp.* wounded R 15/ **iwunded** N(Le) 22.
iwursed *pp.* worsened, impaired N(U) 92.
iwurðe *v. 3 s. pr. subj.* come to pass, be done N(Lo) 145; **iwurden** *pp.* as *adj.* undone, ruined N(Lo) 95.

karlische *adj. pl.* masculine, male W 191.
keiser *n.* emperor W 62(2).
kempe *n.* warrior W 143.
kene *adj.* brave W 24(4).
kin *n.* kin W 177.
kindeliche *adv.* naturally W 218.
kinebearn *n.*: ∼ *of burðe* child of royal birth W 175.
kineʒerde *n.* (royal) sceptre N(Le) 51.
kinesmon *n.* kinsman W 230 (MS. *kinsemon*).
king *n.* king W 170(3), N(Lo) 52; **kinges** *gen. s.* W 169; **kinges** *pl.* W 172.
kissen *v. inf.* kiss W 575; **cusse** *1 s. pr.* N(U) 80, L 66.

ladliche *adv.* loathsomely R 22/ **lodliche** N(Le) 31.

lahe *adj.* (after *prep.*) low L 54/ **lowe** N(U) 63.
lahhen *v. 3 pl. pr.* laugh W 525.
lahter *n.* laughter, laughing-stock W 529, 532.
lai *n.* flame N(Lo) 164.
lamb *n.* lamb W 199.
large *adj.* liberal N(U) 98, L 81; **largere** *compar.* W 103; **largest** *superl.* W 91.
largemen *n. pl.* generous men W 92.
largesce *n.* beneficence W 19(5).
laste *adj. superl.* last W 316(2); **olast** at last, lastly N(Le) 60.
lasted *v. 3 s. pt.* lasted W 445.
lasteles *adj.* flawless W 185; **lastelese** *pl.* W 27.
lates *n. pl.* manners W 28.
laðeliche *adj.* loathsome W 128.
lauerd *n.* lord W title (5); **louerd** L 17(8), N(24); **lauerdes** *pl.* W 172.
lawen *n. pl.* laws N(Lo) 61.
leafdi *n.* lady L 107, N(5); **lefdi** R 1(3); **lauedi** W 554; **lafdi** W 559.
leaue *v. 1 s. pr. subj.* leave W 213; **leaued** *pp.* W 242.
leaste *n.* flaw W 183.
leasunge *n.* lying R 16 (MS. *leasunsunge*)/ **lesunge** N(Le) 23.
leche *n.* physician L 87, N(2), R 9.
lechunge *n.* treatment, cure L 89; **lechnunge** N(U) 109.
leden *v. inf.* lead, bring N(Lo) 81 ?, 86; **ledes** *3 s. pr.* W 492; **leddes** *2 s. pt.* W 146; **ledden** *3 pl. pt.* W 470.
ledunge *n.* leading N(Le) 47.
leitinde *adj.* radiant N(U) 18, L 16.
leof *adj. & n.* dear, beloved W 34(5), N(3), L(2); **lef** W 367(5); **leoue** *wk.* L 44, N(2); **leue** W 54(5); **leuer** *compar.* preferable W 20; **leuere** W 45.
leoflich *adj.* dear N(U) 8/**leoflic** L 7(2); **leoflukest** *superl.* N(U) 88/**leoflucest** L 72.
leofmon *n.* lover W 572, L 17, N(2); **leouemon** N(Lo) 119; **lefmon**

Glossary

W 58(11); **leofmonnes** *gen. s.* N(Lo) 117.
leome *n.* light L 4(3), N(U) 4, 65 ?(4).
leor *n.* countenance W 6(5), L 12; **leore** (after *prep.*) N(U) 13.
leosen *v. inf.* lose N(Lo) 162; **leoseð** *3 s. pr.* N(U) 12, L 11; **leose** *3 s. pr. subj.* N(Lo) 157.
lepen *v. inf.* leap W 596.
ler *v. s. imper.* teach N(U) 19.
lese *v. inf.* release W 89; **lese** *s. imper.* W 385; **lesedes** *2 s. pt.* W 144; **lesed** *pp.* W 381.
lest *conj.* lest W 88; **leste** N(Lo) 37.
lest *adv. superl.* least W 128, NL(o)159.
leten *v. inf.* abandon W 75, N(Lo) 170; **letes** *3 s. pr.* W 163; **let** *s. imper.* let L 16, N(2); **lettest** *2 s. pt.* N(Lo) 95.
lettunge *n.* hindrance N(U) 89, L 74.
leue *v. s. imper.* grant W 56(11), N(Lo) 115; **lef** W 495; **leoue** W 78. See **leof.**
leueð *v. 3 s. pr.* believes, follows W 231; **leued** *3 pl. pr.* N(Lo) 23.
lewe *n.* shelter: *hus* ~ house-room W 324.
lich *n.* body W 478; **like** (after *prep.*) W 571.
licome *n.*: *ilicome* in body R 22/ **licame** N(Le) 32.
licomliche *adj. pl.* bodily L 99/ **licamliche** N(U) 121.
licomliche *adv.* bodily L 19/**licamliche** N(U) 21.
licung *n.* delight, desire L 39, N(Lo) 141; **licunge** L 99, N(U) 46(2); **likinge** W 57(9).
lif *n.* life, living creature W 34(11), N(4), L 4(2); *hwo (hwa)* ~ what living person? N(U) 55, L 47; **liue** (after *prep.*) N(U) 125, N(Lo) 63; **liues** *gen. s.* W 269(5), L 34, N(2); **lifes** L 92.
ligge *v. 1 s. pr.* lie N(Lo) 71(2).
liht *n.* light N(U) 12(2), L 11(2).
lihtliche *adj.* light, easy W 162.
liked *pp.* licked L 31.
likeð *v. 3 s. pr.* pleases N(U) 82, L 68; **likes** W 151.

lim *n.* limb N(U) 118, L 97; **limes** *pl.* W 325(2); **limen** N(Lo) 14(2).
liuien *v. inf.* live L 100, N(2); **liue** W 535; **liuie** *1 s. pr.* L 101(2), N(2); **liuee** N(U) 123; **liue** W 507; **liueð** *3 s. pr.* L 101(2), N(3); **liuie** *1 s. pr. subj.* N(Lo) 67; **liuiinde** *pr. p.* N(U) 20(2); **liuinde** N(Lo) 65; **liuede** *1 s. pt.* N(U) 125; **leuede** L 102; **liuede** *3 s. pt.* W 182.
lo *interj.* lo! W 494.
lokin *v. inf.* look L 9/**logen** N(U) 10; **loken** W 40(2); **loke** *s. imper.* N(Lo) 76.
long *adj.* long W 371; **longe** N(U) 30, L 25.
longe *adv.* long W 209; **lengre** *compar.* W 450, N(Lo) 168, **lengrre** N(Le) 83.
lot *n.* lot, share N(U) 68, L 58.
lowe *adv.* low N(Lo) 71. See **lahe.**
lufsum *adj.* lovable W 14(3), N(2); **lufsume** *wk.* W 395.
luft *adj.* left N(Lo) 117(2).
lure *n.* loss L 60, N(3); **luren** *pl.* N(Lo) 71.
lustes *n. pl.* lusts L 99, N(2).
lusti *adj.* pleasant W 40.
lute *adj.* little L 77; **lutel** W 108, N(2).
luðere *adj. pl.* as *n.* wicked W 529; **luðre** *adj. pl.* N(Le) 12.
luue *n.* love W 33(43), L 65, N(9); **loue** L 2(3); **lou** L 24; perh. *gen.* in *mi luue lif* W 105.
luue-lettres *n. pl.* love messages W 549.
luueleuest *adj.* (as *n.*) dearest love W 34(2).
luueli *adj.* lovely W 6(2).
luueliche *adj.* lovely W 9(3), N(U) 93, L 77; **louelich** N(U) 8; **luuelike** W 533.
luuenesse *n.* love W 613.
luuewurðest *adj.* most worthy of love N(U) 88, L 72.
luuewurði *adj.* worthy of love W 12(3).
luuien *v. inf.* love N(Lo) 108(3);

Glossary

luuie W 615; louien N(U) 20; luuen W 32; luue W 6(12); loue L 17; luuie *1 s. pr.* L 17, N(2); loue L 40; luueð *3 s. pr.* W 230; luues W 219(3); luuieð *3 pl. pr.* N(Lo) 22(2); luuie *1 s. pr. subj.* W 70(2), N(Lo) 65; luue W 212; luuiende *pr. p. (adj.)* L 61; louende L 17; luuedes *2 s. pt.* W 353(3); luued *pp.* W 16(7); iloued N(Le) 21.

maht *n.* might W 23(3).
mahti *adj.* mighty W 150.
make *n.* mate N(Lo) 3.
make *v. inf.* make W 12(4); makes *3 s. pr.* W 15(5); makes *3 pl. pr.* W 263; makien *3 s. pr. subj.* N(U) 122; make *s. imper.* N(U) 17, L 14; makedest *2 s. pt.* N(U) 66(2), L(2); makedes W 84(2); mades W 82; imaket *pp.* R 12; imaked N(2); maked W(3).
martird *pp.* martyred W 557.
me *indef. pron.* one, anyone L 33(2), N(7).
me *conj.* but, however N(U) 36, L 31.
meane *n.* intercourse W 223.
mede *n.* reward N(U) 38, L 34.
medicine *n.* medicine N(U) 107, L 88.
mei *v. 1 s. pr.* may N(U) 95; mai W 71(2); maȝe L 100; meiht *2 s. pr.* N(Lo) 178(2); mei *3 s. pr.* W 5(3), N(U) 127, R 27; mai W 60, 603(10); L 104, N(3); maȝe L 66; maȝen *pl. pr.* L 24; mihte *1 s. pt.* W 301(2); mihtes *2 s. pt.* W 342(6); mahte *3 s. pt.* L 91; mihte W 45(6); mihten *3 pl. pt.* W 41; mihte 77(2). See muhe.
meiden *n.* maiden W 175(3), N(10), R(2); maiden L 107(5), N(Le) 39; meidenes *gen. s.* N(U) 2, N(Lo) 6; maidene L 2; meidnes *pl.* N(Le) 2, R 1.
meidhod *n.* chastity N(Lo) 87.
meister *n.* master W 420.
meknesse *n.* meekness W 196(3).

menged *pp.* mixed W 519.
menske *n.* kindness, humanity, honour W 28(4), N(U) 143, L 116.
mensken *v. inf.* honour W 435; menske W 426.
mensket *n.* virginity W 163.
menskli *adv.* generously W 20.
merci *n.* mercy R 12(2), N(6).
merciable *adj.* merciful N(Lo) 41.
mesaise *n.* hardship W 356.
mete *n.* food W 337, N(Le) 30, R 21.
mid *prep.* with L 95(4), N(9), R 18.
mihte *n.* might L 90, N(4).
mihti *adj.* mighty W 136, N(2), L(2).
milce *n.* mercy W 210(2), L 49, N(7), R 27.
milde *adj. wk.* mild R 26, N(4); mildest *superl.* W 175.
mildeliche *adv.* mildly W 206, N(Lo) 14.
mildeschipe *n.* mildness W 29(2); mildschipe W 196.
mildeu *n.* honey W 5.
milzfule *adj. wk.* merciful R 7, N(4).
mis *adv.* amiss N(Le) 26(2), R(2).
misetholden *pp.* wrongly withheld N(Le) 27.
mishercnet *pp.* wrongly heard R 13/misihercned N(Le) 20.
mishopie *v. 1 s. pr.* mistrust N(Lo) 130.
misifelet *pp.* wrongly felt R 14/misifeled N(Le) 21, L 97; misiueld N(U) 118.
misiliket *pp.* wrongly enjoyed R 14.
misiseien *pp.* wrongly seen N(U) 116/misseien L 95.
misispeken *pp.* wrongly spoken N(Le) 21, R 14.
misliche *adj.* various W 429.
mislicunge *n.* displeasure N(Lo) 72.
misloket *pp.* wrongly beheld R 13/misiloked N(Le) 20.
missware *n.* forswearing R 16.
mod *n.* mood, mind W 175.
moder *n.* mother W 249(4), N(10), L(8), R 27; moderes *gen. s.* N(Lo) 15; moder W 55.
moderliche *adj. wk.* motherly W 557.

Glossary

mon *n.* man (and *indef. pron.* one, etc. in W, though the *n.* and *pron.* cannot always be distinguished) W 15(24), N(8), L(4); man W 120(3), (*dat.*) W 71; **monne** (after *prep.*) N(Lo) 103; **monnes** *gen. s.* W 224(3), N(3), L 38, R 18; **men** *pl.* W 160(3), N(2). See **ei, na.**
moncun *n.* mankind R 2, N(2); **monkin** W 129(3); **moncunne** *gen. s.* N(Lo) 135.
mone *v. 1 s. pr.* complain N(Lo) 77.
mong *n.* company N(U) 24, L21.
monhad *n.* manhood, incarnation W 173.
moni *adj.* many (a), W 15(4), N(2), L 38; **monie** (after *prep.*) N(Lo) 82; **monie** *pl.* R 8, N(2).
monifald *adj.* manifold W 429.
monquellere *n.* murderer W 380.
mot *n.* argument; *nim* ~ intercede N(Le) 36, R 25.
mote *v. 1 s. pr. subj.* must, may N(Lo) 115(3); **mot** *3 s. pr.* N(U) 63(5), L(5).
motild *n.* (female) disputant, advocate N(Le) 7, R 6.
muchel *adj.* great L 69(2), N(2); *pron.* much N(Lo) 113; **muche** W 373, N(2); **muchele** N(U) 142, L 116; **mikel** W 258; **muchele** *wk.* W 156(2), N(5), L(2); **mikle** W 198; **mare** *compar.* W 248(6); **more** N(Lo) 28, 43?; **meast** *superl.* W 298; **measte** *wk.* W 430.
muchel *adv.* greatly, much W 214(3); **mare** *compar.* W 16(2); **more** L 91, N(4); **mest** *superl.* N(Lo) 4(2); see **on.**
muhe *v. 1 s. pr.* may, can W 565; **muwe** N(Lo) 68; **muwe** *3 s. pr.* N(U) 79; **muhen** *pl. pr.* W 12, N(U) 28; **muwen** N(Le) 8; **muhte** *3 s. pt.* N(U) 111; **muhten** *pl. pt.* N(Lo) 138. See **mei.**
munegunge *n.* memory W 4(2), N(U) 81, L 67.
munte *n.* (after *prep.*) mount W 493.
murhðe *n.* (after *prep.*) joy L 26; **murðe** N(U) 30; **murhðes** *pl.* W 67.
muð *n.* mouth W 203(2), L 96; **muðe** (after *prep.*) W 5, N(U) 117.

na, nan *adj.* no, not any; **na** (before cons. except *h*) W 71(6), L 3; **no** L 53, N(5); **nan** (before vowels) W 179(2); (before cons.) L 29(2); **non** (before vowel) N(Lo) 153; **none** *dat.* N(Lo) 172; *onone wise* in no wise N(U) 28, L 24; **nan** *pron.* none W 110(2); *inan* (*in* + *nan*) L 29; **non** N(Lo) 162.
nacnes *v. 3 s. pr.* strips, denudes W 505.
nai *adv.* nay W 123, N(2), L(2).
nailed *pp.* nailed W 137; **neiled** W 591.
naked *adj.* naked W 474.
nawiht *pron.* (usually with additional neg.) nothing, naught W 250; **naut** L 33; **nowitht** N(Lo) 172; **nowt** W 606, N(U) 38; **nout** N(Lo) 65.
nawt *adv.* (usually with additional neg.) not at all, by no means W 124(5), R 27; **naut** L 59(2); **nowt** N(Lo) 130; **noht** W 294(2); **nout** N(13).
ne *adv.* (precedes verb and usually accompanies other negatives) not, W 5(24), N(26), L(15), R 6; coalesced in *narn, nabbe, nis, nulen,* &c.; *ine* (= *ich ne*) W 88, 300. In L 65 the second *ne* is redundant.
ne *conj.* nor W 193(5), N(Lo) 129; *ne ... ne* neither ... nor W 191-2, N(U) 95, L 78.
neauer *adv.* never W 97(7); **neuer** L 9(2), N(3); *neauer mare* W 594.
neb *n.* face W 14(4).
neh *adv.* nearly, almost, nearby W 280(3).
neiles *n. pl.* nails W 469(2), N(5).
neod *n.* need N(Lo) 179; **neoden** *pl.* N(Le) 10, R 8.
neodfulles *adj.* (as *gen. n.*) of the needy N(Lo) 88.
neose *n.* nose L 97/**noese** N(U) 118.

nerre *adj. compar.* nearer W 288; **nehest** *superl.* W 299.
nesche *adj. pl.* tender W 324.
nimen *v. inf.* take, take up N(U) 39, L 34; **nimen** *pl. pr.* N(U) 41/ **neomen** L 36; **nim** *s. imper.* N(Le) 36, R 25; **nam** *1 s. pt.* N(U) 57, L 49; *3 s. pt.* undertook W 222; **inumen** *pp.* N(Le) 26.
nimunge *n.* capture N(Le) 47(2); **niminge** W 463.
noble *adj. pl.* noble W 160.
noblesce *n.* nobility W 25(2).
nohwer *adv.* nowhere W 190; **nowhwer** W 616.
nome *n.* name N(Lo) 176.
nowest: see **ah** *v.*
nowhwider *adv.* nowhere W 475.
nowðer *adv. correl.* (with *ne*) neither ... nor N(Lo) 80; **nouðer** ... **ne** L 114, N(2).
nowðer *pron.* neither W 228.
nu *adv.* now, next W 489(13), N(5); as an introductory word with temporal sense weakened or lost W 32(7).
nunan *adv.* now, at once R 8.
nuðe *adv.* now N(Lo) 78.

o *interj.* oh! L 116/**owe** (an error?) N(U) 142. See **of, on.**
obedience *n.* obedience N(Lo) 127.
of *prep.* of (with various shadings of sense, as: from, by, concerning, among, because of, by means of, on account of, pertaining to, &c.) W 4(84), N(70), L(18), R(4); o W 341.
offeard *pp.* afraid W 131.
offringe *n.* offering N(Le) 72.
ofseruunge *n.* deserving N(Lo) 148(2).
ofte *adv.* often W 161(5), N(3), L 86, R 10.
on *prep.* (before vowels and cons.) on, upon, in W 36(15), N(23), L(4); *on eise* at ease W 651. o (before cons. only, and sometimes joined to following word: as *fluht, rode, none, laste, þe, twa*) W 5(20), N(2), R 8; *o water* with water W 490.

on *adv.* on, upon W 40; **one** at hand? N(Lo) 129.
onde *n.* envy N(Le) 23, R 16.
onont *prep.* anent, compared to W 173(2).
ontenden *v. inf.* kindle N(U) 159; **ontende** *3 s. pr. subj.* N(Lo) 167; **ontend** *s. imper.* N(U) 18, L 15.
openlich *adv.* manifestly, plainly W 550.
openunge *n.* opening N(Le) 55.
oppnes *v. 2 s. pr.* openest W 547; **openeð** *3 s. pr.* L 43; **opne** *3 s. pr. subj.* W 656; **opene** *s. imper.* N(Lo) 51; **opnedes** *2 s. pt.* W 203; **iopened** *pp.* as *adj.* N(Lo) 49, N(U) 50 ? (MS. iopeneð; cf. L 43).
ord *n.* spear-point W 559.
oreisun see **ureisun.**
oðer *adj. & pron.* other, another W 13(4), N(3); *s.* or *pl.* N(U) 46/L 40, R 18; *euchan ... oðer* (each) one ... other W 32(3); **oðre** *pl.* W 75(7), N(2); **oðres** *gen. pl.* N(Lo) 103.
oðer *conj.* or W 302(2), N(3), L(2).
oðer-hwiles *adv.* at other times N(Le) 29/**oderhwiles** R 21.
ouer *prep.* over, above W 85(9), N(2), L 110, R 1.
oueral *adv.* all over, above all N(U) 145; **ouer al** W 30.

paie *v. inf.* pay, repay W 586.
pappe *n.* pap, breast W 332(2).
passiun *n.* passion W 266, N(3), R 4.
paternoster *n.* paternoster W 235.
pik *n.* pitch W 43.
piler *n.* pillar W 474.
pine *n.* pain, torment W 89(7), N(3), L 59; **pinen** *pl.* R 23, N(4); **pines** W 441.
pineful *adj.* painful W 316; **pinefule.** *pl.* W 202.
pinende *pr. p.* as *adj.* torturing W 42; **pinet** *pp.* W 539.
pine-wurðe *adj.* worthy of torment N(Le) 37, R 26.
pleiful *adj.* playful, light-hearted N(Le) 28, R 20.
pouerte *n.* poverty W 310(8).

Glossary

poure *adj.* poor W 314(7); **poure** *pl.* (as *n.*) W 352; **pourere** *compar.* W 330.
poure *adv.* poorly W 327.
praie *n.* prey W 140(2).
prei *v. s. imper.* pray W 645.
preost *n.* priest N(Le) 68.
princes *n. pl.* princes W 467(2).
pris *n.* renown N(Le) 22, R 15.
prisuns *n. pl.* prisoners N 144.
priuete *n.* intimacy N(U) 25, L 22.
prophete *n.* prophet W 64.
prude *n.* pride N(Le) 21, R 14.

quellere: see **monquellere**.
quemen *v. 3 pl. pr.* please W 648.
quene: see **cwene**.
querfaste *adv.* transversely, from side to side W 592.
quiddet: see **cwiddes**.

raise *v. 3 pl. pr.* raise W 503.
rattes *n.pl.* rags: *irattes* in rags W 327.
raðer *adv. compar.* more readily, sooner W 16; **raðeste** *superl.* W 352.
reade *adj.* red W 453; **red** N(Le) 49; **reade** *wk.* W 484.
readi *adj.* ready W 333.
ream *n.* crying N(Lo) 15.
reaues *v. 3 s. pr.* deprives, frees (from) W 601; **reftes** *2 s. pt.* didst seize, take by force W 139.
recches *v. impers. 3 s. pr.*: *ne ~ me* I care not W 245.
red *n.* reed W 486; **rede**? (MS. *rode*) N(Le) 52. See **reade, reden.**
red *n.* counsel N(Lo) 85(2).
reden *v. inf.* read, counsel W 548, N(Lo) 137; **reden** *3 pl. pr.* W 339; **red** *s. imper.* N(Lo) 85.
redleas *adj.* lacking counsel N(Lo) 80; **redles** N(Lo) 86; **redlease** *n. gen. pl.* N(Lo) 85.
reming *n.* lamentation W 500.
reowðe *n.* pity, grief W 460(4); **rewðe** N(Lo) 17.
reste *n.* rest, repose W 596.
reste *v. inf.* rest W 325(2).
rewfule *adj. wk.* sorrowful, pitiful W 539; **rewfulle** *pl.* L 52/**rewðful** N(U) 61.
rewli *adv.* piteously, wretchedly W 86(4).
rewliche *adv.* sorrowfully W 347.
ribauz *n. pl.* ribalds W 410.
riche *adj.* rich, powerful W 318(3); **ricchere** *compar.* W 61.
richesce *n.* riches, wealth W 253.
riddes *v. 2 s. pt.* didst deliver, free from W 145(2).
riht *n.* right(s) W 25.
riht *adj.* right W 101, N(2), L 119; **ritht** N(U) 146.
riht *adv.* rightly, truly W 70(3); **rith** N(Lo) 22.
rihtwise *adj. pl.* as *n.* righteous W 529.
rixlen *v. inf.* rule, reign W 101(2); **rixles** *2 s. pr.* W 61.
robbedes *v. 2 s. pt.* didst rob W 143.
rode *n.* rood, cross W 138(17), N(13), L(4) (never *nom.*). See **red.**
ron *v. 3 s. pt.* ran N(Le) 56; **eorn** W 457.
rug *n.* back W 471.
rune *n.* stream N(Le) 56. See **blod-rune.**

sacrement *n.* sacrament N(Le) 67; **sacremenz** *pl.* N(Le) 69; **sacremens** N(Lo) 27.
sacreð *v. 3 s. pr.* sanctifies N(Le) 68; **isacred** *pp.* N(Lo) 25.
sake *n.* strife W 546; **sake** N(U) 133, L 108.
salmwruhte *n.* psalmist N(Lo) 139; **salmewrihte** W 581.
salue *n.* salve, balm N(U) 105, L 86.
saluen *v. inf.* save N(U) 102(2); **salui** L 108; **sauuin** L 84.
sar *n.* pain, affliction L 62/**sor** N(U) 74, N (3), R 23.
sare *adv.* sorely W 272(2); **sore** N(Le) 22, R 15.
sari *adj.* sorry, bitter R 5; **sori** N(Le) 6, L 38.
sariliche *adv.* sorrowfully W 499.
sawle *n.* soul W 35(5), R(3); **saule** L 3(3); **soule** N(9); **saulen** *pl.* L 83/**soulen** (NU) 101.

Glossary

sawter *n.* psalter N(Lo) 139.
schaftes *n. pl.* creatures, created things W 85(2).
schal *v.* shall (with various sense shadings to represent futurity, fitness, obligation, necessity) *1 s. pr.* W 488(3), N(U) 162; **schal** *3 s. pr.* W 364, N(3); **schule** *1 s. pr. subj.* N(Lo) 86; **schulde** *1 s. pt.* W 358; **schuldi** should I W 551; **schulde** *3 s. pt.* N(U) 161; **schulde we** should we N(Lo) 40.
scharpe *adj. wk.* sharp W 542; *pl.* W 482.
scheadewe *n.* shadow N(U) 12/ **schadwe** L 10.
scheawen *v. inf.* show N(U) 146/ **schawen** L 119; **scheawe** W 130; **schewen** N(Lo) 101; **scheawed** *pp.* W 215.
scheddest *v. 2 s. pt.* didst shed N(Lo) 44, **isched** *pp.* N(U) 97, L 80.
scheld *n.* shield N(Lo) 54.
schendlac *n.* shame, insult W 393.
schene *adj.* bright, fair W 37(3).
schent *pp.* mistreated W 315(2).
scheot *v. 3 s. pr.* shoots N(Lo) 55.
schineð *v. 3 s. pr.* shines N(U) 13.
schome *n.* shame W 200(14), N(Le) 65; **schomen** *pl.* N(Lo) 12; **schomes** W 415. See n. to W 501–2.
schomeð *3 s. pr.* is ashamed L 11; **schomet** *pp.* shamed W 315.
schomeliche *adj.* shameful W 408; **schomeliche** *pl.* W 264.
schomeliche *adv.* shamefully W 368(2).
schop *v. 2 s. pt.* didst create W 85; **ischeapen** *pp.* N(U) 140/**ischapen** L 114.
schrud *n.* garment W 15.
schruddes *v. 2 s. pt.* didst clothe W 219.
schuldi *adj.* guilty R 11. See **schal**.
schuldres *n. pl.* shoulders W 471(2), N(Le) 53.
schuppere *n.* creator W 434.
schurges *n. pl.* scourges W 507.
scornunge *n.* scorning, mockery N(Le) 50(2).

scottin *v. inf.* pay scot L 59(2)/ **scotten** N(U) 71(2).
sec *adj.* sick N(Lo) 83; **seke** *pl.* N(U) 102, L 84.
secheð *v. 3 s. pr.* seeks N(Le) 84; **secheð** *3 pl. pr.* N(Le) 12; **sohten** *3 pl. pt.* : ~ *uppo* assaulted W 284.
secnesse *n.* sickness W 312.
seggen *v. inf.* say W 580, N(5); **segge** L 104; **suggen** L 57; **siggen** N(Lo) 67(2); **seist** *2 s. pr.* W 406; **seið** *3 s. pr.* W 454(2), N(9), L 101; **seie** *3 s. pr. subj.* W 418; **seie** *s. imper.* W 652; **seidest** *2 s. pt.* N(Lo) 94; **seide** *3 s. pt.* W 370, N(2); **saide** L 121; **seide** *3 s. pt. subj.* W 412.
seint *n.* saint W 454, N(2); **seinte** L 100(2), N(5), R(3); **sein** N(Lo) 15 (end of line), N(U) 154.
sel *n.* joy ? L 3 (possibly a defective reading).
selcuðes *adj. pl.* (as *n.*) marvels, strange happenings W 428.
selhðe *n.* happiness N(Lo) 97.
seli *adj.* blessed N(Le) 37(2); **selie** *pl.* N(Lo) 32.
selle *v. inf.* sell W 627.
semeð *v. impers. 3 s. pr.* beseems, is fitting W 115.
semlike *adj.* seemly W 401.
senden *v. inf.* send N(Lo) 136; **sendes** *3 s. pr.* : ~ *his sawle* gives up the ghost W 537; **sendest** *2 s. pt.* N(Lo) 21.
seolf *pron. emph.* (with *pers. pron.*) self N(U) 107, L 88; **self** W 74(5); **seoluen** N(Lo) 40; **seluen** W 74(9); **suluen** N(Le) 75.
seon *v. inf.* see, behold W 42; **seo** W 132(2); **seo** *1 s. pr.* W 508(2); **seh** *2 s. pt.* W 300(3); **sehen** *3 pl. pt.* W 282.
seoruhfulliche *adv.* sorrowfully N(Lo) 50.
seoððen *adv.* next, then N(Le) 59; **siðen** W 473(3); **siðen þ** *conj.* since, seeing that W 553.
seruise *n.* service W 590.
sette *v. inf.* set, put W 167(3);

Glossary

sette *1 s. pr.* W 627; **setis** *3 s.* (or *pl.?) pr.* W 504; **set** *pp.* W 481.
sibbe *adj. pl.* related: ~ *frend* W 31(2).
sibnesse *n.* kinship W 243(2).
side *n.* side W 542, N(4), L 81.
sihðe *n.* sight; *þi* ~ the sight of thee W 49; **sihte** W 402.
siker *adj.* sure, secure, certain N(Lo) 131(2); **sikere** *wk.* N(U) 2, L 2.
sikerliche *adv.* surely N(Lo) 105, N(U) 159.
sikes *n. pl.* sighs N(U) 155.
singen *v. 3 pl. pr.* sing W 235.
slaw *adj.* slow R 19/**slow** N(Le) 27.
smelles *n. pl.* smells N(Le) 21, R 14.
softe *adj.* soft, gentle, mild W 44, N(3), L(2); *pl.* N(Le) 53.
somnedest *v. 2 s. pt.* didst sum up, unite N(Lo) 16.
sone *adv.* soon, at once W 208, N(Lo) 130. See **sune**.
song *n.* song N(Le) 83.
sore *adj.* (after *prep.*) sore N(Le) 60; *pl.* N(Le) 54. See **sare**.
sorhe *n.* sorrow W 307(5); **sorwe** N(Lo) 83; **soruwe** N(Lo) 16; **sorewe** L 62/**seoruwe** N(U) 75.
sorhfule *adj. pl.* sorrowful N(U) 155.
soð *adj.* true L 1(3), N(9); **soðe** (after *prep.*) N(U) 24, L 21; N(Le) 61? (MS. *to-ðe*).
soðe *n.*: *to* ~ in truth N(Lo) 93(2); **soðes** *gen. (adv.)* in truth, truly N(U) 34(3), L(3).
soðliche *adv.* truly W 149, N(Lo)115.
spac *adj.* quick N(Le) 27, R 19.
spatel *n.* spittle W 399.
spateling *n.* spitting W 409; **spotlunge** (after *prep.*) N(Le) 50.
speche *n.* speech N(U) 25(2), L 39.
spekes *v. 3 s. pr.* speaks W 427; **spec** *1 s. pt.* N(Lo) 73; **spec** *3 s. pt.* N(Le) 76; **ispekin** *pp.* L 96/**ispeken** N(U) 117.
spere *n.* spear W 542; **speres** *gen. s.* W 559.
sperred *pp.* enclosed W 591.
spitted *v. 3 s. pt.* spat W 394; *3 pl.* W 390.
spreddest *v. 3 s. pt.* spread N(Lo) 54; **ispred** *pp.* as *adj.* N(U) 58/**isprad** L 50.
spredunge *n.* spreading N(U) 53, L 46.
sprungen *v. 3 pl. pt.* sprang N(U) 114, L 93.
spuse *n.* spouse W 293(3).
stalewurðe *adj.* stalwart W 151.
steapes *n. pl.* steps L 62/**steopes** N(U) 74.
steked *pp.* enclosed, locked W 574.
steorren *n. pl.* stars N(U) 77, L 64.
stepen *v. inf.* step N(Le) 79.
sterke *adj. pl.* strong N(Lo) 46; **starke** W 154.
stihen *v. inf.* ascend N(U) 76, L 64.
stonde *v. inf.* stand W 301; **stont** *3 s. pr.* N(U) 147; **stod** *2 s. pt.* W 554; **stod** *3 s. pt.* L 120; **stode** *impers. 3 s. pt. subj.* N(Lo) 92.
stondunge *n.* standing N(U) 154; **stondunges** *pl.* standing ones N(U) 151.
stowe. See **cwalm**.
streames *n. pl.* streams N(U) 99; **stremes** N(Lo) 46.
streames *v. 3 s. pr.* streams, gushes W 516; **streamed** *3 s. pt.* W 480.
streccheð *v. 3 s. pr.* stretches (out) N(U) 146; **streihtest** *2 s. pt.* N(Lo) 15, N(U) 48/**strahstest** L 41; **strahte** *3 s. pt.* L 119; **istreihte** *pp. (pl.)* as *adj.* N(U) 58/**istrahte** L 50; **strahte** W 527.
strencðe *n.* strength N(Le) 72; **strengðe** W 23(6).
streone *n.* strain, progeny W 178.
strete *n.* street W 326.
striden *v. 3 pl. pt.* flowed N(U) 99.
striken *v. 3 pl. pt.* flowed N(U) 114, L 82; **strike** L 93 (end of line).
strong *adj.* strong W 150(2); **strongest** *superl.* W 153.
strundes *n. pl.* streams N(U) 114; **strunden** L 81; **strondes** L 94.
studen *n. pl.* places N(Le) 57.
sturiunge *n.* stirring, change N(U) 142/**sturunge** L 116.
sumehwile *adv.* sometimes N(Le) 28.

sumhwat *pron.* somewhat W 562.
summe *adj. s.* or *pl.*: ~ *tide* at some time(s) N(Le) 25, R 17; **summe** *pl.* as *pron.* W 16(6); **sume** W 19.
sum-time *adv.* sometime(s) R 20.
sune *n.* son W 55(3), N(7), R 26; **sone** L 1(3).
sune-dai *n.* Sunday N(Lo) 21. See **hwit**.
sunegi *v. 1 s. pr.* sin N(Lo) 74; **suneggeð** *3 s. pr.* N(Lo) 114; **isuneget** *pp.* R 21; **isuneged** N(2), L 97.
sunful *adj.* sinful R 5; **sunfule** N(Le) 6, R 13; **sunfule** *wk.* N(Lo) 48; **sunfule** *pl. adj.* and *n.* R 31, N(7); **sunifule** N(U) 101 (see textual note); **sunefule** W 205(2); **sunfulle** N(Lo) 3, L 110(2); **sinfule** W 376; **sunfules** *gen. pl.* N(U) 129/**sunfulles** L 105.
sunne *n.* sin W 142(5), N(6), L(2), R 11; **sinne** W 296; **sunnen** *pl.* L 73(5), N(12), R(2); **sunnes** W 87.
sunne *n.* sun W 50(2), N(U) 11, L 10.
sur *adj.* sour W 522; **surest** *superl.* W 578.
suster *n.* sister W 250(2).
suti *adj.* foul, besmirched N(U) 17, L 14.
swa *adv.* (manner, result) so, thus W 45(2), L 23; so N(U) 26, N(Lo) 92(2); **swa** (degree: before adj. or adv., frequently followed by *þet*-clause) so, such W 7(30), L(8); **swo** L 7(2); so N(16); **swa** ... **swa** (*correl.*) so much ... so much (with comparatives) W 330(2); **so** ... **so** N(Lo) 168, N(Le) 83; **swa** ... **swa as** (so) ... as W 123(2); **so** ... **so** N(U) 49–50; **swa** ... **as** W 619–20; **swo** ... **ase** L 70; **þer** ... **swa** where ... so (= where ... there) W 297–8; **swa** (relative) as L 43; for **-swa, -so, -se, -soeuer**: see **hwa, hwet, hwuch**.
swanc *v. 2 s. pt.* didst toil W 452.

swat *n.* sweat, moisture W 456; **swote** (after *prep.*) N(Le) 46.
swattes *v. 2 s. pt.* didst sweat W 453.
swepes *n. pl.* whips W 477(2).
swete *adj.* sweet W 1(24), N(14), L(4), R(2); **swet** W 598; **swote** L 7(3), N(Le) 21, R 14; *ðet swete* that sweet (thing) N(Lo) 155; **swetter** *compar.* W 3; **swettere** (after *prep.*) W 72; **swetest** *superl.* N(U) 87, L 72.
sweteli *adv.* sweetly W 575.
sweteliche *adv.* sweetly N(U) 80, L 66.
sweting *n.* sweet one W 69.
swetnesse *n.* sweetness W 36(3), N(3), L(2) (MS. *spetnesse* N(U) 3, L 2); **swotnesse** N(U) 91, L 75.
swetunge *n.* sweating N(Le) 57 (MS. *spetunge*).
swike *n.* deceiver N(Lo) 56.
swing *n.* affliction, hardship W 456.
swink *n.* toil, travail W 449.
swiðe *adv.* exceedingly, quickly W 497, N(U) 49, L 43; **swuðe** N(U) title; **swiðre** *compar.* W 284.
swuch *adj.* such W 426; **swuche** W 230(2), L 117; **swich** N(U)143; **swuche**: *of* ~ *þinge,* s. or pl. N(Lo) 74. For N **swuch ase**/ L **swilc ase**, see **ase**.
swungen *pp.* flogged W 477.

tah *adv.* yet, nevertheless W 319. See **þah**.
tahtes *v. 2 s. pt.* didst teach W 353; **tawhtest** *3 s. pt.* N(Lo) 8.
taken *v. inf.* take W 465; **tac** *s. imper.* W 612; **taken** *pp.* W 374.
teken *prep.* in addition to W 630; **teke** N(U) 7, L 6; **þer teken** N(U) 38/**þer take** L 34 thereunto, in addition (to that).
tellen *v. inf.* tell, reckon W 251(3); **telle** W 459; **telles** *3 s. pr.* W 267.
tend *v. s. imper.* kindle N(Lo) 165.
teone *n.* suffering N(U) 44, L 38.
tide *n.*: *summe* ~ at one time N(Le) 25, R 17.

Glossary

til *prep.* to W 304(2); til þ *conj.* until W 595.

to *prep.* to, towards, into (with various shadings of sense) W 13(25), N(23), L(12), R(6); te R 11; for, as (purpose, function), W 72, 293 (twice), 332, 532, N(Lo) 93, 110; to, in order to (with inf.), W 20(34), N(5), L(5); **for to**: see **for**. On *to-ðe* N(Le) 61, see **soð**.

to *adv.* too L 30, N(9), R(2).

tobreke *v. inf.* break W 422(2).

tocleue *v. inf.* cleave, be cloven W 558.

todrahen *pp.* rent asunder W 509.

todunet *pp.* struck (with resounding blows) W 485.

tomelte *v. inf.* melt W 7.

torent *pp.* rent apart W 479.

tospredde *pp. pl.* as *adj.* spread apart N(U) 50/**tospradde** L 43.

totorn *pp.* torn apart W 479.

tovel see **uuel**.

towart *prep.* toward, to L 77(2); **toward** W(5), N(3); **touwa'rd** N(Lo) 52.

treitur *n.* traitor W 384.

treowe *adj.* true, faithful W 613, N(2); **treoue** N(U) 106; **trewe** W 549, L 59; **trewere** *compar.* W 231.

treowðe *n.* troth, faith R 16; **treouðe** N(Le) 24.

tresun *n.* treason W 387.

treulac *n.* faith N(Lo) 162.

treweliche *adv.* truly, loyally W 239.

truchunge *n.* failing L 115.

trukeð *v. 3 s. pr.* fail, desert N(Lo) 89; **itrukede** *pp. pl.* as *n.* deserters, traitors N(Lo) 96.

trust *n.* trust N(U) 108, L 89.

trusten *v. inf.* N(Lo) 91; **truste** *1 s. pr.* N(Lo) 100(2); **truste** *1 s. pt.* N(Lo) 94(3).

tunʒe *n.* tongue W 458.

tur *n.* tower N(Le) 81.

turnen *v. inf.* turn, turn away W 77, N(Lo) 106; **turn** *s. imper.* L 20, N(2).

tuðe: see **cuið**.

twa *num.* two W 278(3), W 520 (MS. *Ewa*); **otwo** N(U) 155, see **on** *prep.*

twofold *adj.* as *n.* twofold N(Lo) 156.

þa *adv.* then W 563; **þo** N(Lo) 16, L 104.

þa *conj.* then, therefore W 52(3); **ta** W 103.

þah *conj.* though L 121, R 23; **þauh** N(U) 148, N(Lo) 128, N(Le) 33; **tah**: *as* ∼ W 411(2). See **tah**.

þai *pron. 3 pl.* they W 282(5); **þei** W 284; **tai** W 140(2).

þe *art.* the W 8(56), N(76), L(21), R(8); **te** W 50(34), N(2), L(8), R 31 : sometimes joined to *prep.*, as *atte, iþe, oþe*. For inflected forms see **þet**. For *for þe, hwils þe*, see **forþi, hwils**.

þe *pron. rel.* who, which N(Le) 39, L(6), R(2); þ ∼ who L 54–55.

þe *adv.* (with comparatives) the, so much W 288, N(Lo) 90; **te** . . . **te** *correl.* the . . . the W 16.

þeaw *n.* virtue, trait W 27; **þeawes** *pl.* W 611, N(Le) 80.

þen *conj.* than W 4(15), N(8); **þene** L 40; *er þen* before N(Lo) 157.

þenche *v. inf.* think W 403(2); **þenken** W 649; **þenche** *1 s. pr.* N(U) 157; **þenches** *3 s. pr.* W 423; **þenke** *s. imper.* W 406; **þenc** W 653.

þenne *adv.* then, therefore W 90(8), L(3); **þeonne** L 65, N(4); *þeonne forð* thenceforth N(Lo) 125.

þeof *n.* thief W 387(2); **þeofes** *pl.* W 417; **þeoues** W 437.

þeors see **þis** *adj.*

þeosternesse *n.* darkness N(U) 14/ **þesturnesse** L 12.

þeostri *adj.* dark N(U) 15/**þester** L 13.

þer *adv. demonst.* there W 378(4), N(3), L 34 (see **teken**); **þear** L 55(2); *rel.* where W 108(5), N(3), L 100 (see **swa**).

þer-bitweonen *adv.* between those (arms) L 47 (MS. *þe bitweonen*).

Glossary

þerefter *adv.* thereafter N(U) 40/ **þerafter** L 36, W 561; **terafter** W 297.

þerf *v. 3 s. pr.* needs N(U) 104; **derf** L 85.

þerfrom *adv.* therefrom N(U) 42, L 37.

þerinne *adv.* therein N(U) 35, N(Lo) 166 (cf. W 324); **þerin** L 31; **trin** W 66.

þerof *adv.* thereof N(U) 110, L 90–91 ? (MS. *þ̄ of*).

þerto *adv.* thereto, also N(U) 8(3), L(2).

þerþurh *adv.* thereby, from that W 291.

þerupon *adv.* thereupon W 627.

þet (**þ̄**) *pron. rel.* who, which, that R 3(2), N(79); **þat** W 11 (64), N(Lo) 165, L(23); to whom W 20; with which W 496; **þet** *pron. dem.* that, that which, he who, &c. N(U) 7(4), N(Lo)(7); **þat** L 6(5); **tat** W 185(3); **þeo** *pl.* N(Lo) 22; **þoa** W 234. For *þe, þi, þon, þen,* derived from OE. *instr.*, see **forþi, þe** *adv.,* **wið**.

þet (**þ̄**) *adj.* (with force diminishing from *demonst.* that, those, to *def. art.* the; whence inflected forms of both are listed here: see Accidence) L 30 (MS. *þ̄et*), N(5), R(2); **tet** N(U) 35, N(Le) 63; **þat** W 42(11); **tat** W 386(3); **þene** *m. acc. s.* N(U) 146, N(Lo)(3), N(Le)(2); **þen** R 4; **þeo** *f. acc. s.* N(Lo) 93, R 11; **þeo** *pl.* N(U) 49(3), N(Lo)(2); **þa** W 263(10); **ta** W 68(3).

þet (**þ̄**) *conj.* that, so that R 5(3), N(34); **þat** W 7(44), L(7); inasmuch as W 438. Also used in forming compound conj. *forþi þ̄*, and similarly after *gif, hu, hwen, hwer, siðen, swa, til*.

þewe *n.* slave, thrall W 276.

þider *adv.* thither, there W 503.

þing *n.* thing W 192(5), N(7), L(6), R 5; **þinge** (after *prep.*) N(U) 46; *s.* or *pl.* N(Lo) 74, 77; **þing** *pl.* W 621; **þinges** W 11(6), N(Lo) 52; **þinge** *gen. pl.* N(U) 87(2), L 72 (cf. W 519); **þinge** *pl.* (after *prep.*) L 72.

þis *adj.* this W 18(8), N(6), L(2); (after *prep.*) N(Lo) 149; **tis** W 170; **þisse** (after *prep.*) N(Lo) 65, 81 ?; **þeos** *pl.* N(Lo) 116 (MS. *þeors*), 180; **þise** W 93(3).

þis *pron.* this W 31(6), N(8), L(2), R 24; intensive in *he* ~ he himself, he indeed W 418.

þoht *n.* thought N(U) 159.

þolien *v. inf.* suffer, endure W 367; **þolen** W 225(2); **þole** W 226(3); **þolest** *2 s. pr.* W 207; **þolien** *3 pl. pr.* W 357; **þole** *s. imper.* W 189(2); **þolede** *1 s. pt.* W 407; **þoledest** *2 s. pt.* W 201(2), N(Lo) 9; **þoledes** W 265(8); **þolede** *3 s. pt.* N(Le) 45(3).

þonke *n.* thought N(Lo) 83.

þonke *v. 1 s. pr.* thank N(Lo) 98.

þorn *n.* thorn W 483; **þornes** *pl.* W 482, N(U) 35, L 31; **þornene** *gen. pl.* N(Lo) 11, N(Le)(2).

þrasten *v. 3 pl. pr.* press, force W 497.

þreo *num.* three R 10, N(3); **þre** W 270(2).

þridde *adj.* third W 560, N(Lo) 18.

þristes *v. impers. 3 s. pr.* thirsts W 518.

þu *pron. 2 s.* thou W 36(86), N(41), L(14), R(2); **tu** W 85(44), N(3), L(4), R 6; sometimes attached to prec. verb, as: *ertu, wiltu;* **þe** *acc.,* after *prep.,* & *dat.* thee (to, for, from) thee W 9(64), N(53), L(23), R 24; **te**: ~ *in honde* into thy hand W 487; **þe** *reflex. & emph.* thyself (sometimes followed by *self, seluen:* see **seolf**) W 74(12), N(4), L 41; **te** W 220, L 57; **þi** *poss. adj. s.* (before cons.) thy W 6(53), N(22), L(12), R 26; ~ *seolf* N(U) 107, L 88; *iþi* (*in*+*þi*) W 557; (*þi* W 320 prob. = *þu*); **ti** W 38(10), L 112; **þin** (before

Glossary

vowel or *h*, rarely other cons.) W 124(10), N(16), L(7), R(2); **tin** W 95; **þine** *acc. s.* & after *prep.* W 414, N(30), L 59; *ipine (in+ pine)* N(U) 96, N(Lo) 167; *al pine wil* L 118 is subject of passive verb; **þine** *gen.* N(Lo) 15; **þine** *pl.* W 85(7), N(16), L(8); **þin** L 49(2); **tine** W 144(2); **þin** *poss. pron.* thine N(Lo) 104, 165; **tin** W 69, 604.

þunche *v. impers. inf.* seem W 43; **þinche** *3 s. pr.* W 538; **þuhte** *3 s. pt.* W 397(2).

þurh *prep.* through W 112(8), N(4), L(4), R(2); **þuruh** (in full) (NU) 74(10); **þuruh** (MS. þ) N(Lo) 11(17), N(Le) 68(3); **þuruð** N(Le) 4; **þuurh** N(U) 63; **þurch** N(Lo) 17.

þurhdriuen *pp.* transfixed N(U) 152.

þurhut *prep.* through W 209 (4); **þurhhut** W 87.

þurles *v. 3 s. pr.* pierces W 542.

þurlunge *n.* piercing N(Le) 60.

þus *adv.* thus W 569, N(4).

þusandfald *adv.* thousandfold W 605.

ugge *n.* fear N(Lo) 36.

umbe-keoruunge *n.* circumcision N(Le) 57.

under *prep.* under W 14(3).

underȝit *v. 3 s. pr.* understands N(Lo) 157.

vnderstonde *v. inf.* understand W 561; **understonde** *1 s. pr.* W 292, N(Lo) 153; **vnderstond** *s. imper.* W 405.

underuon *v. inf.* receive N(Lo) 127; **underfo** (end of line) *pp.* N(Lo) 140.

unimete *adj.* immeasurable W 68; *adv.* extremely W 39(2).

unimeteliche *adv.* immeasurably W 451.

uniseli *adj.* unhappy N(Lo) 154.

unlusti *adj.* slothful, enervated N(Le) 28, R 20.

unofserued *pp.* as *adj.* undeserved N(Lo) 173.

unrideli *adv.* harshly, roughly W 471.

unriht *n.* injustice N(Le) 26; **unrihte** (after *prep.*) R 18.

unsalued *pp.* unhealed, unsaved N(U) 104/**unsauuet** L 86.

untreowe *adj.* as *n.* disloyal, treacherous W 375.

unþeawe *n.* (after *prep.*) misdemeanour, vice R 13; **unþeawes** *pl.* N(Le) 20.

unweaschen *pp.* unwashed N(U) 102/**unwaschen** L 84.

unwitschipe *n.* ignorance W 227.

unwrest *adj.* unsteadfast, wicked W 609; **unwreste** *pl.* W 531; **unwreastest** *superl.* W 241.

unwrih *v. s. imper.* reveal, make known N(Lo) 143.

unwurð *adj.* unworthy N(U) 82/**unwurhþ** L 68; **unwurðe** *pl.* N(Le) 44, R 31.

unwurði *adj.* unworthy W 409(3).

uorbern *v. s. imper.* burn up N(Lo) 165.

uordriuene *pp. pl.* as *adj.* pierced through N(Lo) 49.

uorloren *pp.* completely lost N(Lo) 135.

uorwunded *pp.* as *adj.* seriously wounded N(Lo) 50.

up *adv.* up W 504(3), N(3).

up-ariste *n.* ascension N(Le) 79.

upon *prep.* (before vowel or *h*) W 494(2); **uppon** N(Lo) 96; **upo** (before cons.) W 166(8); **vpo** W 556; **uppo** W 284, N(Lo) 94.

ureisun *n.* orison N(U) title; **oreisun** R title.

useð *v. 3 s. pr.* uses N(Le) 70.

ut *adv.* out W 145(4), N(Lo) 102.

utewið *adj.* external L 30/**wtewið** N(U) 34.

uttre *adj. pl.* external W 93.

uuel *n.* evil L 90, N(2) and prob. N(Lo) 43, R 19/*tovel* (= *to uvel*) N(Le) 27.

Glossary

vuele *adv.* ill, wickedly N(Le) 23/
  uuele R 16.
uwward *adv.* upwards (for *uppard* ?)
  N(Le) 79.

wa *n.* woe W 46(5), L 18/**woa** N(U)
  20, N(Lo) 106.
wac *adj.* weak W 587, L 32/**woc** N(U)
  36; **wak** W 282. See **wah**.
wacnesse *n.* weakness W 156.
wah ? *adj.* weak ?, slothful ?, woeful ?
  W 279. See note to line.
waheles *adj.* wall-less W 326.
wahes *n. pl.* walls W 593.
wal *n.* wall N(U) 90, L 74.
wallen *v. 3 pl. pr.* well, boil, rage
  W 41.
warant *n.* protection N(Lo) 54.
warhtreo *n.* gallows, cross W 504.
warpe *v. 1 s. pr.* cast, thrust L 42/
  worpe N(U) 48; **warpe** *3 s. pr.*
  L 52/**worpe** N(U) 60; **weorp** *2 s.
  pt.* R 4/**werp** N(Le) 5; **wurpen**
  pp. W 296.
water *n.* water W 490(2).
we *pron. 1 pl.* we W 236(2), N(4),
  L(2); **us** *acc.* & after *prep.* N(U)
  41(3), L(4); *dat.* (to, for) us W 386,
  N(U) 107, L 88; *reflex.* ourselves
  N(U) 42, L 37; *us seoluen* ourselves N(Lo) 40; **ure** *poss. adj.*
  W title (4), N(U) 133, L 108;
  hure N(Lo) 175; **ure** *poss. pron.*
  ours N(Le) 75
wealdes *v. 3 s. pr.* rules W 170;
  welt N(U) 140/ **walt** L 114.
wearnen *v. inf.* refuse, deny W 552;
  wernen R 27; **werne** N(Le) 38;
  werneð *3 pl. pr.* N(U) 91, L 75.
weaschen *v. inf.* wash N(U) 112,
  N(Lo) 45; **waschen** N(U) 101,
  L(2); **wasche** W 400; **wasche**?
  (MS. *waschs*, see fn.) *3 s. pr. subj.*
  N(Lo) 48; **wasche** L 94/ **weasche**
  N(U) 114 (MS. *weaschs*, see fn.) *3
  pl. pr. subj.*; **wesch** *3 s. pt.* W 546.
wei *n.* way N(Lo) 143.
wei *interj.* woe (is me)! alas! N(U)
  88(2), L 73(2).
wel *adv.* very, well L 22(2), N(3);

betere *compar.* better W 104,
  N(4); **bettre** W 616; **best** *superl.*
  best W 623.
welefule *adj. wk.* pleasant W 47;
  welefulle W 394.
welle *v. inf.* well, boil, rage W 46.
wellen *n. pl.* wells, springs N(U) 113/
  wallen L 93.
weneð *v. 3 s. pr.* thinks, intends,
  expects N(U) 58, L 50; **weneð**
  3 pl. pr. N(Le) 61; **wene** *3 s. pr.
  subj.* L 53(2), N(3); **wenden** *3 pl.
  pt.* W 285.
went *v. 3 s. pr.* turns N(Lo) 105;
  wended *1 pl. pr.* N(U) 42, L 37;
  wend *s. imper.* N(U) 22, L 19;
  iwend *pp.* N(U) 22/L 19 is corrupt: the first **iwend** is prob. *pp.*
  (auxil. omitted), the second **iwend**
  s. imper.
weole *n.* weal, happiness L 5(2),
  N(4); **wele** W 80(3).
weouede *n.* altar N(Lo) 25.
wepe *v. inf.* weep W 564; **weopinde**
  pr. p. N(U) 155.
wepmon *n.* man, male W 164(2).
werc *n.* work, deed N(Le) 33, R 23;
  werkes *pl.* N(Lo) 175.
were *v. s. imper.* defend N(Le) 9(2),
  R(2).
westi *adj.* destitute, desolate W
  320(2).
wet *n.* moisture N(U) 103, L 85.
wex *v. 2 s. pt.* didst grow W 330.
wicke *adj.* wicked W 311.
wide *adj. wk.* wide W 544; **wide** *pl.*
  L 43, N(U) 50 (MS. *wiðe*).
widerwines *n. pl.* adversaries N(Le)
  10.
wildernesse *n.* wilderness N(Le) 43,
  R 30.
wilfulle *adj. pl.* wilful, determined
  W 302.
wilfulliche *adv.* willingly, purposely
  W 357.
wille *n.* will W 194(2); **wil** L 118,
  N(2).
willeliche *adv.* willingly N(Le) 44,
  R 31.
wilni *v. inf.* desire N(Lo) 126; **wilni**

Glossary 77

1 s. pr. N(Lo) 144(2); **wilneð** *pl. pr.* L 27/**wilned** N(U) 31.
wilnunge *n.* desire R 15, N(2).
wimmon *n.* woman N(U) 132, L 107 **wummon** W 163(2).
winnen *v. 3 pl. pr.* win, obtain W 161.
wis *adv.* surely, certainly L 91(2), N(2).
wisdom *n.* wisdom W 22(4), N(Lo) 80; **wisedom** W 111(2).
wise *n.* manner, wise W 383, N(2), L 25.
wisere *adj. compar.* wiser W 110.
wit *n.* intelligence, sense W 22(4), N(Lo) 170; **wittes** *pl.* L 94, N(3), R 13.
wite *v. inf.* protect (from) W 274.
witerliche *adv.* truly, indeed W 338(2).
witnesses *v. 3 s. pr.* witnesses, testifies W 117.
wið *prep.* with, &c. (with various shadings of sense chiefly derived from OE. *mid* and defining accompaniment, attendant circumstances or qualities, means and instrument) W 59(52), N(38), L(15), R(2); **wið þen þet** N(U) 41/**wið þon þ** L 36 provided that.
wiðhalde *v. inf.* withhold, retain W 21(2).
wiðinne *prep.* within W 592, N(Lo) 58.
wiðinne *adv.* inwardly W 556.
wiðuten *prep.* without, except W 81(3), N(2); **wiðute** W 414, N(2).
wlite *n.* face, form W 47(2).
wode *adj. pl.* mad, furious W 290(2).
wodschipe *n.* madness N(Lo) 38.
woȝe *v. inf.* woo L 71/**wowen** N(U) 86.
woh *n.* evil, misery, wrong W 200 (2), N(Le) 26, R 18; **wohes** *pl.* W 265, R 31; **wowes** N(Le) 44.
wohunge *n.* wooing W title.
wondred *n.* affliction N(Lo) 109.
wone *n.* lack, want W 337, N(3), L 26.
wonteð *v. 3 s. pr.* is lacking N(Le) 73; **wontes** W 109.

wordes *n. pl.* words W 370(3), N(2).
world *n.* world W 113(11), N(4), L 22, R 11; **werld** W 63(7); **worlde** (after *prep.*) W 310(2), N(6), L 19; **werlde** W 23(2); *werld into werlde* world without end W 634; **worldes** *gen. s.* N(U) 43; **worldles** L 37; **weorldes** W 80.
worldlich *adj.* worldly N(U) 83? (MS. *wordlich*); **worldliche** *pl.* N(Lo) 121.
wot *v. 1 s. pr.* know N(U) 26, N(Lo) 93(3); **wat**? L 22 (MS. *pat*); **wost** *2 s. pr.* N(Lo) 144.
wrange *n.* (after *prep.*) wrong, injustice W 551.
wrecche *n.* wretch W 285(2), N(U) 67/**wreche** L 57; **wrecches** *pl.* N(U) 67/**wreches** L 57.
wrecche *adj.* wretched W 587.
wrecched *adj.* wretched W 320.
wrekes *v. 2 s. pr.* avengest W 207; **wreoke** *2 s. pr. subj.* N(Lo) 38.
wrenche *v. inf.* turn aside W 476.
wreððe *n.* wrath N(Le) 23, R 15, N(Lo) 39 (MS. *preðde*).
wrihe *v. inf.* cover, protect W 345.
writen *pp.* written W 382(2).
wrixlunge *n.* changing N(Le) 48.
wrong *v. 3 s. pt.* pressed, oozed out N(Le) 63; **wrang** W 468(2).
wtewið: see **utewið**.
wulle *v. 1 s. pr.* will (with senses varying from simple future to desire and command) N(U) 149, N(Lo)(2); **chulle** (from *ich wulle*): *ich chulle* I will N(Lo) 91(2); **wile** W 90(5); *iwile* (= *ich wile*) W 53(8); **wult** *2 s. pr.* W 292(2), N(9), L 121; **wilt** W 69(2); *wiltu* (= *wilt tu*) W 631; **wule** *3 s. pr.* L 48(5), N(7); **wolde** *1 s. pt.* N(Lo) 130; **walde** *3 s. pt.* W 43(2); **wolde** N(U) 159, N(Lo)(2). Negative forms: **nule** (*ne*+*wule*) *3 s. pr.* N(U) 71, L 59; **nulen** (*ne*+*wulen*) *3 pl. pr.* W 540.

Glossary

wulues *n. pl.* wolves W 290; **wulues** *gen. pl.* W 383.
wunde *n.* (after *prep.*) wound W 544, N(Le) 61; **wunden** *pl.* L 98(2), N(7), R 8; **wundes** W 202.
wunden *pp.* wrapped, swaddled W 327.
wunder *n.* wonder, marvel W 431 (2), N(U) 94, L 77; **wundres** *pl.* W 428(2).
wundren. See note to W 501–2.
wunie *v. inf.* dwell, remain W 133; **wunieð** *3 s. pr.* N(Lo) 57; **wuneð** W 67; **wunedest** *2 s. pt.* W 187; **wuniinde** *pr. p.* as *adj.* N(U) 126/ **wunende** L 103.

wuninge *n.* dwelling N(U) 18(2)/ **wunninge** L 15(2).
wunne *n.* joy N(U) 6(2), L(2).
wurchen *v. inf.* work N(Lo) 171; **wrahtes** *2 s. pt.* W 63(2); **wrahte** *3 s. pt.* W 113, L 114/**wrohte** N(U) 140, N(Le)(2).
wurschipe *n.* honour N(Lo) 80.
wurð *adj.* worth, worthy W 80(4).
wurðe *adj.* worthy N(U) 17, L 15.
wurðful *adj.* worthy N(Lo) 19; **wurðfule** *wk.* N(Lo) 53.
wurði *adj.* worthy W 619.
wurðliche *adj.* worthy, esteemed L 69. See note to N(U) 83.

INDEX OF NAMES

abrahames *gen. s.* Abraham's W 177.
adames *gen. s.* Adam's W 142, N(Le) 4, R 3.
austin (seint) St. Augustine N(Lo) 153.
barabas Barabbas W 386; **baraban** *acc. s.* W 386.
belleem Bethlehem W 323.
caluarie Calvary W 493.
crist Christ W 91(3), N(6), L(3).
dauiö David N(Lo) 139; **dauid** W 64; **dauiöes** *gen. s.* 177.
iesu Jesu (in W usually iħu) W 1(47), N(19), L(13); **iesus** (MS. iħc) W 384.
iohanes (sein) *gen. s.* St. John's N(U) 154, N(Lo) 16.
iudas scharioth Judas Iscariot W 464.
longis Longinus W 541.
luk (seint) St. Luke W 454.
marie Mary (the Virgin) W 174, N(3), L 107, R(3); **maria** N(Lo) 2.
pawel (seinte) St. Paul L 101/ **powel** N(U) 123, N(Lo) 68.
pilat (Pontius) Pilate W 473.
syon Zion N(Le) 81.

APPENDIX

Oratio ad sanctam Mariam[1]

O SANCTA Virgo virginum! quæ genuisti Dominum
Triumphatorem zabuli, reparatorem sæculi,
Ego peccator nimium a te peto remedium;
Esto patrona misero, et salus, et defensio.
Incumbunt hostes undique, mortem quærentes animæ,
Perversi foris homines, intus maligni dæmones;
Jam mihi multa vulnera inflicta sunt, o Domina!
Quæ nisi tu curaveris sunt mihi causa funeris;
Consensi suadentibus mortale crimen hostibus,
Et ob hoc reus teneor, culpam meam confiteor;
Nam quinque sensus corporis effecti portæ criminis:
Pulchra videndo cupiens, lene tangendo diligens,
Audivi libens turpia, narravi gaudens frivola,
Nares replevi sæpius illicitis odoribus,
Esu potuque dulcium sum delectatus nimium;
Peccavi per superbiam, et per inanem gloriam,
Pollutus sum perjurio, contaminatus otio,
Per iniquum mendacium fefelli [sæpe] proximum,
Et de rapinis pauperum collegi lucrum pessimum;
Iræ vel avaritiæ servivi quasi dominæ;
In corpore vel anima commisi cuncta scelera,
Nam corpus quod non potuit, mens perpetrare voluit.
Me turpis cogitatio, me pestilens locutio,
Me culpa damnat operum, me nequitas consciorum;
Hæc tibi nunc confiteor, o cunctis sanctis sanctior!
Tu causam meam suscipe, tu dignum pœnis eripe;
Exora tuum filium, ut mihi det remedium;
Ex tua carne genitus favebit tuis precibus,
Et matri quæ se peperit negare nihil poterit.
Per ejus natalitium, per ipsius jejunium,
Per asperas injurias, flagella, sputa, alapas,
Quas sponte sua pertulit qui se pro nobis obtulit,
Et per vestem coccineam, et per coronam spineam,
Per clavos, per patibulum, per cicatrices vulnerum,
Per aperturam lateris, per rivum sacri sanguinis,
Per sanctam eucharistiam, et per baptismi gratiam,
Per sacramenta fidei quam corde credens didici,
Imploro te, piissima, pro impetranda venia
Ut mihi Christi passio culparum sit remissio,
Et ejus resurrectio virtutum augmentatio. Amen.

Bishop Marbod of Rennes (1035-1123)

[1] *Patr. Lat.* clxxi. 1651; see Introd., p. xvi, above.

The manufacturer's authorised representative in the EU for product safety is Oxford University Press España S.A. of El Parque Empresarial San Fernando de Henares, Avenida de Castilla, 2 - 28830 Madrid (www.oup.es/en or product.safety@oup.com). OUP España S.A. also acts as importer into Spain of products made by the manufacturer.
Printed and bound by CPI Group (UK) Ltd, Croydon, CR0 4YY

20/03/2026
02075339-0009